RISK SOCIETY

Towards a New Modernity

ULRICH BECK

translated by Mark Ritter

SAGE Publications

London • Newbury Park • New Delhi

Originally published as *Risikogesellschaft: Auf dem Weg in eine andere Moderne* © Suhrkamp Verlag, Frankfurt am Main, 1986

This translation © Sage Publications, 1992

This edition first published 1992, Reprinted 1993 (twice)

Introduction © Scott Lash and Brian Wynne, 1992

SAGE Publications Ltd
6 Bonhill Street
London EC2A 4PU

SAGE Publications Inc
2455 Teller Road
Newbury Park, California 91320

SAGE Publications India Pvt Ltd
32, M-Block Market
Greater Kailash – I
New Delhi 110 048

British Library Cataloguing in Publication Data

Beck, Ulrich
    Risk Society: Towards a New Modernity. –
    (Theory, Culture & Society Series)
    I. Title   II. Ritter, Mark   III. Series
    306

    ISBN 0–8039–8345–x
    ISBN 0–8039–8346–8 (pbk)

Library of Congress catalog card number 92–050272

Typeset by Mayhew Typesetting, Rhayader, Powys
Printed in Great Britain by Redwood Books,
    Trowbridge, Wiltshire

CONTENTS

Ulrich Beck's *Risk Society* is already one of the most influential European works of social analysis in the late twentieth century. *Risikogesellschaft* was published in German in 1986. In its first five years it sold some 60,000 copies. Only a very few books in post-war social science have realized that sort of figure, and most of those have been textbooks. *Risk Society* is most definitely not a textbook. In the German speaking world – in terms of impact both across disciplines and on the lay public – comparison is probably best made with Habermas's *Strukturwandel der Offentlichkeit*, published in German some twenty-five years before Beck's book, though only released in English as *The Transformation of the Public Sphere* in 1989.

But Beck's book has had an enormous influence. First, it had little short of a meteoric impact on institutional social science. In 1990 the biannual conference of the German Sociological Association was entitled 'The Modernization of Modernization?' in oblique reference to Beck's thesis of reflexive modernization. *Risk Society* further played a leading role in the recasting of public debates in German ecological politics. Ulrich Beck is not just a social scientist but what the Germans call a *Schriftsteller*, a word that loses much of its meaning when translated into English as essayist or non-fiction writer. The personal and essayistic style of *Risikogesellschaft* – though it is a quite accessible book in the German – has made it an immensely difficult book to translate. And Mark Ritter, elsewhere a translator of Simmel, has done a heroic job here. Beck, as *Schriftsteller* and public sphere social scientist, writes regularly in the *Frankfurter Allgemeine Zeitung*. There is no equivalent of this in the Anglo-American world, and one is reminded of a continental European tradition in which Walter Benjamin once wrote regularly for the same Frankfurt newspaper and Raymond Aron for *Le Figaro*.

This said, *Risk Society* consists of two central interrelated theses. One concerns reflexive modernization and the other the issue of risk. Let us address these sequentially.

Reflexive Modernization

There is something apt in the above mentioned juxtaposition of Beck's work on risk society and Habermas's on the public sphere. In a very important way Habermas first gave bones in this early seminal work to what would later be his theory of *modernization*. Beck of course makes no claims to the sort of theoretical depth and weight that Habermas has achieved. Yet his theory of reflexive modernization can potentially provide the foundation for the rejection and recasting of Habermas's notion of modernization as Enlightenment project.

Theories of 'simple' modernization, from Habermas to Marx to mainstream Parsonian sociology, all share a sort of utopic evolutionism, whether its motor be communicative rationality, the development of the means of production, or structural differentiation and functional integration. Beck sees another, darker dimension to such developments and especially in the constitutive role assigned to science and knowledge. For Beck the consequences of scientific and industrial development are a set of risks and hazards, the likes of which we have never previously faced. These dangers can, for example, no longer be limited in time – as future generations are affected. Their spatial consequences are equally not amenable to limitation – as they cross national boundaries. Unlike in an earlier modernity, no one can be held accountable for the hazards of the 'risk society'. Further, it is becoming impossible to compensate those whose lives have been touched by those hazards, as their very calculability becomes problematized.

Yet given this seemingly dystopian outcome of rationalization, Beck does not succumb to the pessimism of a Weber, or Foucault or Adorno. His claim is that these *effets pervers* of modernization can potentially be dealt with, not through the negation, but through the *radicalization* of such rationalization. In order for societies really to evolve, he maintains, modernization must become *reflexive*. This sort of reflexivity, for Beck, is not to be abstractly located in some sort of hypothetical ideal speech situation. It is already becoming operative in the critique of science developing not just in the Green movement, but in the broad masses of the lay public. This critique, expressed as it is in diverse forms, is reflexive and can lay a moral claim to rationality which is equal to that of modern science. In the public domain, science inexorably tends to refute itself as its culture of scientism creates false claims and expectations in society at large.

Though Beck's theory of reflexive modernization has its origins in the sociology and critique of scientific knowledge, it is applicable right through society. Modernization involves not just structural change, but a changing relationship between social structures and social agents. When modernization reaches a certain level, agents tend to become more individualized, that is, decreasingly constrained by structures. In effect structural change forces social actors to become progressively more free from structure. And for modernization successfully to advance, these agents must release themselves from structural constraint and actively shape the modernization process.

The historical passage from tradition to modernity was supposed to uncover a social world free of choice, individualism and liberal democracy, based on rational 'enlightened' self-interest. Yet the post-modern critique has exposed how modernity itself imposes constraints of a traditional kind – culturally imposed, not freely chosen – around the quasi-religious modern icon of science. Its cultural form is scientism, which sociologists of science argue is an *intrinsic element* of science as public knowledge. The culture of science ... upon social actors by demanding their identification with particular social institutions and their ideologies, notably in constructions of risk, but also in definitions of sanity, proper sexual behavior, and countless other 'rational' frames of modern social control.

Ulrich Beck's origins are as a hard-working and – until recently – a not particularly celebrated sociologist specializing in research on industry and the family. For him, reflexive modernization is also proceeding in these spheres. Thus structural change in the private sphere results in the individualization of social agents who then are forced to make decisions about whether and whom they shall marry, whether they shall have children, what sort of sexual preference they might have. Individuals must then, free of these structures, reflexively construct their own biographies. In the sphere of work the process of structural change leads to individualization in two senses, through the decline first of class structure and second of the structural order of the Taylorist workplace. The resultant individualization again opens up a situation where individuals reflect upon and flexibly restructure the rules and resources of the workplace and of their leisure time.

The subtitle of Beck's *Risk Society* is *Towards a New Modernity*. He is referring here to an essentially three-stage periodization of social change. This comprises first pre-modernity, then simple modernity, and finally reflexive modernity. On this view, modernity is very much coextensive with industrial society and the new reflexive modernity with the risk society. Industrial society and risk society are for Beck distinct social formations. The axial principle of industrial society is the distribution of goods, while that of the risk society is the distribution of 'bads' or dangers. Further, industrial society is structured through social classes while the risk society is individualized. Yet the risk society, Beck persists in maintaining, is still, and at the same time, an industrial society. And that is because it is mainly industry, in conjunction with science, that is involved in the creation of the risk society's risks.

The Problem of Risk

Risk has become an intellectual and political web across which thread many strands of discourse relating to the slow crisis of modernity and industrial society. Whilst the champions of post-modernity claim triumphantly that the cultural-political hegemony of scientism and its one-dimensional modernity is finished, others question how far this is true, let alone what the societal implications might be of rampant subjectivism in its post-modern form.

The dominant discourses of risk, for all they have taken on the trappings of liberal pluralism, remain firmly instrumentalist and reductionist. To the extent that they allow other forms of experience such as public skepticism into their 'rational' modernist frame, they do so only on sufferance and not as a meeting with other legitimate forms of life.

Indeed the dominant risk paradigms have been able to surround themselves with the appearance (and self-delusion) of critical pluralistic debate and learning, through the growth of a plethora of disciplines, subdisciplines and schools of thought vigorously competing for ascendancy and recognition in the interpretation and 'management' of the risks of modern technological society. Yet the critical force of all this fervent intellectual activity is radically and systematically constrained by its cultural heritage and unreflective idiom (not to mention its forms of patronage and institutional orientations). Risks are defined as the probabilities of physical harm due to given technological or other processes. Hence technical experts are given pole position to define agendas and impose bounding premises *a priori* on risk discourses.

A small group of sociologists and anthropologists from beyond the cultural pale of this hegemony have made three observations in particular. First, such physical risks are always created and effected in social systems, for example by organizations and institutions which are supposed to manage and control the risky activity. Second, the magnitude of the physical risks is therefore a direct function of the quality of social relations and processes. Third, the primary risk, even for the most technically intensive activities (indeed perhaps most especially for them), is therefore that of social dependency upon institutions and actors who may well be – and arguably are increasingly – alien, obscure and inaccessible to most people affected by the risks in question.

Thus the issues of trust and credibility have been raised in the risk field, in a way connected to the trust issue as discussed by Anthony Giddens and others in relation to late modernity and its problems. Yet the treatment of this novel dimension has been itself revealing, as the fuller depth of the problem has been reduced and coopted into the prevailing instrumental terms, as to how institutions can adapt procedures and self-presentation in order to secure or repair credibility, without fundamentally questioning the forms of power or social control involved. The modern sub-field of risk communication exemplifies this baneful defence against reflexivity. Although in the risk field the social dimension of trust has been proposed as crucial for ten years or more, this has been resisted and redefined; now the very different but convergent work of Beck and Giddens has reinforced it.

Reflexivity is excluded from the social and political interactions between experts and social groups over modern risks, because of the systematic assumption of realism in science. Contemporary examples abound. When farm workers claimed that herbicides were causing unacceptable health effects, the British government asked its Pesticides Advisory Committee to investigate. The PAC, composed largely of toxicologists, turned automatically to the scientific literature on laboratory toxicology of the chemicals in question. They concluded unequivocally that there was no risk. When the farm workers returned with an even thicker dossier of cases of medical harm, the PAC dismissed this as merely anecdotal, uncontrolled non-knowledge.

When they were forced by further public objections to return to the question, the PAC again asserted that there was no danger, but this time added an apparently minor, but actually crucial qualification. This was that there was no risk according to the science literature, so long as the herbicide was produced under the correct conditions (dioxins could be produced as contaminants by small variations in production process parameters) and used under the correct conditions. On this latter question the farm workers were the experts. They knew from experience that 'the correct conditions of use' were a scientists' fantasy – 'Cloud-cuckoo-land from behind the laboratory bench' as one farmers' representative put it. The instructions for use were frequently obliterated or lost, the proper spraying equipment was often unavailable, protective clothing was often inadequate, and weather conditions were frequently ignored in the pressure to get the spraying done.

The idealized model of the risk system, reflected in the scientists' exclusive focus on the laboratory knowledge, contained not only question-able physical assumptions but a naive model of that part of society. What is more it was deployed in effect as a social prescription, without any interest or negotiation over its validity or acceptability. The completely unreflective imposition of these bounding premises on the risk debate only polarized the issue around the realist distraction concerning the truth value of scientific propositions, and polemic about the alleged irrationality of the farm workers and corruption of scientists and regulatory institutions. A reflexive learning process would have recognized the conditions under-pinning the scientific conclusions, drawn out the social situational ques-tions which they implied, and examined these with the benefit *inter alia* of the different forms of knowledge held by people other than scientists. This reflexive learning process would have necessarily meant negotiation between different epistemologies and subcultural forms, amongst different discourses; and as such it would have entailed the development of the social or moral identities of the actors involved.

Even in the most apparently technical risk arenas, therefore, there is important sociological work to be done. With a few exceptions, socio-logists have been timid and complacent in the face of this pervasive apologia for the (always temporary but incessantly extended) repair of modernity. Whilst from the well padded armchairs of the seminar rooms of Paris, modernity may appear dead and nearly buried, and reflexivity may be thriving as a collective form of discourse, the conditions of ordinary life for many may call this into question, both as a general account of the present and as a model of the future by diffusion outwards and (it seems) downwards from the vanguard intelligentsia.

Ulrich Beck is one of the few theoretically informed sociologists who have escaped this wider tendency towards timidity or complacent ethnocentrism, and grappled with some central dimensions of the role of risk discourses in structuring, reproducing and repairing the modernist historical project. The theme of reflexive modernization corresponds closely with the outline from the example above, of a reflexive learning process which could be advanced in contemporary risk conflicts instead of deepening the crisis of legitimation of modern institutions, locked as they are in their modernistic delusions. Whereas post-modernism implies the wholesale abandonment of scientific-instrumental modes of thought, and modernism grants them grotesquely inflated and unconditional power, reflexive modernization confronts and tries to accommodate the essential tension between human indeterminacy – as reflected in the incessant but always open attempt to renegotiate coherent narratives of identity – and the inevitable tendency to objectify and naturalize our institutional and cultural productions.

An important issue for sociologists and anthropologists which is raised by Beck's perspective concerns the sources of reflexivity. One approach is to conclude that the religion of science secularizes itself, is pushed through the barriers of its own precommitments by the impetus of criticism built into the social structure. This may seem unduly optimistic, though there is something to be retained here.

Another, widely influential view is that the intellectual class, radically marginalized and alienated from mainstream modernism, acts as the nucleus and vanguard of post-modern critique and reflexivity. This class fraction is seen as uniquely capable of sensing and articulating the new post-paradigmatic culture. However, a skeptical alternative, or at least qualification, to this self-congratulatory theory of intellectuals is suggested by looking more carefully at the discourses of non-intellectual lay public groups in risk conflicts. It is common to suppose that when there is no open public conflict about the risks of some technology, chemical or the like, this is evidence of positive public acceptance of the risks, or of the full social package of risk-technology-institutions. When public opposition emerges into political form, the questions are usually posed in terms of the factors which turned the public negative in its attitudes.

Yet more ethnographic fieldwork frequently shows that people were never particularly positive about the risks in question, or about their controlling institutions. They may not have expressed their criticism or dissent in public form, but that does not mean they were not chronically mistrustful of, skeptical of or alienated from those institutions supposed to be in control. They may simply have been resigned to dependency on that institutional or political nexus, with no perceived power to influence it or make it more accountable.

At this informal, pre-political level, people may well be articulating in their own semi-private social worlds, in their own vernacular, a strong form of critique, whose reflexivity comes not from the critique *per se* but from the occasionally evident sense of self-critique – an awareness of their own self-censorship with respect to the overweening power and hubris of dominant institutions and discourses. This is to be seen in the ambivalence and social reference in what people are prepared to express as belief.

An example can be drawn from fieldwork with Cumbrian sheep farmers after the Chernobyl accident had rained radiocesium down on their fells. The persistence of the contamination way beyond the scientists' predictions led many to ask whether the contamination was not of longer standing – from the nearby Sellafield nuclear plant site. Despite the scientists' confident assertions that they could see a clear scientific difference between the radioactivity from these alternative sources, many farmers continued to express the view that Sellafield was also implicated and that this had been covered up. What is more, they could give cogent reasons competing with the scientists' claims, which had to be taken on trust.

Yet in-depth interviews revealed a profound ambivalence about what to believe, and a reluctance to express the anti-Sellafield view because, it seemed, this would contradict the cherished social and kinship networks which straddled farming families and work dependency on the local economic-technological juggernaut. Quite a number of farming families also have immediate sons, daughters, brothers and friends who work at Sellafield; often they work part-time on the farm and part-time at the nuclear plant. People are struggling to reconcile conflicting identities, fostered in different if overlapping social networks. Their ambivalence about responding to scientific assertion as to the source of the radioactive contamination reflected this multiplex social situation.

It would be possible to interpret this kind of multi-layered response as a form of 'private reflexivity' which must be the prior basis for its more public forms, if and when these develop (which is not inevitable). One would also expect the same private informal ambivalences and attenuated forms of self-reflection to be found within the dominant institutions of science and administration, an important difference being that these are more defended against such ambivalences being made transparent.

Beck's unusually broad-based approach to social constructions of risk and identity in late industrial society would be potentially a rich basis to examine these questions about the sources and social dynamics of forms of reflexivity with which to transform the project of modernism. Perhaps this will be the focus of future work for him, ourselves and others.

This introduction would not be complete without some mention of the remarkable parallel between Professor Beck's work and the recent work of Anthony Giddens. In *Consequences of Modernity* (1990) and *Modernity and Self-Identity* (1991), Giddens has developed themes around the distinctive form reflexivity takes in modernity; about risk and trust; and about the self-creation of identity in late modernity through the reflexive shaping of our own biographical narratives. More remarkable is the fact that, though Beck and Giddens have very recently come fully to appreciate one another's contributions, the major part of this parallel development has been quite independent.

Further, Giddens and Beck write from very divergent backgrounds. The concepts of Giddens now as modernity analyst were already there in his work of the past fifteen years as general social theorist. Thus reflexive modernity for Giddens is very much based in his previous concept of the 'double hermeneutic'. And his notions of risk and trust are grounded in his previously developed notion of 'ontological security'. Finally, the origins of Giddens's theory of modernity lie largely in debates in very general and abstract social theory – in particular in his rejection of structural functionalism via notions of agency from ethnomethodology and Goffman. In contradistinction, Beck's theory stems from experience as a sociologist of institutions, on which he has built a macro-sociology of social change.

One last influence on Beck takes us back to the starting point of this introduction. Even German sociologist's *conscience collective* or even *inconscient collective* is fairly riddled with the assumptions and tenets of the work of Jürgen Habermas. And in the final analysis Beck, like Habermas, does understand social change to be a learning process. He opts, if not for rationality, for a sort of hyper-rationality. He is not the foe but the friend of modernization. But Habermas's benchmark theses on the public sphere were published thirty years ago. If critical theory had to operate in that heyday of the Keynesian welfare state in terms of the fulfillment of the Enlightenment project, times have changed. Today critical theory can no longer proceed on those terms. To operate in a transformed political culture which is at the same time localized – the world of the new (post-traditional) communitarianism, engaged in a seemingly ecumenical, though hopefully pluralist, process of globalization – a new critical theory is needed. Such a theory – if it is to help realize even some of the aims of the Enlightenment – must be reflexively critical and disruptive of the assumptions of the very project of the Enlightenment. In such lies the allure of Beck's work and the theory of reflexive modernization.

Scott Lash
Brian Wynne

PREFACE

The theme of this book is the unremarkable prefix 'post'. It is the key word of our times. Everything is 'post'. We have become used to *post*-industrialism now for some time, and we can still more or less make sense of it. With *post*-modernism things begin to get blurred. The concept of *post*-Enlightenment is so dark even a cat would hesitate to venture in. It hints at a 'beyond' which it cannot name, and in the substantive elements that it names *and* negates it remains tied to the familiar. *Past plus post* – that is the basic recipe with which we confront a reality that is out of joint.

This book is an attempt to track down the word 'post', alternatively called 'late' or 'trans'. It is sustained by the effort to understand the meanings that the historical development of modernity has given to this word over the past two or three decades. This can only succeed through some no-holds-barred wrestling against the old theories and customary ways of thinking, whose life has been artificially prolonged by the word 'post'. Since these are lodged not only in others but within myself, the noise of the wrestling sometimes resounds in this book, deriving its volume in part from the fact that I have also had to grapple with my own objections. Thus some things may have turned out shrill, overly ironic or rash. One cannot resist the gravitational pull of old ways of thinking with the usual academic balancing act.

What is to follow does not at all proceed along the lines of empirical social research. Rather, it pursues a different ambition: to move the future which is just beginning to *take shape* into view against the *still* predominant past. What follows is written in the mode of an early nineteenth century observer, on the lookout for the contours of the as yet unknown industrial age emerging from behind the façade of fading feudal agrarianism. In times of structural transformation, representativity enters an alliance with the past and blocks our view of the peaks of the future that are intruding onto the horizon on all sides. To that extent, this book contains *some empirically oriented, projective social theory* – without any methodological safeguards.

That is based on the assessment that we are eye-witnesses – as subjects and objects – of a break within modernity, which is freeing itself from the contours of the classical industrial society and forging a new form – the (industrial) 'risk society'. This requires a delicate balancing between the contradictions of continuity and rupture within modernity, reflected in the antagonism between modernity and industrial society, and between industrial society and risk society. *That* these epochal distinctions are emerging today is what I claim to show with this book. *How* they can be differentiated in detail is derived from inspection of suggestions for social development. Before clarity can be achieved here, however, a bit more future must come into view.

The exercise in theoretical fence-sitting I shall engage in is matched by a practical one. Those who now cling more tightly than ever to the Enlightenment with the premises of the nineteenth century against the onslaught of 'contemporary irrationality' are challenged every bit as decisively as those who would wash the whole project of modernity, along with its accompanying anomalies, down the river.

There is no need to add anything to the horrific panorama of a self-endangering civilization that has already been sufficiently developed in all sectors of the opinion market. The same applies to the manifestations of a 'new perplexity' which has lost the organizing dichotomies of an industrial world that was 'intact' even in its antagonisms. The present book deals with the ensuing, *second* step. It elevates this step itself to the subject of explanation. The question is how to *understand* and conceptualize in sociologically inspired and informed thought these insecurities of the contemporary spirit, which it would be both ideologically cynical to deny and dangerous to yield to uncritically. The guiding theoretical idea which is developed to this end can once again be best elucidated in a historical analogy. *Just as modernization dissolved the structure of feudal society in the nineteenth century and produced the industrial society, modernization today is dissolving industrial society and another modernity is coming into being.*

The limits of this analogy, however, help to clarify the argument. In the nineteenth century, modernization took place against the background of its opposite: a traditional world of mores, and a nature which was to be known and mastered. Today, at the threshold of the twenty-first century, in the developed Western world, modernization has *consumed and lost its other* and now undermines its own premises as an industrial society along with its functional principles. Modernization within the horizon of experience of *pre*-modernity is being displaced by *reflexive* modernization. In the nineteenth century, privileges of rank and religious world views were being demystified; today the same is happening to the understanding of science and technology in the classical industrial society, as well as to the modes of existence in work, leisure, the family and sexuality. Modernization *within* the paths of industrial society is being replaced by a modernization *of the principles* of industrial society, something not provided for in any of the theoretical scenarios and political recipe books still in use to this day. It is this *antagonism* opening up between industrial society and modernity which distorts our attempts at a 'social mapping', since we are so thoroughly accustomed to conceiving of modernity *within* the categories of industrial society. The thesis of this book is: we are witnessing not the end but the *beginning* of modernity – that is, of a modernity *beyond* its classical industrial design.

This distinction between modernization *of tradition* and modernization *of industrial society*, or expressed differently, between *classical* and *reflexive* modernization, will occupy us for quite some time. In the following pages this will be alluded to in a journey through the various spheres of contemporary life. It is not yet apparent which pillars of the mentality of the industrial society will crumble in this second rationalization that is only just beginning today. But it can be surmised with good reason that this will apply even to the most foundational of these, for example, functional differentiation or factory-bound mass production.

There are two consequences which emerge from this unfamiliar perspective. It maintains what until now seemed unthinkable: that in its mere continuity industrial society *exits the stage of world history on the tip-toes of normality, via the back stairs of side effects*, and not in the manner predicted in the picture books of social theory: with a political explosion (revolution, democratic elections). Furthermore, this perspective implies that the counter-modernistic scenario currently upsetting the world – new social movements and criticism of science, technology and progress – does not stand in contradiction of modernity, but is rather an expression of reflexive modernization beyond the outlines of industrial society.[1]

The global impact of modernity comes into opposition to its limitations and rigidities in the project of industrial society. The access to this view is blocked by an unbroken, as yet barely recognized *myth*, in which the social thought of the nineteenth century was essentially trapped, and which still casts a shadow into the last third of the twentieth century. This myth asserts that developed industrial society with its pattern of work and life, its production sectors, its thinking in categories of economic growth, its understanding of science and technology and its forms of democracy, is a *thoroughly modern* society, a pinnacle of modernity, which it scarcely makes sense even to consider surpassing.

This myth has many forms of expression. Among the most effective is the mad joke of the *end of history*. This idea is especially fascinating to the very epoch in which innovation is set free permanently from traditional burdens. Or, alternatively, we cannot conceive of the coming of another modernity because, as far as our categories go, there cannot be one. The classical theoreticians of industrial society or industrial capitalism have transformed their historical experience into necessities, into hidden apriorities. The Kantian-inspired question – what makes society possible? – has been transformed into a question regarding the functional prerequisites of capitalism and the necessities of modernity in general. The curious way with which it has been thus far alleged in social research that everything essential in industrial society *changes* – family, profession, factory, class, wage labor, science, technology – but simultaneously that these very same things in principle do *not* change, is only further evidence for this fact. In the general view, industrial society is a permanently revolutionary society. But after each industrial revolution what remains is an industrial society, perhaps that bit more industrial. This is the story of modern sociology.

More urgently than ever, we need ideas and theories that will allow us to conceive the new which is rolling over us in a new way, and allow us to live and act within it. At the same time we must retain good relations with the treasures of tradition, without a misconceived and sorrowful turn to the new, which always remains old anyway. Tracking down new categories, which are already beginning to appear with the decay of the old ones, is a difficult undertaking. To some it smacks of 'changing the system' and putting into jeopardy constitutionally guaranteed 'natural rights'. Others have taken refuge in central convictions – which can take many forms: neo-Marxism, feminism, quantitative methods, specialization – and in view of adopted loyalties forced upon themselves against their own wishes they strike out blindly at anything that gives off the scent of deviationism.

Nonetheless, or perhaps for that very reason, the world is not coming to an end, at least not because the world of the nineteenth century is coming to an end today. And even that is exaggerated. As we know, the social world of the nineteenth century was actually never all that stable. It has already perished several times – in thought. In that realm it was already buried before it was properly born. We know today how the late nineteenth century visions of a Nietzsche or how stage productions of the marriage and family dramas of 'classical' (which means: old) literary modernism actually take place every day in our kitchens and bedrooms on the threshold of the twenty-first century. Thus, things thought of long ago are happening now with a delay of, roughly, a half or even a whole century.

We also experience – transcending what was previously conceived in literature – that one must continue to live after the narrative is over. We thus experience so to speak what happens after the curtain has fallen in an Ibsen drama. We experience the off-stage reality of the post-bourgeois epoch. Or, with respect to the risks of civilization: we are the heirs of a cultural criticism that has become rigid, and can thus no longer be satisfied with the diagnoses of cultural criticism, which was always meant more as a kind of admonitory pessimism. An entire epoch cannot slide into a space beyond the previous defining categories, without that 'beyond' being recognized and cast off for what it is: the artificially prolonged authority claim of a past which has seen the present and the future slip out of its hands.

This book is, then, about 'reflexive modernization' of industrial society. This guiding idea is developed from two angles. First, the intermingling of continuity and discontinuity is discussed with the examples of *wealth production* and *risk production*. The argument is that, while in classical industrial society the 'logic' of wealth production dominates the 'logic' of risk production, in the risk society this relationship is reversed (Part I). The productive forces have lost their innocence in the reflexivity of modernization processes. The gain in power from techno-economic 'progress' is being increasingly overshadowed by the production of risks. In an early stage, these can be legitimated as 'latent side effects'. As they become globalized, and subject to public criticism and scientific investigation, they come, so to speak, out of the closet and achieve a central importance in social and political debates. This 'logic' of risk production and distribution is developed in comparison to the 'logic' of the distribution of wealth (which has so far determined social-theoretical thinking). At the center lie the risks and consequences of modernization, which are revealed as irreversible threats to the life of plants, animals, and human beings. Unlike the factory-related or occupational hazards of the nineteenth and the first half of the twentieth centuries, these can no longer be limited to certain localities or groups, but rather exhibit a tendency to globalization which spans production *and* reproduction as much as national borders, and in this sense brings into being *supra*-national and *non*-class-specific *global hazards* with a new type of social and political dynamism (Chapters 1 and 2).

These 'social hazards' and their cultural and political potential are, however, only one side of the risk society. The other side comes into view when one places the *immanent contradictions between modernity and counter-modernity within industrial society* at the center of discussion (Parts II and III). On the one hand, industrial society is planned as an extended group society in the sense of a class or stratified society yesterday, today and for the entire future. On the other hand, classes remain reliant on the validity of social class *cultures* and *traditions*, which in the course of post-war development are in the process of losing their traditional character (Chapter 3).

On the one hand, in industrial society, social life within the framework of the nuclear family becomes normative and standardized. On the other hand, the nuclear family is based on ascribed and, so to speak, 'feudal' sex roles for men and women, which begin to crumble with the continuation of modernization processes (inclusion of women in the work process, increasing frequency of divorce, and so on). But with that the relationship of production and reproduction begins to shift, like everything else connected to the industrial 'tradition of the nuclear family': marriage, parenthood, sexuality, love, and the like (Chapter 4).

On the one hand, industrial society is conceived of in terms of the (*industrial*) *work society*. But, on the other hand, current rationalization takes direct aim at the ordered pattern of that society: flexibilization of work times and places blurs the boundaries between work and non-work. Microelectronics permits a new networking of departments, plants and consumers over and above the production sectors. But with that the previous legal and social premises of the employment system are 'modernized away': mass unemployment is integrated into the occupation system in new forms of *pluralized under*employment, with all the associated hazards and opportunities (Chapter 6).

On the one hand, science and thus *methodical skepticism* are institutionalized in industrial society. On the other hand, this skepticism is (at first) limited to the external, the objects of research, while the foundations and consequences of scientific work remain shielded against internally fomented skepticism. This division of skepticism is just as necessary for the ends of professionalization as it is unstable in the face of the suspicion of fallibility: the continuity of scientific-technical development runs through a discontinuity in its internal and external relations. Reflexive modernization here means that skepticism is extended to the foundations and hazards of scientific work and science is thus both *generalized* and *demystified* (Chapter 7).

On the one hand, the claims and the forms of *parliamentary democracy* are established along with industrial society. On the other, the scope of validity of these principles is *truncated*. Sub-political innovation institutionalized as 'progress' remains under the jurisdiction of business, science and technology, for whom democratic procedures are invalid. This becomes problematic in the continuity of reflexive modernization processes where in the face of increased or hazardous productive forces the sub-politics has taken over the leading role from politics in shaping society (Chapter 8).

In other words: components of a *traditionality inherent in industrialism* are inscribed in varied ways within the architecture of industrial society – in the patterns of 'classes', 'nuclear family', 'professional work', or in the understanding of 'science', 'progress', 'democracy' – and their foundations begin to crumble and disintegrate in the reflexivity of modernization. Strange as it might sound, the epochal irritations aroused by this are all results not of the crisis but of the *success* of modernization. It is successful even against its own industrial assumptions and limitations. Reflexive modernization means not less but more modernity, a modernity radicalized *against* the paths and categories of the classical industrial setting.

We are experiencing a transformation of the foundations of change. To conceive of this presumes, however, that the image of industrial society is revised. According to its blueprint it is a *semi*-modern society, whose built-in counter-modern elements are not something old or traditional but rather the *construct and product of the industrial epoch itself*. The concept of industrial society rests upon a *contradiction* between the *universal* principles of modernity – civil rights, equality, functional differentiation, methods of argumentation and skepticism – and the exclusive structure of its institutions, in which these principles can only be realized on a *partial, sectoral* and *selective* basis. The consequence is that industrial society *destabilizes itself through its very establishment*. Continuity becomes the 'cause' of discontinuity. People are *set free* from the certainties and modes of living of the industrial epoch – just as they were 'freed' from the arms of the Church into society during the age of the Reformation. The shocks unleashed by this constitute the other side of the risk society. The system of coordinates in which life and thinking are fastened in industrial modernity – the axes of gender, family and occupation, the belief in science and progress – begins to shake, and a new twilight of opportunities and hazards comes into existence – the contours of the risk society. Opportunities? In the risk society the principles of modernity are redeemed from their separations and limitations in industrial society.

In many ways this book reflects the discovery and learning process of its author. I was wiser at the end of each chapter than at the beginning. There was a great temptation to rewrite and rethink this book from its conclusion. That I did not do that was not just for lack of time. If I had, a new intermediate stage would only have resulted once again. This emphasizes once more the *process* character of the book's argumentation and should not be understood as a blank check to cover objections. For the reader it offers the advantage of being able to read the chapters in isolation or in a different order, and to think them through with a conscious invitation to employ, oppose and supplement the arguments.

Perhaps everyone who is close to me has been confronted at some point with voluminous predecessors to this text and my requests for their comments. Some of them were not entirely pleased with the variants that continually surfaced. Everything filtered into it. This collaboration with mostly younger scholars in the circle of my research activities cannot be adequately acknowledged either in the text or here in the Preface. It was an incredibly encouraging experience for me. Many parts of this text are virtually plagiarisms of personal conversations and shared life. Without any claims to completeness, I wish to thank: Elisabeth Beck-Gernsheim for our extraordinary everyday life, for ideas mutually lived through and for unimpressible lack of respect; Maria Rerrich for many thoughts, conversations and complicated preparations of material; Renate Schütz for her divinely infectious philosophical curiosity and inspiring visions; Wolfgang Bonß for successful exploratory conversations on almost all parts of the text; Peter Berger for providing me with a copy of his helpful objections; Christoph Lau for thinking through and shoring up wrong-headed lines of argument; Hermann Stumpf and Peter Sopp for many hints and for resourcefully providing literature and empirical material; Angelika Schacht and Gerlinde Müller for their reliability and enthusiasm in typing the text.

I have also experienced wonderfully collegial encouragement from Karl Martin Bolte, Heinz Hartmann and Leopold Rosenmayr. Whatever repetitions and false images remain, I herewith declare to be signs of deliberate imperfection.

Anyone who seems to see the sparkling of a lake between the lines is not mistaken. Extensive parts of this text were written in the open on a hill above the Starnberger See and many a commentary by the light, the wind, or the waves was immediately incorporated. This unusual work-place – favored by a generally sunny sky – was made possible by the hospitable solicitude of Frau Ruhdorfer and her entire family, who even kept their children from playing and their animals from grazing too close to me.

An academy grant from the Volkswagenwerk Foundation created the preconditions for the leisure, without which the adventure of this argument would probably never have been undertaken. My Bamberg colleagues Peter Gross and Laszlo Vaskovics agreed to a postponement of their sabbatical semesters for my benefit. I sincerely thank all these people – they bear no responsibility for my mistakes and exaggerations. Particularly included are those who did not disturb my peace and endured my silence.

Note

1 The concept of reflexive modernization has recently been broadly discussed and further developed by Anthony Giddens (1990; 1991) and by Scott Lash (1992).

PART I

Living on the Volcano of Civilization: the Contours of the Risk Society

1

ON THE LOGIC OF WEALTH DISTRIBUTION AND RISK DISTRIBUTION

In advanced modernity the social production of *wealth* is systematically accompanied by the social production of *risks*. Accordingly, the problems and conflicts relating to distribution in a society of scarcity overlap with the problems and conflicts that arise from the production, definition and distribution of techno-scientifically produced risks.

This change from the logic of wealth distribution in a society of scarcity to the logic of risk distribution in late modernity is connected historically to (at least) two conditions. First, it occurs – as is recognizable today – where and to the extent that *genuine material need* can be objectively reduced and socially isolated through the development of human and technological productivity, as well as through legal and welfare-state protections and regulations. Second, this categorical change is likewise dependent upon the fact that in the course of the exponentially growing productive forces in the modernization process, hazards and potential threats have been unleashed to an extent previously unknown.[1]

To the extent that these conditions occur, one historical type of thinking and acting is relativized or overridden by another. The concepts of 'industrial' or 'class society', in the broadest sense of Marx or Weber, revolved around the issue of how socially produced wealth could be distributed in a socially unequal and *also* 'legitimate' way. This overlaps with the new *paradigm of risk society* which is based on the solution of a similar and yet quite different problem. How can the risks and hazards systematically produced as part of modernization be prevented, minimized, dramatized, or channeled? Where they do finally see the light of day in the shape of 'latent side effects', how can they be limited and distributed away so that they neither hamper the modernization process nor exceed the limits of that which is 'tolerable' – ecologically, medically, psychologically and socially?

We are therefore concerned no longer exclusively with making nature useful, or with releasing mankind from traditional constraints, but also and essentially with problems resulting from techno-economic development itself. Modernization is becoming *reflexive*; it is becoming its own theme. Questions of the development and employment of technologies (in the realms of nature, society and the personality) are being eclipsed by questions of the political and economic 'management' of the risks of actually or potentially utilized technologies – discovering, administering, acknowledging, avoiding or concealing such hazards with respect to specially defined horizons of relevance. The promise of security grows with the risks and destruction and must be reaffirmed over and over again to an alert and critical public through cosmetic or real interventions in the techno-economic development.

Both 'paradigms' of inequality are systematic·lly related to definite periods of modernization. The distribution of socially produced wealth and related conflicts occupy the foreground so long as obvious material need, the 'dictatorship of scarcity', rules the thought and action of people (as today in large parts of the so-called Third World). Under these conditions of 'scarcity society', the modernization process takes place with the claim of opening the gates to hidden sources of social wealth with the keys of techno-scientific development. These promises of emancipation from undeserved poverty and dependence underlie action, thought and research in the categories of social inequality, from the class through the stratified to the individualized society.

In the welfare states of the West a double process is taking place now. On the one hand, the struggle for one's 'daily bread' has lost its urgency as a cardinal problem overshadowing everything else, compared to material subsistence in the first half of this century and to a Third World menaced by hunger. For many people problems of 'overweight' take the place of hunger. This development, however, withdraws the legitimizing basis from the modernization process, the struggle against obvious scarcity, for which one was prepared to accept a few (no longer completely) unseen side effects.

Parallel to that, the knowledge is spreading that the sources of wealth are 'polluted' by growing 'hazardous side effects'. This is not at all new, but it has remained unnoticed for a long time in the efforts to overcome poverty. This dark side is also gaining importance through the over-development of productive forces. In the modernization process, more and more *destructive* forces are also being unleashed, forces before which the human imagination stands in awe. Both sources feed a growing critique of modernization, which loudly and contentiously determines public discussions.

In systematic terms, sooner or later in the continuity of modernization the social positions and conflicts of a 'wealth-distributing' society begin to be joined by those of a 'risk-distributing' society. In West Germany we have faced the beginning of this transition since the early 1970s at the latest – that is my thesis. That means that two types of topics and conflicts overlap here. We do not *yet* live in a risk society, but we also no longer live *only* within the distribution conflicts of scarcity societies. To the extent that this transition occurs, there will be a real transformation of society which will lead us out of the previous modes of thought and action.

Can the concept of risk carry the theoretical and historical significance which is demanded of it here? Is this not a primeval phenomenon of human action? Are not risks already characteristic of the industrial society period, against which they are being differentiated here? It is also true that risks are not an invention of modernity. Anyone who set out to discover new countries and continents – like Columbus – certainly accepted 'risks'. But these were _personal_ risks, not global dangers like those that arise for all of humanity from nuclear fission or the storage of radioactive waste. In that earlier period, the word 'risk' had a note of bravery and adventure, not the threat of self-destruction of all life on Earth.

Forests have also been dying for some centuries now – first through being transformed into fields, then through reckless overcutting. But the death of forests today occurs _globally_, as the _implicit_ consequence of industrialization – with quite different social and political consequences. Heavily wooded countries like Norway and Sweden, which hardly have any pollutant-intensive industries of their own, are also affected. They have to settle up the pollution accounts of other highly industrialized countries with dying trees, plants and animal species.

It is reported that sailors who fell into the Thames in the early nineteenth century did not drown, but rather choked to death inhaling the foul-smelling and poisonous fumes of this London sewer. A walk through the narrow streets of a medieval city would also have been like running the gauntlet for the nose. 'Excrement piles up everywhere, in the streets, at the turnpikes, in the carriages . . . The façades of Parisian houses are decomposing from urine . . . the socially organized constipation threatens to pull all of Paris into the process of putrescent decomposition' (Corbin 1984: 41ff.). It is nevertheless striking that hazards in those days assaulted the nose or the eyes and were thus perceptible to the senses, while the risks of civilization today typically _escape perception_ and are localized in the sphere of _physical and chemical formulas_ (e.g. toxins in foodstuffs or the nuclear threat).

Another difference is directly connected to this. In the past, the hazards could be traced back to an _under_supply of hygienic technology. Today they have their basis in industrial _over_production. The risks and hazards of today thus differ in an essential way from the superficially similar ones in the Middle Ages through the global nature of their threat (people, animals and plants) and through their _modern_ causes. They are risks _of modernization_. They are a _wholesale product_ of industrialization, and are systematically intensified as it becomes global.

The concept of risk is directly bound to the concept of reflexive modernization. _Risk_ may be defined as a _systematic way of dealing with hazards and insecurities induced and introduced by modernization itself_. Risks, as opposed to older dangers, are consequences which relate to the threatening force of modernization and to its globalization of doubt. They are _politically reflexive_.

Risks, in this meaning of the word, are certainly as old as that development itself. The immiseration of large parts of the population – the 'poverty risk' – kept the nineteenth century holding its breath. 'Threats to skills' and 'health risks' have long been a theme of automation processes and the related social conflicts, protections (and research). It did take some time and struggle to establish social welfare state norms and minimize or limit these kinds of risk politically. Nevertheless, the ecological and high-tech risks that have upset the public for some years now, which will be the focus of what follows, have a new quality. In the afflictions they produce they are no longer tied to their place of origin – the industrial plant. By their nature they endanger *all* forms of life on this planet. The normative bases of their calculation – the concept of accident and insurance, medical precautions, and so on – do not fit the basic dimensions of these modern threats. Atomic plants, for example, are not privately insured or insurable. Atomic accidents are accidents no more (in the limited sense of the word 'accident'). They outlast generations. The affected even include those not yet alive at the time or in the place where the accident occurred but born years later and long distances away.

This means that the calculation of risk as it has been established so far by science and legal institutions *collapses*. Dealing with these consequences of modern productive and destructive forces in the normal terms of risk is a false but nevertheless very effective way of legitimizing them. Risk scientists normally do so as if there is not the gap of a century between the local accidents of the nineteenth century and the often creeping, catastrophic potentials at the end of the twentieth century. Indeed, if you distinguish between calculable and non-calculable threats, under the surface of risk calculation new kinds of *industrialized, decision-produced incalculabilities and threats* are spreading within the globalization of high-risk industries, whether for warfare or welfare purposes. Max Weber's concept of 'rationalization' no longer grasps this late modern reality, produced by successful rationalization. *Along with the growing capacity of technical options [Zweckrationalität] grows the incalculability of their consequences.* Compared to these global consequences, the hazards of primary industrialization indeed belonged to a different age. The dangers of highly developed nuclear and chemical productive forces abolish the foundations and categories according to which we have thought and acted to this point, such as space and time, work and leisure time, factory and nation state, indeed even the borders between continents. To put it differently, in the risk society the unknown and unintended consequences come to be a dominant force in history and society.[2]

The social architecture and political dynamics of such potentials for self-endangerment in civilization will occupy the center of these discussions. The argument can be set out in five theses:

(1) Risks such as those produced in the late modernity differ essentially from wealth. By risks I mean above all radioactivity, which completely evades human perceptive abilities, but also toxins and pollutants in the air, the water and foodstuffs, together with the accompanying short- and long-term effects on plants, animals and people. They induce systematic

and often *irreversible* harm, generally remain *invisible*, are based on *causal interpretations*, and thus initially only exist in terms of the (scientific or anti-scientific) *knowledge* about them. They can thus be changed, magnified, dramatized or minimized within knowledge, and to that extent they are particularly *open to social definition and construction*. Hence the mass media and the scientific and legal professions in charge of defining risks become key social and political positions.

(2) Some people are more affected than others by the distribution and growth of risks, that is, *social risk positions* spring up. In some of their dimensions these follow the inequalities of class and strata positions, but they bring a fundamentally different distributional logic into play. Risks of modernization sooner or later also strike those who produce or profit from them. They contain a *boomerang effect*, which breaks up the pattern of class and national society. Ecological disaster and atomic fallout ignore the borders of nations. Even the rich and powerful are not safe from them. These are hazards not only to health, but also to legitimation, property and profit. *Connected* to the recognition of modernization risks are *ecological devaluations and expropriations*, which frequently and systematically enter into contradiction to the profit and property interests which advance the process of industrialization. Simultaneously, risks produce *new international inequalities*, firstly between the Third World and the industrial states, secondly among the industrial states themselves. They undermine the order of national jurisdictions. In view of the universality and supra-nationality of the circulation of pollutants, the life of a blade of grass in the Bavarian Forest ultimately comes to depend on the making and keeping of international agreements. Risk society in this sense is a world risk society.

(3) Nevertheless, the diffusion and commercialization of risks do not break with the logic of capitalist development completely, but instead they raise the latter to a new stage. There are always losers but also winners in risk definitions. The space between them varies in relation to different issues and power differentials. Modernization risks from the winners' points of view are *big business*. They are the insatiable demands long sought by economists. Hunger can be sated, needs can be satisfied, but *civilization* risks are a *bottomless barrel of demands*, unsatisfiable, infinite, self-producible. One could say along with Luhmann that with the advent of risks, the economy becomes 'self-referential', independent of the surrounding satisfaction of human needs. But that means: with the economic exploitation of the risks it sets free, industrial society produces the hazards and the political potential of the risk society.

(4) One can *possess* wealth, but one can only be *afflicted* by risks; they are, so to speak, *ascribed* by civilization. [Bluntly, one might say: in class and stratification positions being determines consciousness, while in risk positions *consciousness determines being*.] Knowledge gains a new political significance. Accordingly the political potential of the risk society

must be elaborated and analyzed in a sociological theory of the origin and diffusion of *knowledge about risks*.

(5) Socially recognized risks, as appears clearly in the discussions of forest destruction, contain a peculiar political explosive: what *was* until now *considered unpolitical becomes political – the elimination of the causes in the industrialization process itself*. Suddenly the public and politics extend their rule into the private sphere of plant management – into product planning and technical equipment. What is at stake in the public dispute over the definition of risks is revealed here in an exemplary fashion: not just secondary health problems for nature and mankind, but the *social, economic and political consequences of these side effects* – collapsing markets, devaluation of capital, bureaucratic checks on plant decisions, the opening of new markets, mammoth costs, legal proceedings and loss of face. In smaller or larger increments – a smog alarm, a toxic spill, etc. – what thus emerges in risk society is the *political potential of catastrophes*. Averting and managing these can include a *reorganization of power and authority*. Risk society is a *catastrophic* society. In it the exceptional condition threatens to become the norm.

Scientific Definition and Distributions of Pollutants

The debate on pollutant and toxic elements in air, water and foodstuffs, as well as on the destruction of nature and the environment in general, is still being conducted exclusively or dominantly in the terms and formulas of *natural* science. It remains unrecognized that a social, cultural and political meaning is inherent in such scientific 'immiseration formulas'. There exists accordingly a danger that an environmental discussion conducted exclusively in chemical, biological and technological terms will inadvertently include human beings in the picture only as *organic material*. Thus the discussion runs the risk of making the same mistake for which it has long and justly reproached the prevailing optimism with respect to industrial progress; it runs the risk of atrophying into a discussion of nature *without* people, without asking about matters of social and cultural significance. Particularly the debates over the last few years, in which all arguments critical of technology and industry were once again deployed, have remained at heart *technocratic* and *naturalistic*. They exhausted themselves in the invocation and publication of the pollutant levels in the air, water and foodstuffs, in relative figures of population growth, energy consumption, food requirements, raw material shortages and so on. They did so with a passion and a singlemindedness as if there had never been people such as a certain Max Weber, who apparently wasted his time showing that without including structures of social power and distribution, bureaucracies, prevailing norms and rationalities, such a debate is either meaningless or absurd, and probably both. An understanding has crept in, according to which modernity is reduced to the frame of reference of technology and nature in the manner of perpetrator and victim. The social, cultural and political risks of modernization remain hidden by this very approach, and from this way of thinking (which is also that of the political environmental movement).

Let us illustrate this with an example. The Rat der Sachverständigen für Umweltfragen (Council of Experts on Environmental Issues) determines in a report that 'in mother's milk beta-hexachlorocyclohexane, hexachlorobenzol and DDT are often found in significant concentrations' (1985: 33). These toxic substances are contained in pesticides and herbicides that have by now been taken off the market. According to the report their origin is undetermined (33). At another point it is stated: 'The exposure of the population to lead is not dangerous on average' (35). What is concealed behind that statement? Perhaps by analogy the following distribution. Two men have two apples. One eats both of them. Thus they have eaten *on average* one each. Transferred to the distribution of foodstuffs on the global scale this statement would mean: 'on average' all the people in the world have enough to eat. The cynicism here is obvious. In one part of the Earth people are dying of hunger, while in the other the consequences of overeating have become a major item of expense. It may be, of course, that this statement about pollutants and toxins is *not* cynical, that the *average* exposure is also the *actual* exposure of *all* groups in the population. But do we know that? In order to defend this statement, is it not a prerequisite that we know what other poisons the people are forced to inhale and ingest? It is astonishing how *as a matter of course* one inquires about 'the average'. A person who inquires about the average already excludes many socially unequal risk positions. But that is exactly what that person cannot know. Perhaps there are groups and living conditions for which the levels of lead and the like that are 'on average harmless' constitute a *mortal danger*?

The next sentence of the report reads: 'Only in the vicinity of industrial emitters are dangerous concentrations of lead sometimes found in children.' What is characteristic is not just the absence of any social differentiations in this and other reports on pollutants and toxins. It is also characteristic *how* differentiations are made – along *regional* lines with regard to emission sources and according to *age* differences – both criteria that are rooted in *biological* (or more generally, natural scientific) thinking. This cannot be blamed on the expert committees. It only reflects the general state of scientific and social thought with regard to environmental problems. These are generally viewed as matters of nature and technology, or of economics and medicine. What is astonishing about that is that the industrial pollution of the environment and the destruction of nature, with their multifarious effects on the health and social life of people, which only arise in highly developed societies, are characterized by a *loss of social thinking*. This loss becomes caricature – this absence seems to strike no one, not even sociologists themselves.

People inquire about and investigate the distribution of pollutants, toxins, contamination of water, air, and foodstuffs. The results are presented to an alarmed public on multi-colored 'environmental maps', differentiated along regional lines. To the extent that the state of the environment is to be presented in this way, this mode of presentation and consideration is obviously appropriate. As soon as *consequences for people* are to be drawn from it, however, the underlying thought *short-circuits*. Either one implies broadly that *all* people are *equally* affected in the identified pollution centers – independent of their income, education, occupation and the associated eating, living and recreational opportunities and habits (which would have to be proved). Or one ultimately excludes people and the extent of their affliction entirely and speaks only about pollutants and their distributions and effects on the region.

The pollution debate conducted in terms of natural science correspondingly moves between the false conclusion of social afflictions based on biological ones, and a view of nature which excludes the selective affliction of people as well as the social and cultural meaning connected to it. At the same time what is not taken into consideration is that *the same* pollutants can have quite *different* meanings for *different* people, according to age, gender, eating habits, type of work, information, education and so on.

What is particularly aggravating is that investigations which start from individual pollutants can *never* determine the concentration of pollutants *in people*. What may seem 'insignificant' for a single product, is perhaps extremely significant when collected in the 'consumer reservoirs' which people have become in the advanced stage of total marketing. We are in the presence here of a *category error*. A pollution analysis oriented to nature and products is incapable of answering questions about safety, at least as long as the 'safety' or 'danger' has anything to do with the people who swallow or breathe the stuff. What is known is that the taking of several medications can nullify or amplify the effect of each individual one. Now people obviously do not (yet) live by medications alone. They also breathe the pollutants in the air, drink those in the water, eat those in the vegetables, and so on. In other words, the insignificances can add up quite significantly. Do they thereby become more and more insignificant – as is usual for sums according to the rules of mathematics?

On the Knowledge Dependence of Modernization Risks

Risks like wealth are the object of distributions, and both constitute positions – risk positions and class positions respectively. In each case, however, one is concerned with a quite different good and a quite different controversy on its distribution. In the case of social wealth, one is dealing with consumer goods, incomes, educational opportunities, property, etc. as desirable items in scarcity. By contrast, risks are an *incidental* problem of modernization in *undesirable abundance*. These must be either eliminated or denied and reinterpreted. The *positive logic of acquisition* contrasts with a *negative logic of disposition*, avoidance, denial, and reinterpretation.

While such things as income and education are consumable goods that can be experienced by the individual, the existence of and distribution of risks and hazards are *mediated on principle through argument*. That which impairs health or destroys nature is not recognizable to one's own feeling or eye, and even where it is seemingly in plain view, qualified expert judgment is still required to determine it 'objectively'. Many of the newer risks (nuclear or chemical contaminations, pollutants in foodstuffs, diseases of civilization) completely escape human powers of direct perception. The focus is more and more on hazards which are neither visible nor perceptible to the victims; hazards that in some cases may not even take effect within the lifespans of those affected, but instead during those of their children; hazards in any case that require the 'sensory organs' of science – *theories, experiments, measuring instruments – in order to become visible or interpretable as hazards at all.* The paradigm of these hazards is the gene-altering effects of radioactivity, which, as the reactor accident at Three Mile Island shows, imperceptibly abandon the victims completely to the judgments, mistakes and controversies of experts, while subjecting them to terrible psychological stresses.

Thinking the Separated Together: Presumptions of Causality

The knowledge dependency and invisibility of civilization's risk positions of course do not suffice to define them conceptually; they also contain additional components. Statements on hazards are never reducible to mere statements of fact. As part of their constitution, they contain both a *theoretical* and a *normative* component. The findings 'significant concentrations of lead in children' or 'pesticide substances in mothers' milk' *as such* are no more risk positions of civilization than the nitrate concentrations in the rivers or the sulfur dioxide content of the air. A causal interpretation must be added, which makes this appear to be a product of the industrial mode of production, a systematic side effect of modernization. In socially recognized risks, therefore, the authorities and agents of the modernization process along with all their particular interests and dependencies are presumed, and are placed in a direct connection, in the pattern of cause and effect, with signs of damage and threats that are socially, substantively, spatially and temporally quite detached. The woman sitting in a three-bedroom apartment in a housing estate of suburban Munich and nursing her three-month-old son Martin is in this way 'directly related' to the chemical industry that produces agricultural chemicals, to the farmers who find themselves forced by EEC rules to engage in specialized mass production with overfertilization and so on. The radius in which one can search for side effects remains largely open. Recently an overdose of DDT was even found in Antarctic penguins.

These examples show two things: firstly, that modernization risks appear in geographically specific areas, as well as unspecifically and universally; secondly, how *erratic* and *unpredictable* the tortuous paths of their deleterious effects can be. In modernization risks, then, things which are substantively-objectively, spatially and temporally disparate are drawn together causally and thus brought into a social and legal context of responsibility. As we have known at least since Hume, however, presumptions of causality escape our perception. They must always be imagined, implied to be true, believed. In this sense too, risks are *in*visible. The implied causality always remains more or less uncertain and tentative. Thus we are dealing with a *theoretical* and hence a *scientized* consciousness, even in the everyday consciousness of risks.

Implicit Ethics

Even this causal linking of the institutionally separated does not suffice. Risks experienced presume a *normative horizon* of lost security and broken trust. Hence, even where they approach us silently, clad in numbers and formulas, risks remain fundamentally *localized*, mathematical condensations of wounded images of a life worth living. These ideas must in turn be *believed*, that is, they cannot be experienced *as such*. In this sense, risks are objectified negative images of utopias, in which the human, or what is left of it, is preserved and revived in the modernization process. Despite all its unrecognizability, this normative horizon, in which the riskiness of the risk first becomes tangible, cannot ultimately be removed by mathematics or experiments. Behind all the objectifications, sooner or later the question of *acceptance* arises and with it anew the old question: *how do we wish to live*? What is the human quality of humankind, the natural quality of nature which is to be preserved? The spreading talk of 'catastrophe' is in this sense an objectivized, pointed, radicalized expression that this development is *not wanted*.

These revived questions – what is humankind? what do we think about nature? – may be shunted back and forth between everyday life, politics and science. In the most advanced developmental stage of civilization they once again occupy a very high place on the agenda, even or *especially* where they were supposed to have been made invisible by their traditional magic cap of mathematical formulas and methodological controversies. Determinations of risks are the form in which ethics, and with it also philosophy, culture and politics, is resurrected *inside* the centers of modernization – in business, the natural sciences and the technical disciplines. They are, one might say, an unwanted means of democratization in the fields of industrial production and management, which somehow does become public discussion, depending on risk reasoning. Risk determinations are an unrecognized, still undeveloped symbiosis of the natural and the human sciences, of everyday and expert rationality, of interest and fact. They are simultaneously neither simply the one nor only the other. They can no longer be isolated from one another through specialization, and developed and set down according to their own standards of rationality. They require a cooperation across the trenches of disciplines, citizens' groups, factories, administration and politics, or – which is more likely – they disintegrate between these into antagonistic definitions and *definitional struggles*.

Scientific and Social Rationality

Herein lies the essential and momentous consequence: in definitions of risks the *sciences' monopoly on rationality is broken.* There are always competing and conflicting claims, interests and viewpoints of the various agents of modernity and affected groups, which are forced together in defining risks in the sense of cause and effect, instigator and injured party. There is no expert on risk. Many scientists do go to work with the entire impetus and pathos of their objective rationality, and their effort to be objective grows in proportion to the political content of their definitions. But at the center of their work they continue to be reliant on social and thus prescribed expectations and values. Where and how does one draw the line between *still* acceptable and *no longer* acceptable exposures? How susceptible to compromise are the presupposed standards? Should the possibility of an ecological catastrophe be accepted, for instance, in order to satisfy economic interests? What are necessities, *supposed* necessities, and necessities *that must be changed*?

Science's rationality claim to be able to investigate objectively the hazardousness of a risk permanently refutes itself. It is based, firstly, on a house of cards of speculative assumptions, and moves exclusively within a framework of *probability statements*, whose prognoses of safety cannot even be refuted, strictly speaking, by *actual* accidents. Secondly, one must assume an *ethical point of view* in order to discuss risks meaningfully at all. Risk determinations are *based* on mathematical *possibilities* and social interests, especially, if they are presented with technical certainty. In dealing with civilization's risks, the sciences have always abandoned their foundation of experimental logic and made a polygamous marriage with business, politics and ethics – or more precisely, they live with the latter in a sort of 'permanent marriage without a license'.

This hidden external determination in risk research becomes a problem at the very least when scientists still appear with a monopoly claim on rationality. The studies of reactor safety restrict themselves to the estimation of certain *quantifiable* risks on the basis of *probable* accidents. The dimensions of the hazard are limited from the very beginning to *technical manageability*. In some circles it is said that risks which are not yet technically manageable do not exist – at least not in scientific calculation or jurisdictional judgment. These uncalculable threats add up to an unknown residual risk which becomes the industrial endowment for everyone everywhere. For large segments of the population and for opponents of nuclear energy, its *catastrophic potential* is central. No matter how small an accident probability is held, it is too large when *one* accident means annihilation. But the quantifiable concepts of risk concentrate on the probable occurrence of an accident and deny the difference, let us say, between a limited aircraft crash and the explosion of an atomic plant, improbable as it might be, which affects nations and generations not yet born. Furthermore, in the public discussions, hazardous qualities have roles which are not dealt with at all in the risk studies, such as the proliferation of nuclear weapons; the changeability of chemical and atomic technologies from civil to military uses and purposes; the gray zone between normal and war production, which expands with expanding risk industries and markets all over the world; the contradiction between humanity (mistakes and failures) and safety; or the length and irreversibility of mega-technological decisions that trifle with the lives of future generations. There is no perfect system, and no perfect human being who fits its necessities. Even trying to establish something like a perfect system would mean to establish perfect control, some kind of dictatorship in everyday life.

In other words, what becomes clear in risk discussions are the fissures and gaps between *scientific* and *social* rationality in dealing with the hazardous potential of civilization. The two sides talk past each other. Social movements raise questions that are not answered by the risk technicians at all, and the technicians answer questions which miss the point of what was really asked and what feeds public anxiety.

Scientific and social rationality do indeed break apart, but they remain at the same time interwoven and interdependent. Strictly speaking, even this distinction is becoming less and less possible. The scientific concern with the risks of industrial development in fact relies on social expectations and value judgments, just as the social discussion and perception of risks depend on scientific arguments. Risk research follows with some embarrassment in the footsteps of 'technophobia' which it was called upon to restrain, and from which, moreover, it has received an undreamed-of material support in recent years. Public criticism and disquiet derive essentially from the dialectic of expertise and counter-expertise. Without scientific arguments and scientific critique of scientific arguments they remain *dull*; indeed, they cannot even perceive the mainly 'invisible' object and event of their critique and fears. To modify a famous phrase: scientific rationality without social rationality remains *empty*, but social rationality without scientific rationality remains *blind*.

The above is not supposed to outline an image of general harmony. On the contrary, what is addressed are frequently competing rationality claims, struggling for acceptance. In both camps quite different things occupy the center of attention and different things are considered variable or held constant. In one camp the primary emphasis for change lies on the industrial mode of production, in the other on the technological manageability of accident probabilities.

The Multiplicity of Definitions: More and More Risks

The theoretical content and the value reference of risks imply additional components: the observable *conflictual pluralization and multiplicity of definitions of civilization's risks*. There occurs, so to speak, an over-production of risks, which sometimes relativize, sometimes supplement and sometimes outdo one another. One hazardous product might be defended by dramatizing the risks of the others (for example, the dramatization of climatic consequences 'minimizes' the risk of nuclear energy). Every interested party attempts to defend itself with risk defini-tions, and in this way to ward off risks which could affect its pocketbook. The endangering of the soil, plants, air, water and animals occupies a special place in this struggle of all against all for the most beneficial risk definition, to the extent that it expresses the *common good* and the vote of those who themselves have neither vote nor voice (perhaps only a passive franchise for grass and earthworms will bring humanity to its senses). This pluralism is evident in the scope of risks; the urgency and existence of risks fluctuate with the variety of values and interests. That this has an effect on the substantive element of risks is less obvious.

The causal nexus produced in risks between actual or potential damag-ing effects and the system of industrial production opens an almost infinite number of individual explanations. Actually, one can relate everything to everything else, at least experimentally, so long as the basic pattern is retained – modernization as the cause, damage as the side effect. Much will not be able to be corroborated. Even what has been corroborated will have to maintain itself against systematic and lasting skepticism. It is essential, however, that even in the incalculable profusion of individual interpretations, *individual* conditions are again and again related to each other. Let us pick out forest destruction. So long as bark beetles, squirrels or the particular responsible forestry office were still being considered as causes and guilty parties, we were seemingly concerned not with a 'risk of modernization', but rather with sloppy forestry or animal voracity.

A quite different spectrum of causes and guilty parties is opened up when this typical local misdiagnosis, which risks always have to break through in order to be acknowledged, is overcome and the destruction of the forest is understood and recognized as an effect of *industrialization*. Only then does it become a long-term, systematically caused problem, which can no longer be alleviated at the local level, but instead requires *political* solutions. Once this change in views has become established, many other things become possible. Is it sulfur dioxide, nitrogen oxides, their photochemical breakdown products, hydrocarbons, or something else as yet totally unknown, which are giving us the final and eternal autumn – the falling leaves? These chemical formulas appear to stand alone. Behind them, however, companies, industrial sectors, business, scientific and professional groups move into the firing line of public criticism. For every socially recognized 'cause' comes under massive pressure for change, and with it, the system of action in which it originated. Even if this public pressure is fended off, sales drop, markets collapse and the 'trust' of customers has to be won back and strengthened by large, expensive advertising campaigns. Is the automobile the 'chief polluter of the nation' and thus the real 'forest killer'? Or is it finally time to install high-quality, state-of-the-art scrubbing apparatus in coal-fired power plants? Or would that too perhaps prove useless, since the pollutants which cause the forest to die are delivered 'free to our doorstep' (or 'free to our forest') from the smokestacks and exhaust pipes of neighboring countries?

Everywhere the spotlight in search of a cause falls, fire breaks out, so to speak, and the hastily assembled and poorly equipped 'argumentation fire company' must try to put it out with a powerful stream of counter-arguments, and save whatever can still be saved. Those who find themselves in the public pillory as risk producers refute the charges as well as they can, with the aid of a 'counter-science' gradually becoming institutionalized in industry, and attempt to bring in other causes and thus other originators. The picture reproduces itself. Access to the media becomes crucial. The insecurity within industry intensifies: no one knows who will be struck next by the anathema of ecological morality. Good arguments, or at least arguments capable of convincing the public, become a condition of business success. Publicity people, the 'argumentation craftsmen', get their opportunity in the organization.

Chains of Causality and Cycles of Damage: the Concept of System

To put it again bluntly, all these effects set in quite independently of how tenable the implied causal interpretations may appear from a possible scientific perspective. Generally, opinions within the sciences and disciplines concerned diverge wildly anyway. *The social effect of risk definitions is therefore not dependent on their scientific validity.*

This diversity of interpretations, however, also has its basis in the logic of modernization risks themselves. After all, the attempt is being made here to relate destructive effects to individual factors that can scarcely be isolated within the complex system of the industrial mode of production. The systemic interdependence of the highly specialized agents of modernization in business, agriculture, the law and politics corresponds to the absence of isolable single causes and responsibilities. Is agriculture contaminating the soil, or are the farmers merely the weakest link in the chain of destructive cycles? Are they perhaps just dependent and subordinate markets for the chemical feed and fertilizer industries, and are they where one should apply leverage for a preventive decontamination of the soil? The authorities could have forbidden or drastically limited the sale of toxic chemicals long ago. But they do not do it. On the contrary, with the support of science they continually issue licenses for the 'harmless' production of toxic chemicals that are cutting us all to the quick (and deeper still). Who will take the hot potato: the authorities, science or politics? But they do not till the soil, after all. So it is the farmers? But they were squeezed by the EEC, they have to practice fertilizer-intensive overproduction in order to survive . . .

In other words, corresponding to the highly differentiated division of labor, there is a general complicity, and the complicity is matched by a general lack of responsibility. Everyone is cause *and* effect, and thus *non-cause.* The causes dribble away into a general amalgam of agents and conditions, reactions and counter-reactions, which brings social certainty and popularity to the concept of system.

This reveals in exemplary fashion the ethical significance of the system concept: *one can do something and continue doing it without having to take personal responsibility for it.* It is as if one were acting while being personally absent. One acts physically, without acting morally or politically. The generalized other – the system – acts within and through oneself: this is the slave morality of civilization, in which people act personally and socially as if they were subject to a natural fate, the 'law of gravitation' of the system. This is the way the 'hot potato' is passed in the face of the threatening ecological disaster.[3]

The Risk Content: the Not-Yet-Event as Stimulus to Action

Risks of course do not exhaust themselves in the effects and damages that have already occurred. There must be a distinction between *already destructive consequences* and the *potential element* of risks. In this second sense, risks essentially express a *future* component. This is based in part on the prolonging of currently calculable damages into the future, and in part on a general loss of confidence or on 'risk multipliers'. By nature, then, risks have something to do with anticipation, with destruction that has not yet happened but is threatening, and of course in that sense risks are already real today. An example from the Rat der Sachverständigen für Umweltfragen (1985): the Council notes that the high nitrate concentrations from nitrogen fertilizers have so far barely if at all seeped down to the deep ground water from which we draw our drinking water. The nitrates are largely broken down in the subsoil. It is not known, though, how this happens or how long it will continue. There are good reasons not to project the filtering effect of this protective layer into the future without reservations. 'It is to be feared that the current leaching of nitrate will also have reached deeper layers of ground water years or decades from now, with a delay corresponding to the flow time' (29). In other words: the time bomb is ticking. In this sense risks signify a future which is to be prevented.

By contrast to the tangible clarity of wealth, risks have something *unreal* about them. In a fundamental sense they are both *real* and *unreal.*

On the one hand, many hazards and damages are already real today: polluted and dying bodies of water, the destruction of the forest, new types of disease, and so on. On the other hand, the actual social impetus of risks lies in the *projected dangers of the future*. In this sense there are hazards which, if they occur, would mean destruction on such a scale that action afterwards would be practically impossible. Therefore, even as conjectures, as threats to the future, as prognoses, they have and develop a practical relevance to preventive actions. The center of risk consciousness lies not in the present, but *in the future*. In the risk society, the past loses the power to determine the present. Its place is taken by the future, thus, something non-existent, invented, fictive as the 'cause' of current experience and action. We become active today in order to prevent, alleviate or take precautions against the problems and crises of tomorrow and the day after tomorrow – or not to do so. Bottlenecks in the labor market projected in mathematical models have a direct effect on educational behavior. Anticipated, threatening unemployment is an essential determinant of the conditions of and attitude towards life today. The predicted destruction of the environment and the nuclear threat upset society and bring large portions of the younger generation into the streets. In the discussion of the future we are dealing with a 'projected variable', a 'projected cause' of present (personal and political) action. The relevance and importance of these variables is directly proportional to their unpredictability and their threat, and we (must) project the latter in order to determine and organize our present actions.

Legitimation: 'Latent Side Effects'

This presupposes, of course, that risks have successfully passed through a process of social recognition. At first, risks are, however, goods to be avoided, *whose non-existence is implied until canceled* – according to the motto *'in dubio pro progress'*, which means *'in dubio pro looking away'*. A mode of legitimation is clearly connected to this, one which differs clearly from the unequal distribution of social wealth. Risks can be legitimated by the fact that one neither *saw nor wanted their consequences*. Risk positions first have to break through the protective shield of taboos surrounding them, and 'be born scientifically' in scientized civilization. This generally happens as the status of a 'latent side effect', which simultaneously admits and legitimates the reality of the hazard. What was not seen could not be prevented, was produced with the best intentions, and is an unwanted problem child of the objective in mind. 'Latent side effect' thus stands for a type of license, a *natural fate* of civilization, which simultaneously confesses to, selectively distributes and justifies undesirable consequences.

Class-Specific Risks

The type, pattern and media for the distribution of risks differ systematically from those of the distribution of wealth. That does not exclude risks from often being distributed in a stratified or class-specific way. In this sense there are broad overlapping areas between class and risk society. The history of risk distribution shows that, like wealth, risks adhere to the class pattern, only inversely: wealth accumulates at the top, risks at the bottom. To that extent, risks seem to *strengthen*, not to abolish, the class society. Poverty attracts an unfortunate abundance of risks. By contrast, the wealthy (in income, power or education) can *purchase* safety and freedom from risk. This 'law' of the class-specific distribution of risks and thus of the intensification of class antagonisms through the concentration of risks among the poor and the weak was valid for a long time and still applies today to some central dimensions of risk. The risk of becoming unemployed is considerably higher for unskilled than for skilled workers. Risks from stress, radiation and toxic chemicals that are connected to working in the corresponding industrial plants are unevenly distributed among specific occupations. It is especially the cheaper residential areas for low-income groups near centers of industrial production that are permanently exposed to various pollutants in the air, the water and the soil. A higher tolerance can be obtained with the threat of a loss of income.

Here it is not just this social filtering or amplification effect which produces class-specific afflictions. The possibilities and abilities to deal with risks, avoid them or compensate for them are probably unequally divided among the various occupational and educational strata. Whoever has the necessary long-term financial cushion at hand can attempt to avoid risk through the choice of a place of residence or the set-up of the residence itself (or through a second house, vacations, etc.). The same is true for nutrition, education and the related behavior patterns in eating and informing oneself. A sufficiently well filled wallet puts one in a position to dine on eggs from 'contented hens' and salads from 'pampered heads of lettuce'. Education and attentiveness to information open up new possibilities of dealing with and avoiding risks. One can avoid certain products (e.g. liver from old steers with high levels of lead), and through sophisticated nutritional techniques one can vary the weekly menu so that the heavy metals in North Sea fish are dissolved, supplemented or neutralized by the toxic chemicals in pork and tea (or maybe they are intensified after all?). Cooking and eating are becoming a kind of *implicit food chemistry*, a kind of witch's cauldron in reverse, meant to minimize harmful effects. Here quite extensive knowledge is required in order use 'nutritional engineering' to play a little private trick on the overproduction of pollutants and toxins in the chemical and agricultural industries. Nonetheless, it is very probable that class-specifically distributed 'anti-chemical' nutritional and living habits *depend on knowledge* and will emerge in reaction to news about pollution in the press and television. In 'nutritionally aware', well heeled segments of the population, this every-day 'anti-chemistry' (often brought neatly packaged to consumers as an offshoot of the chemical industry) will turn every area of subsistence inside out – from food to housing, from illness to leisure behavior (and it has already done that). From this, one could derive the general assess-ment that through these reflective and well financed dealings with risks the old social inequalities are strengthened on a *new* level. But that does *not* strike at the heart of the distributional logic of risks.

Parallel to the intensification of risk positions, the private escape routes and possibilities for compensation shrink and are simultaneously propagated. The exponential growth of risks, the impossibility of escaping from them, political abstinence and the announcement and sale of private escape opportunities *condition* one another. For *some* foods this private evasive action may still help, but already in the water supply all the social strata are connected to the same pipe. When one looks at 'forest skeletons' in 'rural idylls' far removed from industry, it becomes clear that the class-specific barriers fall before the air we all breathe. In these circumstances, only *not* eating, *not* drinking and *not* breathing could provide effective protection. And even that only helps to a degree. After all, we know what is happening to the stone in buildings and the lichens on the ground.

Globalizing the Risks of Civilization

Reduced to a formula: *poverty is hierarchic, smog is democratic.* With the expansion of modernization risks – with the endangering of nature, health, nutrition, and so on – the social differences and limits are relativized. Very different consequences continue to be drawn from this. *Objectively*, however, risks display an *equalizing* effect within their scope and among those affected by them. It is precisely therein that their novel political power resides. In this sense risk societies are *not* exactly class societies; their risk positions cannot be understood as class positions, or their conflicts as class conflicts.

This becomes even clearer when one inspects the particular style, the particular distribution pattern of modernization risks. They possess an *inherent tendency towards globalization.* A universalization of hazards accompanies industrial production, independent of the place where they are produced: food chains connect practically everyone on earth to everyone else. They dip under borders. The acid content of the air is not only nibbling at sculptures and artistic treasures, it also long ago brought about the disintegration of modern customs barriers. Even in Canada the lakes have become acidified, and forests are dying even in the northern reaches of Scandinavia.

The globalization tendency brings about afflictions, which are once again unspecific in their generality. Where everything turns into a hazard, somehow nothing is dangerous anymore. Where there is no escape, people ultimately no longer want to think about it. This eschatological eco-fatalism allows the pendulum of private and political moods to swing in *any* direction. The risk society shifts from hysteria to indifference and vice versa. Action belongs to yesterday anyway. Perhaps one can get at the omnipresent and everlasting pesticides with (in)sects?

The Boomerang Effect

Contained within the globalization and yet clearly differentiated from it is a distribution pattern of risks which contains a considerable amount of political explosive. Sooner or later the risks also catch up with those who produce or profit from them. Risks display a social *boomerang effect* in their diffusion: even the rich and powerful are not safe from them. The formerly 'latent side effects' strike back even at the centers of their production. The agents of modernization themselves are emphatically caught in the maelstrom of hazards that they unleash and profit from. This can happen in a multitude of ways.

Take the example of agriculture once again. In Germany, the consumption of artificial fertilizer grew from 143 to 378 kilograms per hectare over the period 1951 to 1983, and the use of agricultural chemicals rose from 25,000 to 35,000 tonnes between 1975 and 1983. The yields per hectare also rose, but not nearly as fast as the expense for fertilizer and pesticides. Yields doubled for grain and were 20 percent higher for potatoes. A disproportionately *small* increase of yields in relation to the use of fertilizer and chemicals contrasts with a disproportionately *large* increase in the natural destruction that is visible and painful to the farmer.

An outstanding index of this alarming development is the strong decrease in many wild plant and animal species. The 'red lists' that serve as official 'death certificates' to record these threats to existence are growing longer and longer.

Of 680 plant species occurring in Greenland, 519 are endangered. The populations of bird species dependent on meadows, such as the white stork, the curlew, or the whinchat, are decreasing drastically; people are trying to preserve the last flocks in Bavaria through a 'meadow birds program' . . . The affected animals include ground nesting birds, animals at the top of food chains like predatory birds, owls and dragonflies, or those specialized in food which is becoming scarce, for instance large insects or flower nectar available through the whole growing season. (Rat der Sachverständigen für Umweltfragen 1985: 20)

Formerly 'unseen secondary effects' thus become visible primary effects which endanger their causal production centers themselves. The production of modernization risks follows the *boomerang curve*. Intensive industrial agriculture, subsidized with billions, does not just cause the lead content in mothers' milk and children to rise dramatically in distant cities. It also frequently undermines the natural basis of agricultural production itself: the fertility of the soil declines, vitally important animals and plants disappear, and the danger of soil erosion grows.

The circularity of this social endangering can be generalized: under the roof of modernization risks, *perpetrator and victim* sooner or later become *identical*. In the worst, unthinkable case, a nuclear world war, this is evident; it also destroys the aggressor. Here it becomes clear that the Earth has become an ejector seat that no longer recognizes any distinctions between rich and poor, black and white, north and south or east and west. But the effect only exists when it occurs, and when it occurs, it no longer exists, because nothing exists any more. This apocalyptic threat therefore leaves behind no tangible traces *in the now* of its threat (Anders 1983). That is different in the ecological crisis. It undermines even the economic foundations of agriculture, and thus the food supply of the people themselves. Here effects are visible which make their mark not just in nature, but also in the pocketbooks of the wealthy and the health of the powerful. From competent authorities, and not divided along party lines at all, one can hear quite shrill, apocalyptic sounds in this field.

Ecological Devaluation and Expropriation

The boomerang effect need not manifest itself as a direct threat to life; it can also affect secondary media, money, property and legitimation. It does not just strike back directly at the individual source; in a wholesale, egalitarian way it impairs everyone. The destruction of forests does not just cause bird species to disappear, but also makes the economic value of land and forest property shrink. Where a nuclear or coal-fired power plant is being built or planned, land prices fall. Urban and industrial areas, freeways and thoroughfares all pollute their vicinity. It may still be a matter of debate whether 7 percent of the land in Germany is already so polluted from these causes that in good conscience no agriculture should be carried out there, or whether this will not occur until some point in the near future. The principle, however, is the same: property is being devalued, it is undergoing a creeping *ecological expropriation*.

This effect can be generalized. The destruction and endangering of nature and the environment, news of toxic substances in foodstuffs and consumer articles, threatening – and worse yet, actual – chemical, toxic or reactor accidents have the effect of a creeping or galloping devaluation and expropriation of property rights. Through the unrestrained production of modernization risks, a policy of *making the Earth uninhabitable* is being conducted in continuing leaps and bounds, and sometimes in catastrophic intensifications. What is being opposed as a 'communist menace' is occurring as the sum of our own actions via the detour through a contaminated nature. On the battlefield of market opportunities, beyond the doctrinal wars of ideology, everyone is pursuing a 'scorched Earth' policy against everyone else – with resounding but seldom lasting success.

What is contaminated or considered contaminated may belong to whomever you will – for the loss of social and economic value the distinction is inconsequential. Even if legal title to ownership is maintained, it will become useless and worthless. In the case of 'ecological expropriation' we are thus concerned with a *social and economic expropriation while legal ownership continues*. This applies to foodstuffs as much as to the air, the soil and the water. It applies to everything that lives *in* them, and above all, to those who live *from* what lives in them. The talk of 'residential toxins' makes it clear that everything that constitutes the culture of our everyday life can be included here.

The basic insight lying behind all this is as simple as possible: everything which threatens life on this Earth also threatens the property and commercial interests of those who live *from* the commodification of life and its requisites. In this way a genuine and systematically intensifying *contradiction* arises between the profit and property interests that advance the industrialization process and its frequently threatening consequences, which endanger and expropriate possessions and profits (not to mention the possession and profit of life).

With reactor accidents or chemical catastrophes, 'blank spots' on the map arise again in the most advanced stage of civilization. They are monuments of what threatens us. Even toxic accidents, or suddenly discovered toxic waste dumps, transform housing estates into *toxic waste* estates and turn farmland into *waste*land. But there are many preliminary and insidious forms. The fish from the contaminated seas endanger not just the people who eat them, but *because of that*, also all the many people who make a living *from* fishing. During smog alerts the land dies temporarily. Entire industrial regions are transformed into eerie ghost towns. Such is the will of the boomerang effect: even the wheels of the polluting industries come to a halt. But not only theirs. *Smog cares not a jot about the polluter pays principle.* On a wholesale and egalitarian basis it strikes everyone, independently of his or her share in smog production. Thus, smog is certainly not an advertising factor for sanatoriums, certainly not a big seller. The legally established requirement to publicize effectively the maximum smog levels in the air at such establishments (like air and water temperatures) ought to turn the spa administrations and the resort industry into committed supporters of a pollution-fighting policy – even though they have so far advocated policies against setting standards.

Risk Positions are not Class Positions

In this way, with the globalization of risks a social dynamic is set in motion, which can no longer be composed of and understood in class categories. Ownership implies non-ownership and thus a social relationship of tension and conflict, in which reciprocal social identities can continually evolve and solidify – 'them up there, us down here'. The situation is quite different for risk positions. Anyone affected by them is badly off, but deprives the others, the non-affected, of nothing. Expressed in an analogy: the 'class' of the 'affected' does not confront a 'class' that is not affected. It confronts at most a 'class' of not-yet-affected people. The escalating scarcity of health will drive even those still well off today (in health and well-being) into the ranks of the 'soup kitchens' provided by insurance companies tomorrow, and the day after tomorrow into the pariah community of the invalid and the wounded.

The perplexity of authorities in the face of toxic accidents and toxic waste scandals, and the avalanche of legal, jurisdictional and compensation issues that is triggered each time, all speak a clear language. To wit, freedom from risk can turn overnight into irreversible affliction. The conflicts that arise around modernization risks occur around *systematic causes* that coincide with the motor of progress and profit. They relate to the scale and expansion of hazards and the ensuing demands for compensation and/or a fundamental change of course. In those conflicts what is at stake is the issue of whether we can continue the exploitation of nature (including our own), and thus, whether our concepts of 'progress', 'prosperity', 'economic growth', or 'scientific rationality' are still correct. In this sense, the conflicts that erupt here take on the character of *doctrinal struggles* within *civilization* over the proper road for modernity. In many respects, these resemble the doctrinal struggles of the Middle Ages more than the class conflicts of the nineteenth and early twentieth centuries.

Neither do industrial risks and destruction have any respect for national boundaries. They couple the life of a blade of grass in the Bavarian Forest ultimately to effective international agreements on fighting pollution. The *supra*-nationality of the movement of pollution can no longer be dealt with by individual national efforts. The industrial countries must agree from now on to be distinguished according to their *national balances of emissions or immissions*. In other words, *international inequalities* are arising between different industrial nations with 'active', 'even', or 'passive' balances of pollutants, or to put it more clearly, between 'filthy countries' and those who have to clean up, inhale or pay for the filth of others with increasing deaths, expropriations and devaluations. The socialist 'fraternal community' will also soon have to face up to this distinction and the sources of conflict in it.

Risk Position as Fate

The international intractability of modernization risks is matched by the way they spread. At least for the consumer, their invisibility hardly leaves a decision open. They are 'piggy-back products' which are inhaled or ingested *with* other things. They are the *stowaways of normal consumption*. They travel on the wind and in the water. They can be in anything and everything, and along with the absolute necessities of life – air to breathe, food, clothing, home furnishings – they pass through all the otherwise strictly controlled protective areas of modernity. Unlike wealth, which is attractive but can also be repellent, for which selection, purchase and decisions are always possible and necessary, risks and destruction steal in everywhere implicitly and unhindered by free(!) decisions. In this sense they bring about a new kind of risk *ascription* by civilization. This recalls in some respects the *status fate in medieval society*. Now there exists a kind of *risk fate in developed civilization*, into which one is born, which one cannot escape with any amount of achievement, with the 'small difference' (that is the one with the big effect) that we are *all* confronted similarly by that fate.

In developed civilization, which had set out to remove ascriptions, to evolve privacy, and to free people from the constraints of nature and tradition, there is thus emerging a new global ascription of risks, against which individual decisions hardly exist for the simple reason that the toxins and pollutants are interwoven with the natural basis and the elementary life processes of the industrial world. The experience of this victimization by risks which is *closed to decisions* makes understandable much of the shock, the helpless rage and the 'no future' feelings with which many people react ambivalently and with necessarily exploitative criticism to the latest achievements of technical civilization. Is it at all possible to create and maintain a critical distance towards things one cannot escape? Is it permissible to abandon a critical distance just *because* one cannot escape it, and to flee to the inevitable with scorn or cynicism, indifference or jubilation?

New International Inequalities

The worldwide equalization of risk positions must not deceive us about *new* social inequalities *within* the affliction by risk. These arise especially where risk positions and class positions *overlap* – also on an international scale. The proletariat of the global risk society settles beneath the smokestacks, next to the refineries and chemical factories in the industrial centers of the Third World. The 'greatest industrial catastrophe in history' (*Der Spiegel*), the toxic accident in the Indian city of Bhopal, has raised this in the consciousness of the global public. Hazardous industries have been transferred to the low-wage countries of the Third World. This is no coincidence. There is a systematic 'attraction' between extreme poverty and extreme risk. In the shunting yard where risks are distributed, stations in 'underdeveloped provincial holes' enjoy special popularity. And one would have to be a naive fool to continue to assume that the responsible switchmen do not know what they are doing. More evidence for this is the attested 'higher acceptance' of an unemployed provincial population of 'new' (job-creating) technologies.

On the international scale it is emphatically true that material misery and blindness to hazards coincide. 'A German development expert reports on the careless use of pesticides, in Sri Lanka, for instance. "There they spread DDT around with bare hands, the people are powdered white."' On the Antilles island of Trinidad (population 1.2 million) a total of 120 deaths from pesticides were reported. 'A farmer: "If you don't feel sick after spraying, you haven't sprayed enough"' (*Der Spiegel* 1984, no. 50: 119).

For these people the complex installations of the chemical factories with their imposing pipes and tanks are expensive symbols of success. The death threat they contain, by contrast, remains largely invisible. For them, the fertilizers, pesticides and herbicides they produce signify above all emancipation from material need. They are prerequisites of the 'green revolution', which, systematically supported by the Western industrial states, has raised food production by 30 percent, and in some Asian and Latin American countries by 40 percent over the past few years. The fact that every year 'several hundred thousand tonnes of pesticides are sprayed . . . on cotton and rice fields, on tobacco and fruit plantations' (119) recedes behind these tangible successes. In the competition between the visible threat of death from hunger and the invisible threat of death from toxic chemicals, the evident fight against material misery is victorious. *Without* the widespread use of chemical materials the yields of the land would sink and insects and spoilage would consume their part. *With* chemicals the poor countries of the periphery can build up their own stocks of foodstuffs, and gain a bit of independence from the power centers of the industrial world. The chemical factories in the Third World reinforce this impression of independence in production and from expensive imports. The struggle against hunger and for autonomy forms the protective shield behind which the hazards, imperceptible in any case, are suppressed, minimized and, *by virtue of that*, amplified, diffused and eventually returned to the wealthy industrial countries via the food chain.

Safety and protection regulations are insufficiently developed, and where they do exist, they are often just so much paper. The 'industrial naiveté' of the rural population, which often can neither read nor write, much less afford protective clothing, provides management with unimagined opportunities to legitimize the ways of dealing with risks that would be unthinkable in the more risk-conscious milieus of the industrial states. Management can issue strict safety regulations, knowing they will be unenforceable, and insist that they be obeyed. This way they keep their hands clean, and can shift responsibility for accidents and death to the people's cultural blindness to hazards, cheaply and in good conscience. When catastrophes do occur, the jungle of competing jurisdictions and the material interest of the poor countries offer good opportunities for a policy of minimization and obfuscation to limit the devastating consequences by selectively defining the problem. Economic conditions of production, freed from the constraints of legitimation, attract industrial concerns like magnets, and combine with the particular interests of the countries in overcoming material poverty and gaining national autonomy into an explosive mixture, in the truest sense of the word. *The devil of hunger is fought with the Beelzebub of multiplying risks*. Particularly hazardous industries are transferred to the poor countries of the periphery. The poverty of the Third World is joined by horror at the unleashed destructive powers of the developed risk industry. The pictures and reports from Bhopal and Latin America speak a language of their own.

Villa Parisi

The dirtiest chemical town in the world is located in Brazil . . . Every year the slum residents have to redo their corrugated iron roofs, because the acidic rain eats them away. Anyone who lives here for some time develops rashes, 'alligator skin', as the Brazilians say.

The worst affected are the residents of Villa Parisi, a slum of 15,000 people, most of whom have been able to build modest little houses of gray stone. Here they even sell gas masks in supermarkets. Most of the children have asthma, bronchitis, diseases of the nose and throat, and skin rashes.

In Villa Parisi, it's easy to find your way by smell. On one corner an open sewer is bubbling, on the other a slimy green stream runs. A smell like burnt chicken feathers indicates the steel works, while the odor of rotten eggs marks the chemical factory. An emission meter set up by the town's authorities failed in 1977, after one and a half years of service. It apparently could not withstand the pollution.

The history of the dirtiest town in the world began in 1954, when Pegropràs, the Brazilian oil company, selected the coastal marsh as the site for its refinery. Soon Cosipa, Brazil's largest steel concern, and Copegràs, a Brazilian-American fertilizer company, arrived, followed by multinationals like Fiat, Dow Chemical and Union Carbide. It was the boom phase of Brazilian capitalism. The military government invited foreign enterprises to produce environmentally harmful products there. 'Brazil can still afford to import pollution', boasted Planning Minister Paulo Vellosa in 1972, the year of the environmental conference in Stockholm. Brazil's only ecological problem was poverty, he claimed.

'The main causes of disease are malnutrition, alcohol and cigarettes', the spokesman for Pegropràs says. 'The people are already ill when they come from Copataò', agrees Paulo Figueiredo, boss of Union Carbide, 'and if they get worse, they blame it on us. That's simply illogical.' For years, the governor of São Paulo has been attempting to bring a fresh breeze into polluted Copataò. He fired thirteen officials of the lax environmental agency and employed computers to monitor emissions. But the minor fines of a few thousand dollars didn't bother the environmental violators.

The catastrophe happened on 25 February of this year. Through the sloppiness of Pegropràs, 700,000 liters of oil flowed into the swamp on which the pile buildings of Villa Soco stand. Within two minutes a fire storm raced through the *favela*. Over 500 people were burnt to death. The corpses of small children were never found. 'They just evaporated from the heat', a Brazilian official said. (*Der Spiegel* 1984, no. 50: 110)

Bhopal

The birds fell from the skies. Water buffaloes, cows and dogs lay dead in the streets and fields – bloated after a few hours in the sun of Central Asia [*sic*]. And everywhere the asphyxiated people, curled up, foam at the lips, their cramped hands dug into the earth. There were 3000 of them by the end of last week and new victims were still being found; the authorities stopped counting. 20,000 people will probably go blind. As many as 200,000 were injured.

> In the city of Bhopal an industrial apocalypse without parallel in history occurred last Sunday night and Monday morning. A toxic cloud escaped from a chemical factory and settled like a shroud over sixty-five thickly settled square kilometers; when it finally dissipated, the sickly sweet smell of decay was spreading. The city had turned into a battlefield, in the midst of peace. Hindus burned their dead on cremation pyres, twenty-five at a time. Soon there was a shortage of wood for the ritual cremation – thus kerosene flames licked around the corpses. The Moslem cemetery became too crowded. Earlier graves had to be opened, breaking holy commandments of Islam. 'I know it's a sin to bury two people in a single grave', one of the grave-diggers complains. 'May Allah forgive us. We're putting three, four and even more in.' (110)

In contrast to material poverty, however, the pauperization of the Third World through hazards is contagious for the wealthy. The multiplication of risks causes world society to contract into a community of danger. The boomerang effect strikes precisely those wealthy countries which had hoped to get rid of hazards by transferring them overseas, but then had to import cheaper foodstuffs. The pesticides return to their highly industrialized homeland in the fruit, cacao beans and tea leaves. The extreme international inequalities and the interconnections of the world markets move the poor neighborhoods in the peripheral countries to the doorsteps of the rich industrial centers. They become the breeding grounds of an international contamination, which – like the infectious diseases of the poor in the cramped medieval cities – does not spare even the wealthy neighborhoods of the world community.

Two Epochs, Two Cultures: on the Relationship between the Perception and the Production of Risks

Inequalities in class and risk society can therefore overlap and condition one another; the latter can produce the former. The unequal distribution of social wealth offers almost impregnable defensive walls and justifications for the production of risks. Here a precise distinction must be made between the cultural and political *attention* to risks and their actual *diffusion*.

Class societies are societies where, across all the gaps between classes, the main concern is the visible satisfaction of material needs. Here, hunger and surplus or power and weakness confront each other. Misery needs no self-confirmation. It exists. Its directness and visibility correspond to the material evidence of wealth and power. The certainties of class societies are in this sense the certainties of a culture of *visibility*: emaciated hunger contrasts with plump satiety; palaces with hovels, splendor with rags.

These evident qualities of the tangible no longer hold in risk societies. What escapes perceptibility no longer coincides with the unreal, but can instead even possess a higher degree of hazardous reality. Immediate need competes with the known element of risk. The world of visible scarcity or surplus grows dim under the predominance of risks.

The race between perceptible wealth and imperceptible risks cannot be won by the latter. The visible cannot compete with the invisible. Paradox decrees that *for that very reason* the invisible risks win the race.

The ignoring of risks that are in any case imperceptible, which always finds its justification in the elimination of tangible need – and in fact actually *has* that justification (see the Third World!) – is the cultural and political soil on which the risks and hazards *grow, bloom and thrive.* In the overlap and competition between the problems of class, industrial and market society on one side and those of the risk society on the other, the logic of wealth production always wins, in accordance with the power relationships and standards of relevance – *and for that very reason the risk society is ultimately victorious.* The tangibility of need suppresses the *perception* of risks, but only the perception, not their reality or their effects; risks denied grow especially quickly and well. At a certain stage of social production, characterized by the development of the chemical industry, but also by reactor technology, microelectronics, and genetic technology, the predominance of the logic and conflicts of wealth production, and thus the social invisibility of the risk society, is no proof of its unreality; on the contrary, it is a motor for the origin of the risk society and thus a proof that it is becoming real.

This is what the overlapping and amplification of class and risk positions in the Third World teaches; the same can be said, however, of action and thought in the wealthy industrial countries. Protecting economic recovery and growth still enjoys unchallenged first priority. The threatening loss of jobs is played up, in order to keep the loopholes in prescribed emissions regulations wide and their enforcement lax, or to prevent any investigation into certain toxic residues in foodstuffs. No records are kept on entire families of chemicals out of consideration for the economic consequences; they do not exist legally and can be freely circulated for that very reason. The contradiction that fighting environmental risks has itself become a flourishing branch of industry that guarantees many millions of people secure (all too secure) jobs in Germany is passed over in silence.

At the same time the instruments of *definitional* risk 'management' are being sharpened and the relevant axes are being swung. Those who point out risks are defamed as 'alarmists' and risk producers. Their presentation of the hazards is considered 'unproven'. The effects on man and animals they demonstrate are called 'outrageously exaggerated'. More research is required, they say, before one can be sure what the situation is and take the appropriate measures. Only a rapidly growing gross national product could create the prerequisites for improved environmental protection. They invoke trust in science and research. Their rationality has so far found solutions to every problem, the argument goes. Critique of science and anxieties about the future are stigmatized in contrast as 'irrationalism'. They are supposed to be the real roots of the evils. Risk belongs to progress as much as a bow-wave belongs to a speeding ship.

Risk is no invention of modern times. It is tolerated in many areas of social life. The deaths from traffic accidents, for instance. Every year a middle-sized city in Germany disappears without a trace, so to speak. People have even got used to that. So there is plenty of free space and air for little mini-catastrophes with radioactive material or waste or such (these are in any case extremely unlikely, considering German safety technology).

Even the dominance of this interpretation cannot delude us as to its loss of reality. Its victory is a Pyrrhic one. Where it prevails it produces what it denies, the risk society. But there is no consolation in that; on the contrary there is a growing danger.

The Utopia of a World Society

Thus it is also and especially in denial and non-perception that the *objective community* of a global risk comes into being. Behind the variety of interests, the reality of risk threatens and grows, knowing no social or national differences anymore. Behind the walls of indifference, danger runs wild. Of course, this does not mean that a grand harmony will break out in the face of the growing risks of civilization. Precisely *in* dealing with risks, a variety of new social differentiations and conflicts emerge. These no longer adhere to the plan of class society. They arise above all from the double face of risks in late industrial society: risks are no longer the dark side of opportunities, they are also *market opportunities*. As the risk society develops, so does the antagonism between those *afflicted* by risks and those who *profit* from them. The social and economic importance of *knowledge* grows similarly, and with it the power over the media to structure knowledge (science and research) and disseminate it (mass media). The risk society is in this sense also the *science, media and information* society. Thus new antagonisms open up between those who *produce* risk definitions and those who *consume* them.

These tensions between business and the elimination of risks, and between the consumption and the production of risk definitions, range across all areas of social action. Here lie the essential sources of the *definitional struggles over the scale, degree and urgency of risks*. In the fixing of acceptable levels, the numbers of people afflicted as patients or victims increase or decrease. By drawing lines of causation, companies and occupations are caught in the firing line of accusation. Politicians and politics release pressure by holding individuals and not systems responsible for the accidents and damage. On the other hand, the viewers of risk definition take over and expand their market opportunities. Some, like chemists, are on both sides at the same time; they make people sick and then feed them pills to cure their secondary sickness (allergy medication, for example).

The market-expanding exploitation of risks favors a general to and fro between revealing and concealing risks – with the effect that ultimately no one quite knows whether the 'problem' might not be the 'solution' or vice versa, who profits from what, where responsibilities for creation are being covered up or concealed through causal speculations, and whether the whole talk about risk is not the expression of a displaced political drama, which in reality intends something quite different.

But unlike wealth, risks *always* produce *only partial polarization*, based on the advantages, which they *also* produce, at least while they are not yet fully developed. As soon as the growing element of damage moves into view, the advantages and differences melt away. Sooner or later risks simply present us with threats, which in turn relativize and undermine the associated advantages, and precisely with the growth of the danger they make the commonality of risk a reality, through all the variety of interests. In that way, under the canopy of risk affliction – no matter how much this covers – commonalities behind all the antagonisms also come into being. In order to prevent hazards from nuclear energy or toxic waste or obvious destruction of nature, members of divergent classes, parties, occupational groups and age groups organize into citizens' movements.

In this sense, the risk society produces new antagonisms of interest *and* a new type of community of the endangered whose political carrying capacity remains, however, an open question. To the extent to which modernization hazards generalize and thus abolish the remaining zones of non-involvement, the risk society (in contrast to class society) develops a tendency to unify the victims in global risk positions. In the limiting case, then, friend and foe, east and west, above and below, city and country, south and north are all exposed to the leveling pressure of the exponentially increasing risks of civilization. Risk societies are not class societies – that is not saying enough. They contain within themselves a grass-roots *developmental dynamics that destroys boundaries*, through which the people are forced together in the uniform position of civilization's self-endangering.

To that extent the risk society controls new sources of conflict and consensus. The place of *eliminating scarcity* is taken by *eliminating risk*. Even if the consciousness and the forms of political organization for this are still lacking, one can say that risk society, through the dynamic of endangerment it sets in motion, *undermines the borders of nation states as much as those of military alliances and economic blocs*. While class societies are capable of being organized as national states, risk societies bring about 'communities of danger' that ultimately can only be comprised in the United Nations.

The potential for self-endangering developed by civilization in the modernization process thus also makes the utopia of a world society a little more real or at least more urgent. People in the nineteenth century had to learn, on penalty of economic ruin, to subject themselves to the conditions of industrial society and wage labor. In just the same way, they also have to learn today as in the future, under the shadow of an apocalypse of civilization, to sit down at a table to find and enforce solutions to the self-inflicted endangering that crosses all borders. Pressure in this direction can already be perceived today. Environmental problems can only be solved in an objectively meaningful way in border-spanning negotiations and international agreements, and the way to them accordingly leads to conferences and agreements crossing military alliances. The threat from the storage of nuclear weapons with unimaginable destructive power upsets people in all military spheres and creates a community of threat, whose viability must still prove itself.

The Political Vacuum

But such attempts to gain at least a political meaning from the terror that cannot be understood, cannot blind us to the fact that these newly arising objective commonalities of danger have so far been floating in thin air in the political and economic sense. On the contrary, they collide with national-state egoisms and the prevailing intrasocial party, industrial and interest organizations of industrial societies. There is no place in the jungle of corporatist society for such global risks that span groups. Here every organization has its clientele and its social milieu, consisting of opponents and allies, who are to be activated and played off against one another. The commonality of dangers confronts the pluralistic structure of interest group organizations with almost insoluble problems. It confuses the mutually worked out and well worn compromise routines.

It is true: the dangers grow, but they are not politically reforged into a *preventive* risk management policy. What is more, it is unclear what sort of politics or political institutions would even be capable of that. An incomprehensible community emerges corresponding to the incomprehensibility of the problem. But it remains more an ideal than a reality. At the same time as this gap, a vacuum of institutionalized political competence, or even of ideas about it, emerges. The openness of the question as to how the dangers are to be handled politically stands in stark contrast to the growing need for action and policy-making.

Among the many questions concealed behind this is also that of the *political subject*. Theoreticians of the class societies of the nineteenth century chose the proletariat for this role with good reason. They had their difficulties with it and still have them today. The social and political obviousness of this assumption is retrograde, precisely because it was so right. The achievements of the workers' political and trade union movement were great, so great that they have even undermined its former role as leader into the future. It has become more a preserver of what has already been attained and is being eroded by the future, than a source of political imagination that seeks and finds the answers to the hazards of the risk society.

What corresponds to the political subject of class society – the proletariat – in risk society is only the *victimization of all by more or less tangible massive dangers*. One need not be a Freudian to believe that such overwhelming anxiety can be easily repressed. Everyone and no one is responsible for it. In classical industrial society, everyone is engaged in the struggle for *his* job (income, family, little house, automobile, hobbies, vacation wishes, etc. If those are lost, then you are in a tight spot in any case – pollution or no). But can intangible, universal afflictions be organized politically at all? Is 'everyone' capable of being a political subject? Is this not jumping much too casually from the global nature of the dangers to the commonality of political will and action? Is not globalized and universal victimization a reason *not* to take notice of problem situations or to do so only *indirectly*, to shift them onto others? Are not these the roots that lead to the creation of scapegoats?[4]

From the Solidarity of Need to Solidarity Motivated by Anxiety

Even if the political expression is open and the political consequences ambiguous, in the transition from class to risk society, the *quality of community* begins to change. Schematically, two totally different value systems are expressed in these two types of modern society. Class societies remain related to the ideal of *equality* in their developmental dynamics (in its various formulations from 'equal opportunity' to the variants of socialist models of society). Not so the risk society. Its normative counter-project, which is its basis and motive force, is *safety*. The place of the value system of the 'unequal' society is taken by the value system of the 'unsafe' society. Whereas the utopia of equality contains a wealth of substantial and *positive* goals of social change, the utopia of the risk society remains peculiarly *negative* and *defensive*. Basically, one is no longer concerned with attaining something 'good', but rather with *preventing* the worst; *self-limitation* is the goal which emerges. The dream of class society is that everyone wants and ought to have a *share* of the pie. The utopia of the risk society is that everyone should be *spared* from poisoning.

There are corresponding differences in the basic social situation in which people in both societies live and join together, and which moves them, divides them or fuses them. The driving force in the class society can be summarized in the phrase: *I am hungry!* The movement set in motion by the risk society, on the other hand, is expressed in the statement: *I am afraid!* The *commonality of anxiety* takes the place of the *commonality of need*. The type of the risk society marks in this sense a social epoch in which solidarity from anxiety arises and becomes a political force. But it is still completely unclear how the binding force of anxiety operates, even whether it works. To what extent can anxiety communities withstand stress? What motives and forces for action do they set in motion? Will the social power of anxiety actually break individual judgments of utility? How capable of compromise are anxiety-producing communities of danger? In what forms of action will they organize? Will anxiety drive people to irrationalism, extremism, or fanaticism? So far, anxiety has not been a foundation for rational action. Is this assumption no longer valid either? Is anxiety – unlike material need – perhaps a very shaky foundation for political movements? Can the community of anxiety perhaps even be blown apart by the weak draft of counter-information?

Notes

1 *Modernization* means surges of technological rationalization and changes in work and organization, but beyond that it includes much more: the change in societal characteristics and normal biographies, changes of lifestyle and forms of love, change in the structures of power and influence, in the forms of political repression and participation, in views of reality and in norms of knowledge. In social science's understanding of modernity, the plough, the steam locomotive and the microchip are visible indicators of a much deeper process, which comprises and reshapes the entire social structure. Ultimately the *sources of certainty* on which life feeds are changed (Etzioni 1968; Koselleck 1977; Lepsius 1977; Eisenstadt 1979). In the last year (after the third edition of this book in Germany) there has been a new wave of modernization theory. Now the discussion centers on the possible post-modern problematization of modernity (Berger 1986; Bauman 1989; Alexander and Sztompka 1990).
2 For more sophisticated distinctions between risk in industrial society and risk in risk society see Beck (1988) and (1992).
3 Political strategies against this 'organized irresponsibility' are discussed in Beck (1988).
4 This argument is incomplete; it denies the reflexive politicization of risk conflicts. See Beck (1988: Part II, 1991; and 1992, p. 113ff).

2

THE POLITICS OF KNOWLEDGE IN THE RISK SOCIETY

Anyone moved by these questions must be interested in the *social and political dynamics* of the risk society – alongside its technical, chemical, biological and medical expertise. That is what will be pursued here. An analogy to the nineteenth century offers itself as a starting point to that end. My thesis is that in the risk society we are concerned with a type of *immiseration* which is comparable to that of the working masses in the nineteenth century, and yet not comparable at all. Why 'immiseration' and in what sense?

Immiseration of Civilization?

Both in the nineteenth century and today, consequences experienced by the bulk of humanity as devastating are connected with the social process of industrialization and modernization. With both epochs we are concerned with drastic and threatening interventions in human living conditions. These appear in connection with definite stages in the development of productive forces, of market integration, and of the relationships of property and power. There may be different material consequences each time – back then, material immiseration, poverty, hunger, crowding; today, the threatening and destruction of the natural foundations of life. There are also comparable aspects, such as the amount of danger and the *systematic nature* of modernization with which it is produced and grows. Therein lies its internal dynamic – not malevolence, but the market, competition, division of labor, all of it just a bit more global today. Just as before, the latency (side effects) can in both cases only be broken through in conflict. Then as now, people went into the streets to protest, there was and is loud criticism of progress and technology, there was Luddism – and its counter-arguments.

Then came the gradual admission to the problems, as can still be observed today. Systematically produced suffering and oppression become more and more visible and must be recognized by those who have denied them. The law sets its sails to the prevailing wind, by no means voluntarily, but with the powerful support of politics and the streets: universal suffrage, social welfare laws, labor laws and codetermination. The parallels to today are obvious; harmless things, wine, tea, pasta, etc., turn out to be dangerous. Fertilizers become long-term toxins with worldwide consequences. The once highly praised sources of wealth (the atom, chemistry, genetic technology and so on) are transformed into unpredictable sources of danger. The obviousness of the danger places more and more obstacles in the way of the customary routines of minimizing and covering up. The agents of modernization in science, business and politics find themselves placed in the uncomfortable position of a denying defendant breaking into a real sweat because of the chain of circumstantial evidence.

One could almost say, we have seen it all before, there is nothing new. But the systematic differences stick out just as much. The immediacy of personally and socially experienced misery contrasts today with the intangibility of threats from civilization, which only come to consciousness in scientized thought, and cannot be directly related to primary experience. These are the hazards that employ the language of chemical formulas, biological contexts and medical, diagnostic concepts. This constitution of knowledge does not make them any less hazardous, of course. On the contrary, intentionally or not, through accident or catastrophes, in war or peace, a large group of the population faces devastation and destruction today, for which language and the powers of our imagination fail us, for which we lack any moral or medical category. We are concerned with the absolute and unlimited NOT, which threatens us here, the *un- in general*, unimaginable, unthinkable, un-, un-, un-.

But it only *threatens*. Only? Here another essential difference is revealed; we are dealing today with a *threatening possibility*, which sometimes shows a horrified humanity that it is not just a possibility, but a fact *in abeyance* (and not just a chimera of dreamers).

This difference in kind between reality and possibility is further supplemented by the fact that – in the most developed countries with high levels of social security – the immiseration through hazards coincides with the *opposite* of material immiseration (at least if one looks at the images of the nineteenth century and the starving countries in the Third World). The people are not impoverished, but often prosperous; they live in a society of mass consumption and affluence (which can certainly move in tandem with an intensification of social antagonisms); they are mostly well educated and informed but they are afraid, feel threatened and organize themselves in order not to let the only possible test of their realistic-pessimistic visions of the future even happen, or to actually prevent it. A confirmation of the danger would mean irreversible self-annihilation, and this is the argument that actively transforms the projected threat into a *concrete* one. In that sense, the problems emerging here cannot be mastered by increased production, redistribution or expansion of social protection – as in the nineteenth century – but instead require either a focused and massive 'policy of counter-interpretation' or a fundamental rethinking and reprograming of the prevailing paradigm of modernization.

These differences also make it appear understandable how quite different groups are affected then and now. In the past, the affliction was dictated along with one's class fate. One was born into it. It stuck to one. It lasted from youth to old age. It was contained in everything, what one ate, how and with whom one lived, what kind of coworkers and friends one had, and whom one cursed and, if necessary, went into the streets to protest against.

Risk positions, on the contrary, contain a quite different type of victimization. There is nothing taken for granted about them. They are somehow universal and unspecific. One hears of them or reads of them. This transmission through knowledge means that those groups that tend to be afflicted are *better educated* and *actively inform themselves*. The competition with material need refers to another feature: risk consciousness and activism are more likely to occur where the direct pressure to make a living has been relaxed or broken, that is, among the wealthier and more protected groups (and countries). The spell of the invisibility of risks can also be broken by personal experiences, such as fatal signs on a beloved tree, the planned nuclear power plant in the area, a toxic waste accident, media reporting on it, and similar things, which in turn sensitize one to new symptoms, toxic residues in foodstuffs, and the like. This type of affliction produces no social unity that would be visible on its own and to others, nothing that could be designated or organized as a social class or stratum.

This difference in how people are affected by class and risk positions is essential. To put it bluntly, in class positions, being determines consciousness, while in risk positions, conversely, *consciousness (knowledge) determines being.* Crucial for this is the type of knowledge, specifically the lack of personal experience and the depth of dependency on knowledge, which surrounds all dimensions of defining hazards. The threatening potential that resides in the determinants of the class situation – the loss of a job, for instance – is evident to everyone affected. No special cognitive means are required for this, no measuring procedures, no statistical survey, no reflections on validity, and no consideration of tolerance thresholds. The affliction is clear and in that sense *in*dependent of knowledge.

People who find out that their daily tea contains DDT and their newly bought cake formaldehyde, are in a quite different situation. Their victimization is *not determinable* by their own cognitive means and potential experiences. Whether DDT is contained in the tea or formaldehyde in the cake, and in what dose, remains outside the reach of their own knowledge just as much as does the question of whether and in what concentrations these substances have a long- or short-term deleterious effect. *How* these questions are decided, however, decides a person's affliction one way or the other. Whether yes or no, the degree, the extent and the symptoms of people's endangerment are fundamentally *dependent on external knowledge*. In this way, risk positions create dependencies which are unknown in class situations; the affected parties are becoming *incompetent* in matters of their own affliction. They lose an essential part of their cognitive sovereignty. The harmful, threatening, inimical lies in wait everywhere, but whether it is inimical or friendly is beyond one's own power of judgment, is reserved for the assumptions, methods and controversies of external knowledge producers. In risk positions, accordingly, features of daily life can change *overnight*, so to speak, into 'Trojan horses', which disgorge dangers and with them risk experts, arguing with each other even as they announce what one must fear and what not. Even the decision of whether one will let them in or ask them for advice at all does not lie in the hands of the afflicted parties. They no longer pick the experts, but instead the latter choose the victims. They can barge in and out at will. For hazards can be projected onto all the objects of daily life. And that is where they are now lodged – invisible and yet all too present – and they now call for experts as sources of answers to the questions they loudly raise. Risk positions in this sense are *springs, from which questions rise to the surface, to which the victims have no answer.*

On the other hand, this also means that all decisions on the risks and hazards of civilization falling within the compass of knowledge production are never just questions of the substance of knowledge (inquiries, hypotheses, methods, procedures, acceptable values, etc.). They are *at the same time* also decisions on *who is afflicted*, the extent and type of hazard, the elements of the threat, the population concerned, delayed effects, measures to be taken, those responsible, and claims for compensation. If it is determined today in a socially binding way that, for example, DDT or formaldehyde are dangerous to health in the concentrations in which they appear in ordinary products and foodstuffs, this would be the equivalent of a catastrophe, since they are present everywhere.

This makes it clear *that the margins for scientific research become narrower and narrower as the threatening potential increases.* To admit today that one had been mistaken in setting the acceptable values for the safety of pesticides – which actually would be a normal case in science – amounts to the unleashing of a *political* (or economic) catastrophe, and must be prevented for that reason alone. The destructive forces scientists deal with in all fields today impose on them the inhuman law of *infallibility*. Not only is it one of the most human of all qualities to break this law, but the law itself stands in clear contradiction to science's ideals of progress and critique (on this, see Chapter 7).

Unlike news of losses in income and the like, news of toxic substances in foods, consumer goods, and so on contain a *double shock*. The threat itself is joined by the *loss of sovereignty* over assessing the dangers, to which one is directly subjected. The whole bureaucracy of knowledge opens up, with its long corridors, waiting benches, responsible, semi-responsible, and incomprehensible shoulder-shruggers and poseurs. There are front entrances, side entrances, secret exits, tips and (counter-)information: how one gets access to knowledge, how it should be done, but actually how it is twisted to fit, turned inside and outside, and finally neatly presented so that it does not say what it really means, and signifies what people should rather keep to themselves. All of that would not be so dramatic and could be easily ignored if only one were not dealing with very real and personal hazards.

On the other hand, the investigations of risk researchers also take place with a parallel displacement in everyone's kitchen, tea room or wine cellar. Each one of their central cognitive decisions causes the toxin level in the blood of the population to shoot up or plunge, so to speak – if one first short-circuits the entire division of labor. In risk positions then, unlike class positions, quality of life and the production of knowledge are locked together.

From this it follows that the political sociology and theory of the risk society is in essence *cognitive sociology*, not only the sociology of science, but in fact the sociology of all the admixtures, amalgams and agents of knowledge in their combination and opposition, their foundations, their claims, their mistakes, their irrationalities, their truth and in the impossibility of their knowing the knowledge they lay claim to. To summarize, the current crisis of the future is not visible, it is a possibility on the way to reality. But as just happens to be the case with possibilities: it is an *imputation* one hopes will *not* occur. The falsity of the claim thus lies in the intention of the prognosis. It is an invisible immiseration in the face of flourishing wealth, ultimately with global extent, but without a political subject. And yet: it is clearly and unambiguously an *immiseration*, if one looks correctly at both the similarities to and the differences from the nineteenth century. Alongside lists of casualties, pollutant balances and accident statistics, other indicators also speak in favor of the immiseration thesis.

The latency phase of risk threats is coming to an end. The invisible hazards are becoming *visible*. Damage to and destruction of nature no longer occur outside our personal experience in the sphere of chemical, physical or biological chains of effects; instead they strike more and more clearly our eyes, ears and noses. To list only the most conspicuous phenomena: the rapid transformation of forests into skeletons, inland waterways and seas crowned with foam, animal bodies smeared with oil, erosion of buildings and artistic monuments by pollution, the chain of toxic accidents, scandals and catastrophes, and the reporting about these things in the media. The lists of toxins and pollutants in foodstuffs and articles of daily use grow longer and longer. The barriers provided by 'acceptable values' seem better suited to the requirements for Swiss cheese than to the protection of the public (the more holes the better). The denials of the responsible parties grow ever *higher* in volume and *weaker* substance. While some of this thesis remains to be demonstrated, it should already be clear from this list that the *end of latency* has two sides, the risk itself *and public perception of it.* It is not clear whether it is the risks that have intensified, or our *view* of them. Both sides converge, condition each other, strengthen each other, and because risks are risks in *knowledge*, perceptions of risks and risks are not different things, but one and the same.

The death list for plants and animals is joined by the more acute *public* consciousness, the increased sensibility to the hazards of civilization, which by the way must not be confused with hostility to technology and demonized as such. It is predominantly young people *interested* in technology who see and speak of these hazards. This increased consciousness of risk can be seen from international comparative surveys of the population in the Western industrial states, as well as from the greater relative importance of corresponding news and reportage in the mass media. This loss of latency, this growing awareness of modernization risks, was a totally unimaginable phenomenon a generation ago, and is now already a political factor of the first rank. It is not the result of a general awakening, however, but is based in turn on a number of key developments.

First, the *scientization* of risks is increasing; secondly – and mutually related – the *commerce* with risks is growing. Far from being just critique, the demonstration of the hazards and risks of modernization is also an *economic development factor of the first rank*. This becomes all too clear in the development of the various branches of the economy, and equally in the increasing public expenditures for environmental protection, for combating the diseases of civilization and so forth. The industrial system *profits* from the abuses it produces, and very nicely, thank you (Jänicke 1979).

Through the production of risks, needs are definitively removed from their residual mooring in natural factors, and hence from their finiteness, their satisfiability. Hunger can be assuaged, needs can be satisfied; risks are a 'bottomless barrel of demands', unsatisfiable, infinite. Unlike demands, risks can be more than just called forth (by advertising and the like), prolonged in conformity to sales needs, and in short: manipulated. Demands, and thus markets, of a completely new type can be *created* by varying the definition of risk, especially demand for the avoidance of risk – open to interpretation, causally designable and infinitely reproducible. Production and consumption are thus elevated to a completely new level with the triumph of the risk society. The position of pre-given and manipulable demands as the reference point of commodity production is taken over by the *self-producible* risk.

If one is not afraid of a rather bold comparison, one can say that in risk production, developed capitalism has absorbed, generalized and normalized the destructive force of war. Similarly to war, the risks of civilization which people become aware of can 'destroy' modes of production (for instance, heavily polluting cars or agricultural surpluses), and therefore overcome sales crises and create new markets, which are expandable to boot. Risk production and its cognitive agents – critique of civilization, critique of technology, critique of the environment, risk dramatization and risk research in the mass media – are a system-immanent normal form of the revolutionizing of needs. With risks, one could say with Luhmann, the economy becomes *self-referential*, independent of its context of satisfying human needs.

An essential factor for this, however, is a 'coping' with the *symptoms and symbols* of risks. As they are dealt with in this way, the risks must *grow*, they must not actually be eliminated as causes or sources. Everything must take place in the context of a *cosmetics* of risk, packaging, reducing the symptoms of pollutants, installing filters while retaining the source of the filth. Hence, we have not a *preventive* but a symbolic industry and policy of eliminating the increase in risks. The 'as if' must win and become programmatic. 'Radical protesters' are needed just as much for that as technologically oriented scientists and alternative scientists who study hazards. Sometimes self-financed ('self-help'!), sometimes publicly financed, these groups are generally 'advertising agencies in advance' for the creation of new sales markets for risks, one might say.

Fiction? Polemic? A trend in this direction can already be seen today. If it should win out, then this too would be a *Pyhrric victory*, for the risks would actually emerge through all the cosmetics and with them *the global threat to everyone*. A society would come into being here in which the explosive force of risks would spoil and poison *everyone's* taste for profits. Nevertheless, even the *possibility* illustrates the dynamics of reflexive modernization. Industrial society *systematically* produces its own endangerment and a questioning of itself through the multiplication and the economic exploitation of hazards. The socio-historical situation and its dynamic is comparable to the situation during the waning of the age of feudalism at the threshold of the industrial society. The feudal nobility lived off the commercial bourgeoisie (through the fief-dependent granting of rights to trade and economic use, as well as from business taxes), and encouraged it in its own interests. In this way, the nobility involuntarily and necessarily created a successor which grew steadily in power. In the same way, developed industrial society 'nourishes' itself from the hazards it produces, and so creates the social risk positions and political potentials which call into question the foundations of modernization as it has so far been known.

Mistakes, Deceptions, Errors and Truths: on the Competition of Rationalities

Where the surplus of risks far overshadows the surplus in wealth, the seemingly harmless distinction between risks and the *perception* of risks gains importance – and simultaneously loses its justification. The monopoly on rationality enjoyed by scientific hazard definition stands and falls with this distinction. For it puts forward the possibility of objectively and obligatorily determining hazards in a specialized fashion and through expert authority. Science 'determines risks' and the population 'perceives risks'. Deviations from this pattern indicate the extent of 'irrationality' and 'hostility to technology'.

This division of the world between experts and non-experts also contains an image of the public sphere. The 'irrationality' of 'deviating' public risk 'perception' lies in the fact that, in the eyes of the technological elite, the majority of the public still behaves like engineering students in their first semester. They are ignorant, of course, but well intentioned; hard-working, but without a clue. In this view, the population is composed of nothing but would-be engineers, who do not yet possess sufficient knowledge. They only need be stuffed full of technical details, and then they will share the experts' viewpoint and assessment of the technical manageability of risks, and thus their lack of risk. Protests, fears, criticism, or resistance in the public sphere are a *pure problem of information*. If the public only knew what the technical people know, they would be put at ease – otherwise they are just hopelessly irrational.

This perception is *wrong*. Even in their highly mathematical or technical garb, statements on risks contain statements of the type *that is how we want to live* – statements, that is, to which the natural and engineering sciences *alone* can provide answers only by overstepping the bounds of their disciplines. But then the tables are turned. The non-acceptance of the scientific definition of risks is not something to be reproached as 'irrationality' in the population; but quite to the contrary, it indicates that the cultural premises of acceptability contained in scientific and technical statements on risks *are wrong*. The technical risk experts *are mistaken* in the empirical accuracy of their implicit value premises, specifically in their assumptions of what appears acceptable to the population. The talk of a 'false, irrational' perception of risk in the population, however, crowns this mistake; the scientists withdraw their *borrowed* notions of cultural acceptance from empirical criticism, elevate their views of other people's notions to a dogma and mount this shaky throne to serve as judges of the 'irrationality' of the population, whose ideas they ought to ascertain and make the foundation of their work.

One can also view it another way: in their concern with risks, the natural sciences have involuntarily and invisibly *disempowered themselves somewhat, forced themselves toward democracy*. In their implicit cultural value notions of a life worth living, statements on risks contain *a bit of codetermination*. Techno-scientific risk perception may resist this through the inversion of the presumption of irrationality, just as the feudal lords resisted the introduction of universal suffrage, but at the same time it has made a decision for them. If not, it would be permanently and systematically arguing in contradiction of its own claims to the empirical correctness of its assumptions.

The distinction between (rational) *determination* of risks and (irrational) *perception* of them also inverts the role of scientific and social rationality in the origin of a civilizational risk consciousness. It contains a falsification of history. Today's recognized knowledge of the risks and threats of techno-scientific civilization has only been able to become established *against the massive denials*, against the often bitter *resistance* of a self-satisfied 'techno-scientific rationality' that was trapped in a narrow-minded belief in progress. The scientific investigation of risks everywhere is limping along behind the social critique of the industrial system from the perspectives of the environment, progress and culture. In this sense, there is always a good bit of the unavowed *cultural critical zeal of a convert* in the techno-scientific concern with risks, and the engineering sciences' claim to a monopoly on rationality in risk perception is equivalent to the claim to infallibility of a Pope who has converted to Lutheranism.

The growing awareness of risks must be reconstructed as a struggle among rationality claims, some competing and some overlapping. One cannot impute a hierarchy of credibility and rationality, but must ask how, in the example of risk perception, 'rationality' *arises socially*, that is how it is believed, becomes dubious, is defined, redefined, acquired and frittered away. In this sense, the *(il)logic* as well as the cooperation and opposition of the scientific and social perception of civilizational risks should be displayed. In the process, one can pursue the questions: what systematic sources of mistakes and errors are built into the *scientific* perception of risks, which only become visible in the reference horizon of a social risk perception? And conversely, to what extent does the social perception of risks remain dependent on scientific rationality, even where it systematically disavows and criticizes science, and hence threatens to turn into a revitalization of pre-civilizational doctrines?

My *thesis* is that the origin of the critique of science and technology lies not in the 'irrationality' of the critics, but in the *failure* of techno-scientific rationality in the face of growing risks and threats from civilization. This failure is not mere past, but acute present and threatening future. In fact it is only gradually becoming visible to its full extent. Nor is it the failure of individual scientists or disciplines; instead it is systematically grounded in the institutional and methodological approach of the sciences to risks. As they are constituted – with their overspecialized division of labor, their concentration on methodology and theory, their externally determined abstinence from practice – the sciences are *entirely incapable* of reacting adequately to civilizational risks, since they are prominently involved in the origin and growth of those very risks. Instead – sometimes with the clear conscience of 'pure scientific method', sometimes with increasing pangs of guilt – the sciences become the *legitimating patrons* of a global industrial pollution and contamination of air, water, foodstuffs, etc., as well as the related generalized sickness and death of plants, animals and people.

How can that be shown? The consciousness of modernization risks has established itself against the *resistance* of scientific rationality. A broad trail of scientific mistakes, misjudgments and minimizations leads to it. The history of the growing consciousness and social recognition of risks coincides with the history of the demystification of the sciences. The other side of recognition is the refutation of the scientific 'see no evil, hear no evil, smell no evil, know no evil'.

also medical

Economic Blindness to Risks

> The original mistake over the risk element of a technology lies in the unparalleled misunderstanding and trivialization of the *nuclear* risks. The contemporary reader does not believe his eyes when he reads what found its way in 1959 into an official instruction sheet issued by the [West German] federal government:
>
> 'A strong, blinding flash of light is the first sign of the detonation of an atomic bomb. Its thermal effects can produce burns.
>
> Therefore: immediately cover sensitive body parts like eyes, face, neck and hands!
>
> Immediately jump into a hole, a pit or a ditch!
>
> In an automobile, immediately duck beneath the dashboard, stop the car, fall to the floor of the vehicle and protect your face and hands by curling up!
>
> If possible look for protection behind a heavy table, desk, workbench, bed or other furniture!
>
> You have a better chance of surviving in a cellar than in upper floors. Not every cellar has to cave in!
>
> If chemical or biological weapons are used, immediately put on your protective mask!
>
> If you don't have a protective mask, don't breathe deeply and protect your breathing passages by holding a moist handkerchief over your mouth and nose.
>
> Clean up and decontaminate yourself from radiation or poisons as circumstances warrant.
>
> Prevent panic, avoid unthinking haste, but act![1]

The apocalyptic catastrophe is euphemized for public consumption. The 'travesty of measurement' (Anders 1983) inherent in every nuclear threat is completely misunderstood and trivialized. The suggestions involuntarily follow a humorous horror logic: 'If you're dead, caution! Delay is dangerous!' (133).

This fall from grace of nuclear physics and technology is no coincidence. It is also neither individually conditioned nor the unique 'operating accident' of a scientific discipline. Rather, in its very radicalness it makes us conscious of the central institutional source of errors of engineering science in dealing with self-produced risk: *in the effort to increase productivity, the associated risks have always been and still are being neglected.* The first priority of techno-scientific curiosity is *utility for productivity*, and the hazards connected with it are considered only later and often not at all.

The production of risks and their misunderstanding, then, has its origin in the economic Cyclopia of techno-scientific rationality. Its view is directed at the advantages for productivity. Hence it is also stricken with a systematically conditioned *blindness to risk*. The very people who predict, develop, test and explore possibilities of economic utility with all the tricks of the trade, always fight shy of risks and are then deeply shocked and surprised at their 'unforeseen' or even 'unforeseeable' arrival. The alternative idea that advantages for productivity might be noticed 'unseen' and 'undesired' as 'latent side effects' of a conscious monitoring of hazards only subsequently and against the wishes of risk-oriented natural science, seems totally absurd. This once again clarifies how self-evidently a type of *productivity-raising knowledge interest* (to put it in Habermas's (1971) terms) prevails historically in scientifically directed technological development, an interest which is related to the logic of wealth production and remains embedded in it.

The Voices of the 'Side Effects'

While on the one hand this induces opportunities, it makes people *ill* on the other. Parents whose children suffer attacks of pseudo-croup bang their heads against the walls of scientific denials of the existence of modernization risks. All those who have seen the way their child hacks and coughs at night, lying in bed, eyes wide with terror and fighting for air, can only speak of infinite fear. Now that they have learned that pollutants in the air threaten not just trees, soil and water, but also infants and young children, they no longer accept the coughing fits as acts of fate. They have joined together across Germany in more than 100 citizens' initiative groups. Their demand is, 'Reduce sulfur dioxide instead of just gassing about it!' (König, *Der Stern*, April 1985).

They no longer need to ponder the problems of their situation. What scientists call 'latent side effects' and 'unproven connections' are for them their 'coughing children' who turn blue in foggy weather and gasp for air, with a rattle in their throat. On their side of the fence, 'side effects' have *voices, faces, eyes* and *tears*. And yet they must soon learn that their own statements and experiences are worth nothing so long as they collide with the established scientific naiveté. The farmers' cows can turn yellow next to the newly built chemical factory, but until that is 'scientifically proven' it is not questioned.

Therefore people themselves become small, private alternative experts in risks of modernization. For them, risks are not risks, but pitifully suffering, screaming children turning blue. It is the children they fight for. Modernization risks, for which no one is responsible in a highly professionalized system where everyone has his own small responsibility, now have an *advocate*. The parents begin to collect data and arguments. The 'blank spots' of modernization risks, which remain 'unseen' and 'unproven' for the experts, very quickly take form under their cognitive approach. They discover, for instance, that the established acceptable values for pollutants in Germany are much too high. Although investigations have shown that children suffer pseudo-croup surprisingly often even at a short-term level of 200 micrograms of sulfur dioxide per cubic meter of air, twice that amount is permissible according to the prevailing prescribed values in Germany. This is four times as much as the World Health Organization considers acceptable as a short-term value. Parents prove that measurement results only fall within the 'acceptable' scope because the peak values from heavily impacted neighborhoods are averaged in with values from wooded residential neighborhoods and so 'calculated away'. 'But our children', they say, 'are not getting sick from the average value.'

The uncovered 'cheating tactics' of the scientists point to categorical differences between scientific and social rationality in their dealings with risks.

Causal Denial of Risks

In the beginning were the *varied afflictions*. People found themselves on both sides of the same fence. If the scientist lets a mistake slip through, the worst that can happen is a blemish on his reputation (if the 'mistake' is what the right people want, it could even bring him a promotion). On the side of the afflicted, the same thing takes on very different forms. Here, a mistake in determining the acceptable value means irreversible liver damage or danger of cancer. Accordingly, the urgencies, time horizons and norms against which the erroneousness of the errors are measured are different.

Scientists insist on the 'quality' of their work and keep their theoretical and methodological standards high in order to assure their careers and material success. From that very fact, a peculiar non-logic results in their dealings with risks. The insistence that connections are not established may look good for a scientist and be praiseworthy in general. When dealing with risks, the contrary is the case for the victims; *they multiply the risks*. One is concerned here with dangers to be avoided, which even at low probability have a threatening effect. If the recognition of a risk is denied on the basis of an 'unclear' state of information, this means that the necessary counteractions are neglected and *the danger grows*. By turning up the standard of scientific accuracy, the circle of recognized risks justifying action is *minimized*, and consequently, *scientific license is* implicitly *granted for the multiplication of risks*. To put it bluntly: insisting on the *purity* of the scientific analysis leads to the *pollution and contamination* of air, foodstuffs, water, soil, plants, animals and people. What results then is a covert coalition between strict scientific practice and the threats to life encouraged or tolerated *by it*.

This is no longer just a general and thus abstract connection, there are scientific and methodological instruments for it. A vital character is assumed here by the determination of the presumption of *causality* contained in modernization risks, a presumption it is difficult if not impossible to prove for theoretical reasons (for a summary, see Stegmüller 1970). We are interested here in the controllability of the recognition process by means of validity criteria of the proof of causality. The higher these criteria are set, the smaller is the circle of recognized risks, and the larger becomes the accumulation of unrecognized risks. Of course, it is also true that the walls of recognition in front of the risks only grow higher. The insistence on elevated validity criteria, then, is a *highly effective and thoroughly legitimized construction* meant to dam and channel the flood of risks, but with a built-in screen that increases the growth of risks in inverse proportion to the successful 'derecognition' of them.

Under these circumstances, a liberalization of the causality proof would be like a bursting dam and thus would imply a flood of risks and damages to be recognized that would rock the entire social and political structure through its broader effects. And so – in a beautiful harmony of science and law – we continue to use the so-called *polluter pays principle as the channel for recognizing and dismissing* risks. It is known that modernization risks, because of their structure, *cannot* generally be adequately interpreted according to this principle. There is usually not *one* polluter, but just pollutants in the air from many smokestacks, and in addition these are correlated with unspecific illnesses, for which one can always consider a number of 'causes'. Anyone who insists on *strict* proof of causality under these circumstances is maximizing the dismissal and minimizing the recognition of industrially caused contaminations and diseases of civilization. With the innocence of 'pure' science, risk researchers defend the 'high art of proving causality', thus blocking citizens' protests, choking them in infancy for lack of a causal link. They seem to keep down costs for industry, and to keep the politicians' backs off the wall, but in reality they open the floodgates for a general endangering of life.

This is also a good example of how 'rationality' can become 'irrationality', according to whether the same thought and action is seen through the frame of reference of wealth or risk production. The insistence on strict proof of causality is a central element of scientific rationality. Being accurate and 'not conceding anything' to oneself or others is one of the central values of the scientific ethos. At the same time, though, these principles stem from other contexts and perhaps even from a different intellectual epoch. In any case, they are *basically inadequate* for modernization risks. Where pollution exposures can only be understood and measured within international exchange patterns and the corresponding balances, it is obviously impossible to bring individual producers of individual substances into a direct, causal connection with definite illnesses, which may also be caused or advanced by other factors as well. This is equivalent to the attempt to calculate the mathematical potential of a computer using just five fingers. Anyone who insists on strict causality *denies* the reality of connections that exist nonetheless. Just because the scientists cannot identify any individual causes for individual damage, the pollutant levels in the air and in foodstuffs do not decrease, the swelling of the air passages under exposure to smog does not go down and neither do the mortality rates, which rise significantly with sulfur dioxide levels above 300 micrograms per cubic meter.

In other countries, quite different norms apply to the validity of causal proofs. Often, of course, they have only been established through social conflicts. In view of the globally intermeshed risks of modernization, the judges in Japan have decided they will no longer interpret the impossibility of a rigorous proof of causality to the detriment of the victims and thus ultimately against everyone. They already recognize a causal connection if *statistical correlations* can be established between pollution levels and certain diseases. Those plants that emit such pollutants can then be made legally responsible and sentenced to corresponding damage payments. In Japan, a number of firms were obliged to make enormous payments to injured parties in a series of spectacular environmental trials. For the victims in Germany, the *causal denial* of the injuries and illnesses they have experienced must seem like sheer scorn. As the arguments they collect and advance are blocked, they experience the *loss of reality* in a scientific rationality and practice that have always confronted their self-produced risks and dangers blindly and like a stranger.

A Phony Trick: Acceptable Levels

There are other 'cognitive toxic floodgates' under the control of risk scientists. They also have really great magic at their command: abracadabra!, shimsalabim! This is celebrated in certain areas as the 'acid rain dance' – in plain language, acceptable level determination or maximum concentration regulation, both expressions for not having a clue. But since that never happens to scientists, they have many words for it, many methods, many figures. A central term for 'I don't know either' is 'acceptable level'. Let us spell out this term.

In connection with risk distribution, acceptable levels for 'permissible' traces of pollutants and toxins in air, water and food have a meaning similar to that of the principle of efficiency for the distribution of wealth: they permit the emission of toxins *and* legitimate it to just that limited degree. Whoever *limits* pollution has *also concurred* in it. Whatever is still possible is, by social definition, 'harmless' – no matter how harmful it might be. Acceptable values may indeed prevent the very worst from happening, but they are at the same time 'blank checks' to poison nature and mankind *a bit*. How big this 'bit' can be is what is at stake here. The question of whether plants, animals and people can withstand a *large* or a *small* bit of toxin, and *how* large a bit, and what 'withstand' means in this context – such are the delightful horror questions from the toxin and antitoxin factories of advanced civilization which are at stake in the determination of acceptable levels.

We do not wish to concern ourselves here with the fact that values [*Werte*], even acceptable values [*Grenzwerte*] at one time were a matter for ethics, not chemistry. Thus we are dealing with the 'Decree on Maximum Amounts of Agricultural and Other Chemicals as Well as of Other Pesticides in or on Foodstuffs and Tobacco Products', to quote the clumsy official language, that is, with the *residual biological ethics* of developed industrial civilization. This remains, however, peculiarly negative. It expresses the formerly self-evident principle that people should not poison one another. More accurately it should have read: not *completely* poison. For ironically, it permits the famous and controversial bit. The subject of this decree then, is not the prevention of, but the *permissible extent* of poisoning. *That* it is permissible is no longer an issue on the basis of this decree. Acceptable levels in this sense are the retreat lines of a civilization supplying itself in surplus with pollutants and toxic substances. The really rather obvious demand for non-poisoning is rejected as *utopian*. At the same time, the bit of poisoning being set down becomes *normality*. It disappears behind the acceptable values. Acceptable values make possible a *permanent ration of collective standardized poisoning*. They also cause the poisoning they allow not to have occurred, by declaring the poisoning that did occur harm*less*. If one has adhered to the acceptable values, then in this sense one has not poisoned anyone or anything – no matter how much toxin is actually contained in the foodstuffs one produces. This indicates that production of toxins and so on is not only a question of which industries, but of fixing acceptable levels. It is, then, a matter of coproduction across institutional and systemic boundaries, political, bureaucratic and industrial.

If people could agree to the not totally absurd premise of *not* poisoning *at all*, then there would not be any problems. There would also be no more need for a maximum concentration decree. The problems therefore lie in the concessional character, in the double moral standard, in the yes-and-no of a *maximum* concentration decree. Here one is no longer concerned with questions of ethics at all but with how far one of the most minimal rules of social life – not to poison each other – may be *violated*. It ultimately comes down to how long poisoning will not be called poisoning and when it will begin to be called poisoning. This is doubtless an important question, a much too important question to be left completely to experts on toxins. Life on Earth depends on it, and not only in the figurative sense. Once one has stepped onto the slippery slope of a 'permissible toxic effect', the question of how much toxicity is 'permissible' gains the importance that the young Hamlet – with a bit of pathos – reduced to the alternative: 'to be or not to be?' This is concealed in the maximum concentration decree – a peculiar document of this era. That will not be discussed here. We wish to move onto the ground of the acceptable value determination itself and inquire into its logic or non-logic, that is to say, we will ask whether it could possibly know what it purports to know.

If one permits toxicity at all, then one needs an acceptable level decree. But then that which is *not* contained in it becomes more important than what is in it. Because what is not in, not covered by it, *is not considered toxic*, and can *freely be introduced into circulation, without any restraints*. The silence of the acceptable level decree, its 'blank spots', are its most dangerous statements. What it does not discuss is what threatens us the most. With the maximum level decree, the *definition of pesticides* and of what is excluded from its scope as 'non-pesticide toxins' become the first switch thrown on the track to a long-term and permanent toxification of nature and humankind. The battle over definitions, no matter how much it seems to be conducted just within academia, thus has a more or less toxic consequence for everyone.

Whatever does not fit into the conceptual order, because the phenomena are not yet registered clearly enough or are too complex, whatever lies across the lines of the conceptual plan – all this is covered by the definition-making claims of the order, and *absolved of the suspicion of toxicity by going unmentioned*. The maximum concentration decree is based, then, on a most dubious and dangerous *technocratic fallacy*: that what has not (yet) been covered or cannot be covered is not toxic. Put somewhat differently, in case of doubt please protect toxins from the dangerous interference of human beings.

As chance would have it, the maximum concentration decree in Germany exhibits *gigantic holes* – even by comparison to other industrial countries. Entire families of toxins do not even appear in the work, since they are not pesticides in the eyes of the law. The continuation of the list of pollutants is limping hopelessly behind the production and use of chemical substances. The American Council on Environmental Quality warned years ago against overrating the *known* pollutant parameters in comparison with the untold number of chemicals whose toxicity is unclear, whose concentrations are unknown and whose potential polluting effects are not being diminished by any regulation. Reference is made to the more than four million chemical compounds, whose number is continually growing. 'We know very little about the possible health effects of these compounds . . . but their mere number . . . the diversity of their application, and the negative effects of some of them that have already occurred, make it increasingly likely that chemical pollutants are becoming a significant determining factor of human health and life expectancy.'[2]

If any notice is taken of new compounds at all, then appraisal takes three or four years as a rule. For that amount of time the potentially toxic substances can be employed without restraint, in any case.

These voids of silence can be pursued further. It remains the secret of the architects of acceptable values how *acceptable values* can be *determined for individual substances*. It is not completely fanciful to claim that acceptable values have to do with notions of the toleration of substances *by people and nature*. The latter, however, are the *collecting vessels* for all sorts of pollutants and toxins in the air, the water, the soil, food, furniture, etc. Whoever would determine threshold values of toleration must take account of this *summation*. Those who nonetheless set acceptable levels for individual toxic substances, either proceed from the completely erroneous assumption that people ingest only a particular toxin, or from the very starting point of their thought they completely miss the opportunity to speak of acceptable values *for people*. The more pollutants are put in circulation, the more acceptable levels related to individual substances are set, the more liberally this occurs, and the more *insane* the entire hocus-pocus becomes, because the overall toxic threat to the population grows – presuming the simple equation that the total volume of various toxic substances means a higher degree of overall toxicity.

One can argue quite similarly for the *synergism* of individual toxic substances. How does it help me to know that this or that toxin in this or that concentration is harmful or harmless, if I do not know what reactions the synergy of these multiple toxins provokes? It is already known from the field of internal medicine that medications can minimize or multiply each other's effects. It is not completely misguided to surmise the same for the innumerable partial toxic effects permitted through acceptable levels. The decree does not contain an answer to this central question either.

Both of the logical flaws here are not coincidental, but rather are based on problems which systematically result when one moves onto the cock-eyed plane of possible partial toxic effects. For it seems scornful if not cynical, to determine acceptable levels on the one hand and thus to permit toxic effects to some degree, and on the other to devote no intellectual effort whatsoever to the question of what effects the *summation* of toxins have in their *synergy*. This reminds one of the story about a gang of poisoners who stand before their victim and assure the judge with an innocent look that each of them was well under the acceptable levels and thus should be acquitted!

Now many will say, those are fine demands, but that is not possible, and for fundamental reasons. We have only a specialized knowledge of individual pollutants. Even that is dragging miserably far behind the industrial multiplication of chemical compounds and materials. We have a lack of personnel, research experts, and so on. But do people know what they are saying here? The proffered knowledge on acceptable levels does not become one jot better because of that. It remains eye-wash to set acceptable levels for individual pollutants, if at the same time one releases thousands of other harmful materials, whose synergistic effects one says nothing about!

If this is really not possible any other way, then that means nothing less than that the system of professional overspecialization and its official organization *fails* in the face of the risks set in motion by industrial development. It may be suited to the development of productivity, but not to the limitation of dangers. Of necessity, people are threatened in their civilizational risk positions not by individual pollutants, but *holistically.* To respond to their forced questions regarding their *holistic* endangerment with tables of acceptable values for individual substances amounts to collective ridicule with consequences that are no longer only latently murderous. It may be that one could make this mistake in times of a general belief in progress. But to stick to it today in the face of widespread protests and statistical evidence of morbidity and mortality, under the legitimating protection of scientific 'acceptable value rationality', far exceeds the dimensions of a crisis of faith, and is enough to call for the public prosecutor.

But let us put these considerations aside for a moment. Let us take a look at the scientific construction of an acceptable level. In a purely logical way, of course. To abbreviate this, every determination of an acceptable value is based on *at least* the following two false conclusions.

First, *false conclusions on the reaction of people are drawn* from the *results of animal experiments.* Let us select the toxin TCDD, which wreaked havoc in Seveso (Umweltbundesamt, (Federal Office of the Environment) 1985; Urban 1985). It arises in the production of a large number of chemical products, for instance, wood preservatives, herbicides and disinfection agents. It also develops during waste incineration, and in fact in larger amounts the lower the incineration temperature. The carcinogenic effect of TCDD has been proven for two animal species. They were fed the stuff. But now comes the key methodological issue from civilization's poison cauldron: how much can a human being tolerate? Even small animals react *very differently*: guinea pigs, for instance, are *ten to twenty times* more sensitive than mice and *three to five thousand times* more sensitive than hamsters. The results for lions are not yet available, elephants are already being selected . . .

It remains the as yet unaired secret of the acceptable level jugglers how one can draw conclusions on the toleration of this toxin in people on the basis of such results. Let us assume that it is possible to speak of 'the' person. Let us pack infants, children, pensioners, epileptics, merchants, pregnant women, people living near smokestacks and those far away, Alpine farmers and Berliners into the big gray sack of 'the' person. Let us assume that the laboratory mouse reacts just like the church mouse. The question still remains, how does one get from A to B, from the extremely varying animal reactions to the completely unknown reactions in people, which are never derivable from the animal ones?

To put it briefly, only by following the *lotto model*: mark a box and wait. As in lotto, people do have their method. In the acceptable level lotto it is known as *safety factor*. What is a safety factor? We are taught what it is by 'practice' ('Höchstmengen', *Natur* 1985, no. 4: 46–51). So one cannot just mark a box, one really does have to wait. But one could have done that immediately. There would have been no need to torture animals for that. To say it one more time: from the results of animal experiments, which in any case only provide answers to very *limited* questions under *artificial* conditions and often display extremely varied reactions, only the abilities of a *clairvoyant* could lead to the 'tolerable' dose of a toxin for 'people'. The designers of acceptable levels are seers, they have the ability of the 'third eye', they are late industrial chemical magicians using the apparatus of experimental series and coefficients. No matter how benevolently one looks at it, the whole affair remains a very complicated, verbose and number-intensive way of saying: we do not know *either*. Just wait. Practice will show us. With that we reach the second point.

Acceptable levels certainly fulfill the function of a *symbolic* detoxification. They are a sort of symbolic tranquilizer pill against the mounting news reports on toxins. They signal that someone is making an effort and paying attention. *In actual fact* they have the effect of raising the threshold of experiments on people somewhat higher. There is no way around it, *only when the substance is put into circulation can one find out what its effects are.* And that is exactly where the second wrong conclusion lies, which is not really a wrong conclusion at all, but a scandal.

The effect *on* people can ultimately only be studied reliably *with* people. Society is becoming a laboratory. Once again, we find no desire to discuss ethical questions, but rather we limit ourselves completely to the experimental logic. Substances are disseminated in the population in all imaginable ways: air, water, food chains, product chains, etc. So what? Where is the mistaken conclusion? Just this: nothing happens. *The experiment on people that takes place does not take place.* More precisely, it takes place by administering the substance to people, as with research animals, in small doses. It fails to take place in the sense that the reactions in people are not systematically surveyed and recorded. The mode of action among experimental animals had no validity for people, but it was very carefully recorded and correlated. For the sake of caution, the reactions in people themselves are not even noted, unless someone reports and can *prove* that it is actually *this* toxin which is harming him. The experiment on people does take place, but invisibly, *without* scientific checking, *without* surveys, *without* statistics, *without* correlation analysis, under the condition that the victims are *not* informed – and with an *inverted* burden of proof, if they should happen to detect something.

It is not that one *could not* know how the toxic rations affect people individually or in total. *One does not want to know it.* People are supposed to find that out for themselves. A permanent experiment is being conducted, so to speak, in which people serving as laboratory animals in a self-help movement have to collect and report data on their own toxic symptoms *against* the experts sitting there with their deeply furrowed brows. Even the already published statistics on such things as diseases or dying forests apparently do not appear eloquent enough to the acceptable level magicians.

We are concerned, then, with a permanent large-scale experiment, requiring the involuntary human subjects to report on the accumulating symptoms of toxicity among themselves, with a reversed and elevated burden of proof. Their arguments need not be heeded, because, after all, *there are acceptable levels that were met!* Those levels, which really could only be determined from the reactions of people, are held up to deny the fears and diseases of the afflicted! And all of this in the name of 'scientific rationality'! The problem is not that the acceptable level acrobats do not know. The admission of 'not knowing either' would be comforting. That they do not know, and yet act as if they did, is the annoying and dangerous thing, as well as the fact that they continue to insist on their impossible 'knowledge' even where they should have known better long ago.

Scientific Rationality in Rupture

The origin of risk consciousness in highly industrialized civilization is truly not a page of honor in the history of (natural) scientists. It came into being against a continuing barrage of scientific denial, and is still suppressed by it. To this day the majority of the scientists sympathize with the other side. Science has *become the protector of a global contamination of people and nature.* In that respect, it is no exaggeration to say that in the way they deal with risks in many areas, the sciences *have squandered until further notice their historic reputation for rationality.* 'Until further notice', i.e. until they perceive the institutional and theoretical sources of their errors and deficits in dealing with risks, and until they have learned self-critically and practically to accept the consequences from this.

The increase of productivity is married to the ever more fine-grained division of labor. Risks display an *encroaching* relation to this trend. They bring the substantively, spatially and temporally disparate into a direct, threatening connection. They fall through the sieve of overspecialization. They are what lies *between* the specializations. Coping with risks compels a general view, a cooperation over and above all the carefully established and cultivated borders. Risks lie *across* the distinction between theory and practice, *across* the borders of specialties and disciplines, *across* specialized competences and institutional responsibilities, *across* the distinction between value and fact (and thus between ethics and science), and *across* the realms of politics, the public sphere, science and the economy, which are seemingly divided by institutions. In that respect, the *de*differentiation of subsystems and functional spheres, the *re*networking of specialists and the risk-reducing *unification* of work become the cardinal problems of system theory and organization.

At the same time the unrestrained production of risks inherently erodes the ideals of *productivity* towards which scientific rationality is oriented.

> The traditional environmental policy attacking symptoms and concerned with facts can meet *neither* ecological *nor* economic standards in the long run. Ecologically, it always runs behind the advancing production processes that damage the environment; economically, the problem arises of increasing cleanup costs with decreasing ecological success. What are the reasons for this double inefficiency?
>
> A major reason must reside in the fact that traditional environmental policy starts at the end of the production process, and not at the beginning, that is, in the choice of technologies, sites, raw materials, ingredients, fuels, or products to be produced . . . It is the *ex post facto* cleanup of environmental damage utilizing end-of-the-pipe technologies. Starting from the existing environmentally damaging technology, a diffusion of the accumulated pollutants and waste materials is supposed to be avoided to a certain extent. Through the installation of decontaminating technologies at the end of the production process, potential emissions are retained in the plant and collected in concentrated form. Typical examples of this are filtering units that capture pollutants before they enter the outside air, such as scrubbers to remove sulfur

dioxide and nitrogen oxides, furthermore, waste disposal and sewage treatment plants, but also the catalytic converter technologies for automobile exhausts, which are currently so controversial . . .

Now, in almost all areas of environmental protection it is true that the cleanup costs (in the sense of the costs for retaining and collecting pollutants) rise *disproportionately* with *increasing* degrees of cleaning – something, by the way, which also applies to recycling as a production method. And from the perspective of the economy as a whole this means that with continued economic growth a continually increasing portion of the economy's resources must be diverted in order to guarantee a given level of emissions, resources which then are no longer available for consumption purposes. Here there is a danger of a counter-productive overall development of the industrial system. (Leipert and Simonis 1985)

It is increasingly apparent that the engineering sciences face a *historic turning point*: they can continue to think and work in the worn-out ways of the nineteenth century. Then they will confuse the problems of the risk society with those of early industrial society. Or they can face the challenges of a genuine, preventive management of risks. Then they must rethink and change their own conceptions of rationality, knowledge and practice, as well as the institutional structures in which these are put to work (see Chapter 7 on this).

The Public Consciousness of Risks: Second-Hand Non-Experience

For the cultural criticism of science, the converse applies that one must finally appeal to what one argues against, scientific rationality. Sooner rather than later, one comes up against the law that so long as risks are not recognized scientifically, *they do not exist* – at least not legally, medically, technologically, or socially, and they are thus not prevented, treated or compensated for. No amount of collective moaning can change this, only science. Scientific judgment's monopoly on truth therefore forces the victims themselves to make use of all the methods and means of scientific analysis in order to succeed with their claims. But they are also forced to *modify* the analysis immediately. The demystification of scientific rationality which they undertake therefore acquires a highly ambivalent meaning for the critics of industrialism.

On the one hand, the softening of scientific knowledge claims is necessary in order to gain space for their own viewpoints. They get to know the levers necessary to set the switches in scientific arguments, so that sometimes the train heads towards trivialization, other times towards taking risks seriously. On the other hand, as the uncertainties of scientific judgments grow, so does the gray area of unrecognized suspected risks. If it is impossible anyway to determine causal relationships finally and unambiguously, if science is only a disguised mistake in abeyance, if 'anything goes', then where does anyone derive the right to believe only in certain risks? It is this very crisis of scientific authority which can favor a general *obfuscation of risks*. Criticism of science is also *counter-productive* for the recognition of risks.

Accordingly, the risk consciousness of the afflicted, which is frequently expressed in the environmental movement, and in criticism of industry, experts and culture, is usually both *critical* and *credulous* of science. A solid background of faith in science is part of the paradoxical basic equipment of the critique of modernization. Thus, risk consciousness is neither a traditional nor a lay person's consciousness, but is essentially determined by and oriented to science. For, in order to recognize risks at all and make them the reference point of one's own thought and action, it is necessary on principle that invisible causality relationships between objectively, temporally, and spatially very divergent conditions, as well as more or less speculative projections, be *believed*, that they be *immunized* against the objections that are always possible. But that means that the invisible – even more, that which is by nature beyond perception, that which is only connected or calculated theoretically – *becomes the unproblematic element of personal thought, perception and experience.* The 'experiential logic' of everyday thought is reversed, as it were. One no longer ascends merely from personal experience to general judgments, but rather general knowledge devoid of personal experience becomes the central determinant of personal experience. Chemical formulas and reactions, invisible pollutant levels, biological cycles and chain reactions have to rule seeing and thinking if one wishes to go to the barricades against risks. In this sense, we are dealing not with 'second-hand experience', in risk consciousness, but with 'second-hand non-experience'. Furthermore, ultimately *no one* can know about risks, so long as to know means to have consciously experienced.

A Speculative Age

This fundamental theoretical trait of risk consciousness is of *anthropological* importance. Threats from civilization are bringing about a kind of new 'shadow kingdom', comparable to the realm of the gods and demons in antiquity, which is hidden behind the visible world and threatens human life on this Earth. People no longer correspond today with spirits residing in things, but find themselves exposed to 'radiation', ingest 'toxic levels', and are pursued into their very dreams by the anxieties of a 'nuclear holocaust'. The place of the anthropomorphic interpretation of nature and the environment has been taken by the modern risk consciousness of civilization with its imperceptible and yet omnipresent latent causality. Dangerous, hostile substances lie concealed behind the harmless façades. Everything must be viewed with a double gaze, and can only be correctly understood and judged through this doubling. The world of the visible must be investigated, relativized and evaluated with respect to a second reality, only existent in thought and yet concealed in the world. The standards for evaluation lie only in the second, not in the visible world.

Those who simply use things, take them as they appear, who only breathe and eat, without an inquiry into the background toxic reality, are not only naive but they also misunderstand the hazards that threaten them, and thus expose themselves to such hazards with no protection. Abandonment, direct enjoyment, simple being-so are broken. Everywhere, pollutants and toxins laugh and play their tricks like devils in the Middle Ages. People are almost inescapably bound over to them. Breathing, eating, dwelling, wearing clothes – everything has been penetrated by them. Going away on a trip ultimately helps no more than eating muesli. The hazards are also waiting at the destination and they are hidden in the grain. Like the tortoise in the race with the hare, they have always been there. Their invisibility is no proof of their non-existence; instead, since their reality takes place in the realm of the invisible anyway, it gives their suspected mischief almost unlimited space.

Along with the critical risk consciousness of culture then, in almost all realms of everyday existence, a theoretically determined consciousness of reality enters the stage of world history. Like the gaze of the exorcist, the gaze of the pollution-plagued contemporary is directed at something invisible. The risk society marks the dawning of a *speculative* age in everyday perception and thought. People have always quarreled over contrasting interpretations of reality. In the development of philosophy and the theory of science, reality was brought more and more into the theoretical interpretation.

Today, however, something quite different is happening. In Plato's 'Allegory of the Cave', the visible world becomes a mere shadow, a reflection of a reality that by nature escapes our possible knowledge. The world of the visible is thus devalued *en bloc*, but is not lost as a point of reference. Something similar applies to Kant's view that 'things in themselves' are *by nature* beyond our knowledge. This is directed against 'naive realism', which duplicates individual perception into a 'world itself'. But this does not change the fact that the world appears to us in this way or that way. Even if it is only a thing *for me*, the apple I hold in my hand is no less red, round, toxic, juicy, etc.

Not until the step to cultural risk consciousness is everyday thought and imagination *removed from its moorings in the world of the visible*. In the struggle over risks of modernization we are no longer concerned with the specific value of that which appears to us in perception. What becomes the subject of controversy as to its degree of reality is instead what everyday consciousness does *not* see, and *cannot perceive*: radioactivity, pollutants and threats in the future. With this relation to theory devoid of personal experience, the controversy over risks has always been balanced on a knife's edge, and threatens to turn into a sort of *modern seance* by means of (counter-)scientific analysis.

The role of the spirits would be taken over by invisible but omnipresent pollutants and toxins. All people have their own personal hostile relationships to special subordinate toxins, their own evasion rituals, incantations, intuition, suspicions and certainties. *Once the invisible has been let in, it will soon not be just the spirits of pollutants that determine the thought and the life of people.* This can all be disputed, it can polarize, or it can fuse together. New communities and alternative communities arise, whose world views, norms and certainties are grouped around the center of invisible threats.

The Solidarity of Living Things

Their center is *fear*. What type of fear? In what way does fear have a group-forming effect? In what world view does it originate? The sensibility and morality, the rationality and responsibility that are sometimes taught and sometimes violated in the process of becoming aware of risks can no longer be understood by means of the interlocking interests of the *market*, as was still possible in the bourgeois and industrial societies. What is being articulated here are not competition-oriented individual interests sworn to the common welfare of all by the 'invisible hand' of the market. This fear and its political forms of expression are not based on any judgment of utility. It would probably also be too easy and too hasty to see in this a self-grounded interest of reason in reason, this time reformulated directly in the context of the natural and human foundations of life.

In the generalized consciousness of affliction that is quite broadly expressed in the environmental and peace movement, but also in the ecological critique of the industrial system, it is most likely other layers of experience that are spoken about. Where trees are cut down and animal species destroyed, people feel victimized *themselves* in a certain sense. The threats to life in the development of civilization touch commonalities of the experience of organic life that connect the human vital necessities to those of plants and animals. In the dying forest, people experience themselves as 'natural creatures with moral claims', as movable, vulnerable things among things, as natural parts of a threatened natural *whole*, for which they bear responsibility. Levels of a *human consciousness of nature* are wounded and awakened which undermine the dualism of body and spirit, or nature and humankind. In the threat, people have the experience that they breathe like the plants, and live *from* water as the fish live *in* water. The toxic threat makes them sense that they participate with their bodies in things – 'a metabolic process with consciousness and morality' – and consequently, that they can be eroded like the stones and the trees in the acid rain. A community among Earth, plant, animal and human being becomes visible, a *solidarity of living things*, that affects everyone and everything equally in the threat (Schütz 1984).

The 'Scapegoat Society'

denial of risk

Affliction by hazards need not result in an awareness of the hazard; it can also provoke the opposite, *denial from fear*. Wealth and risk distribution differ and overlap in this possibility of repressing the victimization oneself. Hunger cannot be satisfied by denial. Dangers, on the other hand, can always be interpreted away (as long they have not already occurred). In the experience of material need, actual affliction and subjective experience or suffering are indissolubly linked. Not so with risks. On the contrary, it is characteristic of them that it is precisely affliction that *can cause* a lack of consciousness. The possibility of denying and trivializing the danger *grows* with its extent.

There are always reasons for this. Risks originate after all in knowledge and norms, and they can thus be enlarged or reduced in knowledge and norms, or simply displaced from the screen of consciousness. What food is for hunger, eliminating risks, *or interpreting them away*, is for the consciousness of risks. The importance of the latter increases to the extent that the former is (personally) impossible. The process of becoming aware of risks is therefore always *reversible.* Troubled times and generations can be succeeded by others for which fear, tamed by interpretations, is a basic element of thought and experience. Here the threats are held captive in the cognitive cage of their always unstable 'non-existence', and in that sense one has the right of later generations to make fun at what so upset the 'old folks'. The threat from nuclear weapons with unimaginable destructive force does not change. The perception of it fluctuates wildly. For decades the phrase was: 'Live with the bomb.' Then once again it drove millions into the streets. Agitation and calming down can have *the same cause*: the unimaginability of a danger with which one must nonetheless live.

For risks, *interpretative diversions* of stirred-up insecurities and fears are more easily possible than for hunger and poverty. What is happening here need not be overcome here, but can be deflected in one direction or another and can seek and find symbolic places, persons, and objects for overcoming its fear. In risk consciousness then, *displaced* thought and action, or *displaced* social conflicts are especially possible and in demand. In that sense, precisely as the dangers increase along with political inaction, the risk society contains an inherent tendency to become a *scapegoat society*: suddenly it is not the hazards, but those who point them out that provoke the general uneasiness. Does not visible wealth always confront invisible risks? Is not the whole thing an *intellectual fantasy*, a canard from the desks of intellectual nervous nellies and risk promoters? Is it not spies, communists, Jews, Turks, or asylum seekers from the Third World who are ultimately behind it? The very intangibility of the threat and people's helplessness as it grows promote *radical and fanatical reactions and political tendencies* that make social stereotypes and the groups afflicted by them into 'lightning rods' for the invisible threats which are inaccessible to direct action.

Dealing with Insecurity: an Essential Qualification

For survival in the old industrial society, a person's skill in combating material poverty and avoiding social decline was essential. This was the focus of action and thought with the collective goal of 'class solidarity', just as much as the individual goals of educational behavior and career planning. In the risk society, additional skills become vitally necessary. Here the *ability to anticipate and endure dangers, to deal with them biographically and politically* acquires importance. In place of fears of losing status, class consciousness and orientation to upward mobility, which we have more or less learned to handle, other central questions appear. How do we handle *ascribed* outcomes of danger and the fears and insecurities residing in them? How can we cope with the fear, if we cannot overcome the causes of the fear? How can we live on the volcano of civilization without deliberately forgetting about it, but also without suffocating on the fears – and not just on the vapors that the volcano exudes?

Traditional and institutional forms of coping with fear and insecurity in the family, in marriage, sex roles, and class consciousness, as well as in the parties and institutions related to them, lose meaning. In equal measure it comes to be demanded of the individuals that they cope with fear and anxiety. Sooner or later, new demands on social institutions in education, therapy and politics are bound to arise from these increasing pressures to work out insecurity by oneself (see Part II on this). In the risk society, therefore, handling fear and insecurity becomes an *essential cultural qualification,* and the cultivation of the abilities demanded for it become an essential mission of pedagogical institutions.

The Political Dynamics of Recognized Modernization Risks

As poisoned eggs, wine, steaks, mushrooms or furniture, as well as explosions in nuclear or chemical plants demonstrate, where modernization risks have successfully passed through the process of social (re)cognition, *the order of the world changes* – even if little activity occurs at first. The limits of specialized responsibility fall. The constructions for neglecting the dangers collapse. The public gets a say in technical details. Businesses that had long been pampered in a cozy capitalist consensus because of their fiscal benefactions and their charitable creation of jobs, suddenly find themselves on the witness bench, or more precisely, locked in the pillory, and confronted with the kind of questions that were previously used to prosecute poisoners caught red-handed.

If it were only limited to that! In fact, however, markets collapse, costs become due, prohibitions and trials loom, pressure develops to renew the technical production system from the ground up – and the voters run away, no one quite knows where. Where people had felt they were alone among their own kind – in the technical, economic and legal details –

everyone suddenly wants to get a word in, and ultimately not with comparable precepts, but from a totally different system of reference. Economic and technological details are investigated in the light of a *new ecological morality*. Anyone on a crusade against pollutants must scrutinize the industrial operations from the eco-moral point of view. Before that, they must give the same scrutiny to those who controlled the operations, or better, were supposed to control them. And then to those who profit from the mistakes that systematically happen there.

Where modernization risks have been 'recognized' – and there is a lot involved in that, not just knowledge, but *collective* knowledge of them, belief in them, and the political illumination of the associated chains of cause and effect – where this happens the risks develop an incredible political dynamic. They forfeit everything, their latency, their pacifying 'side effect structure', their inevitability. Suddenly the problems are simply there, without justification, as pure, explosive challenges to action. People emerge from behind the conditions and objective constraints. *Causes* turn into *causators* and issue statements. 'Side effects' speak up, organize, go to court, assert themselves, refuse to be diverted any longer. As was said, the world has changed. These are the dynamics of *reflexive politicization* producing risk consciousness and conflict. This does not automatically help to counteract danger, but it opens up previously closed areas and opportunities for action. It produces the sudden melting point of the industrial order, where the unthinkable and unmakeable become possibilities for a short period.

What begins to happen here, is of course supposed to be prevented through resisting recognition. This once again throws characteristic light on what is really at stake in the process of recognition for modernization risks. The decisive factor here is not, or at least not only, the health consequences, the consequences for the life of plants, animals and people, but *the social, economic and political side effects of these side effects*: market collapses, devaluation of capital, creeping expropriation, new responsibilities, market shifts, political pressures, checks on plant decisions, recognition of compensation claims, gigantic costs, legal proceedings, and loss of face.

The ecological and health consequences may be as hypothetical, as justified, as minimized, or as dramatized as they wish. Where they are *believed* they have the social, economic, political and legal consequences just mentioned. To put it in the well known sociological sentence: if people experience risks as real, *they are real* as a consequence. If they are *real* in this sense, however, they completely mix up the structure of social, political and economic (ir)responsibility. Thus, a political explosive accumulates with the recognition of modernization risks. Things that were still possible yesterday suddenly face limits today. Anyone who still trivializes the exportation of chemical factories and possibly military technologies to Iraq after the Gulf War must obviously be prepared to be accused publicly of cynicism. 'Acceptable exposures' turn into 'intolerable sources of hazards'. What was recently still beyond the possibilities of human intervention, now becomes part of the scope of political influence. The *relativity* of acceptable levels and of *variables inaccessible to policy-making* becomes manifest. The checks and balances of the political and the non-political, the necessary and the possible, the given and the changeable are redetermined. Solid techno-economic 'constants' – the emission of pollutants, for instance, the 'indispensability' of nuclear energy, or the gap between civilian and military production – are recast into politically malleable variables.

Here we are no longer concerned only with the established repertoire of politics – controlling the market through economic policy, redistributions of income, social security measures – but rather with the *non-political: the elimination of the causes of hazards in the modernization process itself becomes political*. Questions that fall within the sovereignty of industrial management, such as details of product planning, production processes, types of energy and disposal of wastes are no longer just questions for plant management. They become instead *hot potatoes for governmental policy-making*, which can even compete with the problems of unemployment in voters' opinions. As the threat grows, the old priorities melt away, and parallel to that the *interventionist policy of the state of emergency* grows, drawing its expanded authorities and possibilities for intervention from the threatening condition. Where danger becomes normalcy, it assumes permanent institutional form. In that respect, modernization risks prepare the field for a partial *redistribution of power* – partially retaining the old formal responsibilities, partially expressly altering them.

The accustomed structure of (ir)responsibilities in the relationship between business, politics and the public is increasingly shaken; the more emphatically the dangers in the modernization process increase, the more obviously central values of the public are threatened in this, and the more clearly it enters everyone's consciousness. It is also that much more likely that under the influence of the threatening danger responsibilities will be redefined, authorities to act centralized, and all the details of the modernization process encrusted with bureaucratic controls and planning. In *their effect*, with the recognition of modernization risks and the increase of the dangers they contain, *some changes to the system* occur. This, of course, happens in the form not of an open but of a *silent* revolution, as a consequence of *everyone's* change in consciousness, as an upheaval *without* a subject, without an exchange of elites and while the old order is maintained.

In the unbridled development of civilization, quasi-revolutionary situations are virtually *ascribed*. They come into being as a civilizational *fate* occasioned by modernization. Hence they possess on the one hand the pretense of *normality*, and on the other, the *enabling power of catastrophes*, which can quite well achieve and exceed the political significance of revolutions. The risk society is thus not a revolutionary society, but more than that, a *catastrophic society*. In it the *state of emergency* threatens *to become the normal state*.

We know all too well from the history of Germany in this century that an actual or potential catastrophe is no teacher of democracy. How ambivalent and scandalous the accumulating explosive already is becomes perfectly clear in the report of the 'environmental experts', despite themselves (Rat der Sachverständigen für Umweltfragen 1985). The urgency of the environmental dangers to the lives of plants, animals, and people depicted there 'legitimates' these experts with a confessional ecological morality typical of the turn of the twenty-first century. It gives birth to a language that fairly crawls with expressions like 'control', 'official approval', and 'official supervision'. Characteristically, far-reaching intervention, planning and control possibilities and rights are demanded there, on a graduated scale depending on the severity of the insults to the environment (45). There is discussion of an 'expansion of the surveillance and information system for agriculture' (45). They dramatize the challenges to 'comprehensive land planning' with 'biotopic surveys' and 'plans for protection of an area', based on 'scientifically exact surveys down to the level of individual plots' to be 'imposed against competing utilization demands' (48f.). In order to accomplish its plan of 'renaturation' (51), the Council recommends 'removing the most important areas . . . completely from the cultivation interests of their owners' (49). The farmers should 'be motivated by compensation to forgo certain usage rights or to adopt required protective measures' (49). They discuss 'fertilization permits subject to official approval', 'legally binding fertilization plans with concrete provisions on type, extent, and time of application' (53). This 'planned fertilization' (59), like other protective measures, requires a differentiated system of 'environmental surveillance' that is to be set up nationally, regionally and on the scale of individual operations (61), and will 'require a revision and further development of the basic legal provisions' (64). In short, the panorama of a *scientific and bureaucratic authoritarianism* is being laid out.

Farmers were viewed for centuries as the 'peasantry' wresting the 'fruits' from the soil, on which the life and survival of everyone depended, but this image is beginning to be transformed into its opposite. In this new view, agriculture becomes a distribution point for the toxins that threaten the lives of animals, plants and people. To turn aside the threatening dangers at the currently achieved high level of agricultural productivity, people demand expropriation and/or plans and controls governing every detail of work, all under the patronage of science and bureaucracy. It is not just these demands (or even the matter-of-fact way they are raised) that is the disturbing element here. Instead it is that they *are part of the logic of hazard prevention*, and that, considering the impending hazards, it will not likely prove to be at all easy to point to *political alternatives* that really prevent what must be prevented under the dictatorship of dangers.

With the increase of hazards *totally new types of challenges to democracy* arise in the risk society. It harbors a tendency to a *legitimate totalitarianism of hazard prevention*, which takes the right to prevent the worst and, in an all too familiar manner, creates something even worse. The political 'side effects' of civilization's 'side effects' threaten the continued existence of the democratic political system. That system is caught in the unpleasant dilemma of either failing in the face of systematically produced hazards, or suspending fundamental democratic principles through the addition of authoritarian, repressive 'buttresses'. Breaking through this alternative is among the essential tasks of democratic thought and action in the already apparent future of the risk society.

Outlook: Nature and Society at the End of the Twentieth Century

With the industrially forced degradation of the ecological and natural foundations of life, a historically unparalleled and so far completely uncomprehended social and political dynamic is set in motion, which also forces a rethinking of the relationship between nature and society. This point requires some theoretical explication. A few points of orientation will be suggested here in conclusion, necessary for the courage to venture into a tentative future.

The preceding discussion meant in sum: *the end of the antithesis between nature and society*. That means that nature can no longer be understood *outside of* society, or society *outside of* nature. The social theories of the nineteenth century (and also their modified versions in the twentieth century) understood nature as something given, ascribed, to be subdued, and therefore always as something opposing us, alien to us, as *non*-society. These imputations have been nullified by the industrialization process itself, *historically falsified*, one could say. At the end of the twentieth century, nature is *neither* given *nor* ascribed, but has instead become a historical product, the *interior* furnishings of the civilizational world, destroyed or endangered in the natural conditions of its reproduction. But that means that the destruction of nature, integrated into the universal circulation of industrial production, ceases to be 'mere' destruction of nature and becomes an integral component of the social, political and economic dynamic. The unseen side effect of the societalization [*Vergesellschaftung*] of nature is the *societalization of the destruction and threats to nature*, their transformation into economic, social and political contradictions and conflicts. Violations of the natural conditions of life turn into global social, economic and medical threats to people – with completely new sorts of challenges to the social and political institutions of highly industrialized global society.

This very transformation of threats to nature from culture into threats to the social, economic and political order is the concrete challenge of the present and the future which once again justifies the concept of risk society. Whereas the concept of the classical industrial society is based on the antithesis between nature and society (in the nineteenth century sense), the concept of the (industrial) risk society proceeds from 'nature' as integrated by culture, and the metamorphosis of injuries to it is traced through the social subsystems. What 'injury' means here is subject, under the conditions of industrialized secondary nature, to scientific, counter-scientific and social definitions – as has been shown. This controversy has been retraced here using the origin and awareness of *modernization risks* as a guide. That means that 'modernization risks' are the conceptual arrangement, the categorical setting, in which injuries to and destruction of nature, as immanent in civilization, are seized upon socially. In this scenario of conflict, decisions are made as to the validity and urgency of risks, and the way they will be repressed or dealt with is decided. Modernization risks are the scientized 'second morality' in which negotiations are conducted on the injuries of the industrially exhausted ex-nature in a socially 'legitimate' way, that is, with a claim to effective remedy.

The central consequence is that in advanced modernity, society with all its subsystems of the economy, politics, culture and the family can no longer be understood as autonomous of nature. Environmental problems are *not* problems of our surroundings, but – in their origins and through their consequences – are thoroughly *social* problems, *problems of people*, their history, their living conditions, their relation to the world and reality, their social, cultural and political situations. The industrially transformed 'domestic nature' of the cultural world must frankly be understood as an exemplary *non*-environment, as an *inner* environment, in the face of which all of our highly bred possibilities of distancing and excluding ourselves *fail*. At the end of the twentieth century nature *is* society and society is also *'nature'*. Anyone who continues to speak of nature as non-society is speaking in terms from a different century, which no longer capture our reality.

In nature, we are concerned today with a highly synthetic product everywhere, an artificial 'nature'. Not a hair or a crumb of it is still 'natural', if 'natural' means nature being left to itself. Even the scientists do not confront the artifact of 'nature', which they investigate with professional scientific patience, in a purely scientific manner. In their actions and their knowledge they are *executors* of the generalized social claim to the mastery of nature. When they bend over their material, alone or in regional research laboratories, in a certain sense everyone is looking over their shoulder. When they move their hands, these are the hands of an institution, and in that sense, the hands of all of us. What is treated there as 'nature' is the internal 'second nature' brought into the cultural process, and thus burdened and overburdened with not very 'natural' system functions and meanings. Under these conditions, whatever scientists do, measure, ask, assume, or check, they *advance or impair* health, economic interests, property rights, responsibilities, or jurisdictions. In other words, *because* it is a nature circulating and utilized within the system, nature has become *political*, even at the objective hands of objective (natural) scientists. Results of measurements, unburdened by a single evaluative word or even the smallest normative exclamation mark, proceeding with the utmost objectivity in a linguistic desert of figures, which would have been a pure joy to good old Max Weber, can contain a political explosive power never reached by the most apocalyptic formulations of social scientists, philosophers or moralists.

Because their object is 'charged' in this way, natural scientists work in a *powerful political, economic and cultural magnetic field*. They notice this and react to it *in* their work: in the development of measuring procedures, in decisions on thresholds of tolerance, the pursuit of causal hypotheses and so on. The lines of force from this magnetic field can even direct their pens on occasion. They allow the questioning to settle into tracks which must of course then be justified on a purely substantive basis. And they probably also form the energy source which feeds the red lights that flash on against career prospects when certain decisions are taken in the course of the argumentation. These are all just indications that under the conditions of a societalized nature, the natural and engineering sciences *have become a branch office of politics, ethics, business and judicial practice in the garb of numbers*, despite the external preservation of all their objectivity (see Chapter 7 on this).

Thus, the natural sciences have slipped into a historical situation of work and experience which the social sciences have always known, given the obviously political character of their 'subject'. It is as if a uniform scientific convergence takes place, but one where the convergence ironically stems from the politicization of the subject, and not what might have at first been suspected, the approach of the semi-scientific character of the social sciences to the super-ego provided by natural science. In the future, it will become a central insight for the role of *all* sciences that one requires an *institutionally strengthened and protected moral and political backbone in order to be able to conduct respectable research at all*. Then, however, research will consciously have to assume and settle the burden of its political implications. In a certain way, the substantive quality and the political significance of scientific work could someday be harmonized. This would have to mean above all that as taboo zones inspired by political sensibilities grow, there would be a proportionally increasing, institutionally enabled willingness to break out of them relentlessly and competently by asserting the primacy of knowledge. This could shed light on the well worn institutional, scientifically mediated routines and rituals for obscuring the risks to our continued existence from civilization.

The socio-cultural critique of modernity must always struggle against the (sociological) platitude that traditional norms just simply get violated in the course of modernity. Contradictions between even the most proven norms and social development are central to even the most mundane everyday life. In that sense, the cutting edge of social-scientific cultural criticism has been blunted from the start by the social sciences themselves. Yet only a bad sociologist could repeatedly argue against the dark side of modernity with that evolutionary optimism which we know culminates in the repeated triumph of rational reason.

It is somewhat different with the sociological demonstration that groups are being neglected, that social inequalities are intensifying, and economic crises overtaking one another. Considering organized campaigning groups, this contains a great deal of explosive power, as we know. Nevertheless, there is also a parallel here that connects these figures of thought with those previously mentioned, and differentiates them from the scientific risk report: the transgression of values is *selective* and can be *permanently institutionalized*. The same is true for social inequality. It *does not* apply to the consequences of modernization, which threaten *survival*. These follow a universalized, egalitarian basic pattern. Their institutionalization, which is of course possible, as we have experienced, interferes irreversibly with everyone's health. 'Health' is certainly also a culturally elevated value, but it is – in addition to that – the prerequisite for survival. The universalization of health threats create threats to existence, everywhere and eternally, which now penetrate the economic and political system with corresponding rigor.

But not only cultural and social premises are being threatened here, which one can live with after all, despite all the tears shed over them on the path of modernity. At least at the underlying level that is being violated, the question arises as to how long the list of endangered plant and animal species can be confined to plants and animals. It may be that we are situated at the beginning of a historical process of habituation. It may be that the next generation, or the one after that, will no longer be upset at pictures of birth defects, like those of tumor-covered fish and birds that now circulate around the world, just as we are no longer upset today by violated values, the new poverty and a constant high level of mass unemployment. It would not be the first time that standards disappear as a result of their violation. The well founded opinion still endures that it will not happen this way, that on the contrary, as nature is increasingly industrialized, its destruction will be universalized and perceived as such. (This is a fact at which no one can rejoice, especially not in the interest of a professionalization of criticism.)

It may sound paradoxical to sociologists' ears, not used to formulas, but the recourse to chemical, biological or medical hazard formulas – whether justified scientifically or in some other way – may very well be able to provide social-science research with critical, normative premises. Conversely, the implicit content of those premises will probably first become recognizable in their extension into the social and political. That also means, of course, that as modernization risks develop, social scientists, like everyone else, are dependent on *second-hand non-experience controlled by professionals outside their field*, with all the damage that does to their battered ideals of professional autonomy. What the social scientists can offer from their own efforts can hardly compete with that.[3]

Notes

1 *Wehrpolitische Information, Wehrberichterstattung aus aller Welt*, Cologne, 1959; quoted in Anders (1983: 133).
2 *Environmental Quality 1975*, 6th report of the CEQU, Washington: 326; quoted Jänicke (1979: 60).
3 For further argument on this point see Beck (1988: Part II).

PART II

The Individualization of Social Inequality: Life Forms and the Demise of Tradition

The distributional logic of modernization risks, as elaborated in the preceding chapter, is an essential dimension of the risk society, but only *one*. The global risk situations that come into being and the social and political dynamism of development and conflict they contain are new and considerable. But they overlap with social, biographical and cultural risks and insecurities. In advanced modernity, the latter have disembodied and reshaped the inner social structure of industrial society and its grounded and basic certainties of life conduct – social classes, familial forms, gender status, marriage, parenthood, and occupations.

This second feature will be the center of attention from now on. Both sides together, the sum of risks and insecurities, their mutual reinforcement or neutralization, constitute the social and political dynamic of industrial society. In sweeping terms, one can formulate the theory of reflexive modernization: at the turn of the twenty-first century the unleashed process of modernization is overrunning and overcoming its own coordinate system. This coordinate system had fixed understandings about the separation of nature and society, the understanding of science and technology and the cultural reality of social class. It featured a stable mapping of the axes between which the life of its people is suspended – family and occupation. It assumed a certain distribution and separation of democratically legitimated politics on the one hand, and the 'sub-politics' of business, science and technology on the other.

Ambivalences: Individuals and the Developed Labor Market

At the core of this section lies the assessment that we are eye witnesses to a social transformation within modernity, in the course of which people will be *set free* from the social forms of industrial society – class, stratification, family, gender status of men and women – just as during the course of the Reformation people were 'released' from the secular rule of the Church into society. The argument can be outlined in seven theses.

(1) In the welfare states of the West, reflexive modernization dissolves the traditional parameters of industrial society: class culture and consciousness, gender and family roles. It dissolves these forms of the conscience collective, on which depend and to which refer the social and political organizations and institutions in industrial society. These detraditionalizations happen in a *social surge of individualization*. At the same time the *relations* of inequality remain stable. How is this possible? Against the background of a comparatively high material standard of living and advanced social security systems, the people have been removed from class commitments and have to refer to themselves in planning their individual labor market biographies.

The process of individualization has previously been claimed largely for the developing bourgeoisie. In a different form, however, it is also characteristic of the 'free wage laborer' in modern capitalism, of the dynamics of labor market processes, labor mobility, education and changing occupation. The entry into the labor market dissolves such bindings and is connected over and over again with 'liberations' [*Freisetzungen*] in a double sense from traditional networks and the constraints of the labor market. Family, neighborhood, even friendship, as well as ties to a regional culture and landscape, contradict the individual mobility and the mobile individual required by the labor market. These surges of individualization do compete with the experiences of a collective fate (mass unemployment and deskilling); however, under the conditions of a welfare state, class biographies, which are somehow ascribed, become transformed into reflexive biographies which depend on the decisions of the actor.

(2) With respect to the interpretation of *social inequality*, therefore, an ambivalent situation arises. For the Marxist theoretician of classes as well as for the investigator of stratification, it may be that not much has changed. The separations in the hierarchy of income and the fundamental conditions of wage labor have remained the same. On the other hand, ties to a social class recede mysteriously into the background for the actions of people. Status-based social milieus and lifestyles typical of a class culture lose their luster. The tendency is towards the emergence of individualized forms and conditions of existence, which compel people – for the sake of their own material survival – to make themselves the center of their own planning and conduct of life. Increasingly, everyone has to choose between different options, including as to which group or subculture one wants to be identified with. In fact, one has to choose and change one's social identity as well and take the risks in doing so. In this sense, individualization means the variation and differentiation of lifestyles and forms of life, opposing the thinking behind the traditional categories of large-group societies – which is to say, classes, estates, and social stratification.

In Marxist theories the antagonism between classes was linked once and for all to the 'essence' of industrial capitalism. This conceptualizing of historical experience into a permanent form can be expressed as the *law of the excluded middle*: *either* capitalism exits the stage of world history through the only door open to it – the intensifying class struggle – with the 'big bang of revolution', and then reappears through the back door, with transformed relationships of ownership, as socialist society; *or* the classes struggle and struggle and struggle. The individualization thesis asserts the excluded middle, that the dynamism of the labor market backed up by the welfare state has diluted or dissolved the social classes *within* capitalism. To put it in Marxist terms, we increasingly confront the phenomenon of a capitalism *without* classes, but with individualized social inequality and all the related social and political problems.

(3) This tendency to the 'classlessness' of social inequality appears as a textbook example in the distribution of mass unemployment. On the one hand, the proportion of the unemployed who have been without work for a long time is rising, as is the proportion of people who have left the

labor market, or never entered it at all. On the other hand, the constancy of the number of unemployed by no means implies a constancy of registered cases and affected persons. In Germany during the years from 1974 to 1983, roughly 12.5 million people, or *every third* gainfully employed German, were unemployed at least once. Simultaneously there are growing gray zones between registered and unregistered unemployment (among housewives, youths, early retirers) as well as between employment and underemployment (flexibilized work hours and forms of employment). The broad distribution of more or less temporary unemployment thus coincides with a growing number of long-term unemployed and with new hybrids between unemployment and employment. The culture of social classes is unable to provide a context of orientation for this. Intensification *and* individualization of social inequalities interlock. As a consequence, problems of the system are lessened politically and transformed into personal failure. In the detraditionalized modes of living, a *new immediacy for individual and society* arises, the immediacy of *crisis and sickness*, in the sense that social crises appear to be of individual origin, and are perceived as social only indirectly and to a very limited extent.

(4) The 'freeing' relative to status-like social classes is joined by a 'freeing' relative to *gender status,* as reflected primarily in the changed condition of *women*. The most recent data speak clearly: it is not social position or lack of education but *divorce* which is the trap-door through which women fall into the 'new poverty'. This is an expression of the extent to which women are being cut loose from support as spouses and housewives, a process which can no longer be checked. The spiral of individualization is thus taking hold *inside* the family: labor market, education, mobility – everything is doubled and trebled. Families become the scene of a continuous juggling of diverging multiple ambitions among occupational necessities, educational constraints, parental duties and the monotony of housework. The type of the 'negotiated family' comes into being, in which individuals of both genders enter into a more or less regulated exchange of emotional comfort, which is always cancellable.

(5) Even these quarrels between the sexes, which occur as matters for the individuals involved, have another dimension. From a theoretical point of view, what happens between a man and a woman, both inside and outside the family, follows a general pattern. These are the consequences of reflexive modernization and the private parameters of industrial society, since the industrial social order has always divided the indivisible principles of modernity – individual freedom and equality – and has ascribed them by birth to only one gender and withheld them from the other. Industrial society *never* is and *never* was possible *only* as industrial society, but always as half industrial and half *feudal* society, whose feudal side is not a relic of tradition, but the *product* and *foundation* of industrial society. In that way, as industrial society triumphs, it has always promoted the dissolution of its family morality, its gender fates, its taboos relative to marriage, parenthood and sexuality, even the reunification of housework and wage labor.

what about Race?

(6) This brings out clearly the special features of present-day individualization (by comparison to apparently similar ones in the Renaissance or the early industrial age). The new aspect results from the consequences. The place of hereditary estates is no longer taken by social classes, nor does the stable frame of reference of gender and the family take the place of social classes. *The individual himself or herself becomes the reproduction unit of the social in the lifeworld.* What the social is and does has to be involved with individual decisions. Or put another way, both within and outside the family, the individuals become the agents of their educational and market-mediated subsistence and the related life planning and organization. Biography itself is acquiring a reflexive project.

This differentiation of individual conditions in the developed labor market society must not, however, be equated with successful emancipation. In this sense, individualism does not signify the beginning of the self-creation of the world by the resurrected individual. Instead it accompanies tendencies toward the *institutionalization* and *standardization* of ways of life. The detraditionalized individuals become dependent on the labor market, and *with that*, dependent on education, consumption, regulations and support from social laws, traffic planning, product offers, possibilities and fashions in medical, psychological and pedagogical counseling and care. All of this points to the special forms of control which are being established here.

(7) Correspondingly, individualization is understood here as a historically contradictory *process of societalization*. The collectivity and standardization of the resulting 'individual' modes of living are of course difficult to grasp. Nevertheless, it is precisely the eruption and the growing awareness of these contradictions which can lead to *new socio-cultural commonalities*. It may be that social movements and citizens' groups are formed in relation to modernization risks and risk situations. It may be that in the course of individualization expectations are aroused in the form of a desire for a 'life of one's own' (in material, temporal and spatial terms, and in structuring social relationships) – expectations which however face social and political resistance. In this way *new social movements* come into existence again and again. On the one hand, these react to the increasing risks and the growing risk consciousness and risk conflicts; on the other hand, they experiment with social relationships, personal life and one's own body in the numerous variants of the alternative and youth subcultures. Not least of all, therefore, communities are produced from the forms and experiences of the protest that is ignited by administrative and industrial interference in private 'personal life', and develop their aggressive stance in opposition to these encroachments. In this sense, on the one hand the new social movements (ecology, peace, feminism) are expressions of the new risk situations in the risk society. On the other, they result from the search for social and personal identities and commitments in detraditionalized culture.

3

Beyond Status and Class?

Are advanced societies class societies? In looking for an answer to this question, we immediately confront apparently contradictory facts. When examining the situation from a socio-historical perspective, we find that the structure of social inequality in the developed countries displays an amazing stability. Research on this clearly indicates that, especially in Germany, the inequalities between the major social groups *have not changed* appreciably, except for some relatively minor shifts and reallocations, despite all the technological and economic transformations and in the face of the many efforts in the past two or three decades to introduce changes.[1]

Nevertheless, it is during precisely this period that the topic of inequality disappeared almost completely from the agenda of daily life, of politics, and of scholarship. It may well be that, under conditions of economic stagnation and consistently high or even rising unemployment, it will once again turn into a socially explosive issue. It is surprising, however, how much inequality has lost significance as an issue during the past two decades. Now and again questions may be raised about inequality in other contexts or in the form of new confrontations (e.g. in the struggle for women's rights, grassroots initiatives against nuclear power plants, intergenerational inequality, even regional and religious conflicts). But if public and political discussion is taken as an accurate indication of the actual developments one could easily be led to the conclusion that in the Western countries, especially Germany, we have moved beyond class society. The notion of a class society remains useful only as an image of the past. It only stays alive because there is not yet any suitable alternative.[2]

The analysis that follows therefore aims to explain a paradoxical state of affairs. My thesis is that in the history of Germany patterns of social inequality have remained relatively *stable*. Yet at the same time the *living conditions of the population have changed dramatically*. Changes in income and education, in addition to other social changes, have contributed to this. These changes have been taken account of in a number of sociological investigations but they have never been analyzed systematically or explained as important social structural developments in their own right. I would therefore like to show that, as a result of shifts in the standard of living, subcultural class identities have dissipated, class distinctions based on status have lost their traditional support, and processes for the 'diversification' and individualization of lifestyles and ways of life have been set in motion. As a result, the hierarchical model of social classes and stratification has increasingly been subverted. It no longer corresponds to reality (Weber 1972).

During the past three decades, almost unnoticed by social stratification research, the social meaning of inequality has changed. In all wealthy Western and industrialized countries, a *process of individualization* has taken place. And while this process still continues, persistent inequalities have concealed it from our view. To put it more concisely, there have been specific historical developments leading to individualization. They have disrupted the experience of historical continuity; as a consequence people have lost their traditional support networks and have had to rely on themselves and their own individual (labor market) fate with all its attendant risks, opportunities, and contradictions (Berger et al. 1975; Touraine 1983).

Processes of individualization are very dynamic; they make it difficult to avoid ambiguities in the interpretation of social structure. Empirical stratification research or Marxist class analysis probably detect no significant changes; income inequalities, the structure of the division of labor, and the basic determinants of wage labor have, after all, remained relatively unchanged. The attachment of people to a 'social class' (in Max Weber's sense) has nevertheless become weaker. It now has much less influence on their actions. They develop ways of life that tend to become individualized. For the sake of economic survival, individuals are now compelled to make themselves the center of their own life plans and conduct.

The Labor Market as 'Motor' of Individualization

'Individualization of social inequality' – does this not suggest that everything important is being forgotten, misunderstood, or simply dismissed, including everything we have learned about the class character of society, its nature as a system, about mass society and capital concentration, about ideological distortions and alienation, about unchanging human traits and the complexity of social and historical reality? And does not the concept of individualization also spell the premature end of sociology, leading to the tolling of its bell?

This requires more precise arguments. The existence of individualization has been empirically verified in numerous qualitative interviews and studies. They all point to one central concern, the demand for control of one's own money, time, living space, and body. In other words, people demand the right to develop their own perspective on life and to be able to act upon it. However illusory and ideological these claims may turn out to be, they are a reality which cannot be overlooked. And they arise from the actual conditions of life in Germany as they have developed in the past three decades (Mooser 1983; Fuchs 1983).

But today it is also becoming apparent that such processes of individualization can be quite precarious, especially where groups suddenly face or are threatened by unemployment and forced to confront radical disruptions of their lifestyle precisely because of the individualization they have experienced, and despite the protections provided by the welfare state.

Among the negative effects of individualization processes are the separation of the individual from traditional support networks (e.g. family or neighborhood), the loss of supplementary sources of income (e.g. part-time farming), and, along with this, the experience of an increased wage and consumption dependency in all spheres of life. To the extent that the main income security of this new condition of life, steady employment, is lost – regardless of the availability of social security – people are suddenly confronting an abyss. We already receive rather disturbing news from the United States: more than twelve million unemployed, more than thirty million living below the poverty line. But there are also alarming upheavals within Germany among welfare recipients and the so-called 'transient population'. Women may face particular threats in the future. Because of individualization processes, on the one hand, they have extricated themselves from the traditional network of support offered by the family, and the new divorce laws also force them to stand on their own feet economically. On the other hand, their position in the labor market is especially uncertain and the percentage of unemployed women is known to be much higher than that of men, in spite of a good deal of underreporting (Beck-Gernsheim 1983; see also Chapter 4).

How can these developments be distinguished from the rise of bourgeois individualism in the eighteenth and nineteenth centuries? Processes of individualization among the bourgeoisie derived essentially from the ownership and accumulation of capital. The bourgeoisie developed its social and political identity in the struggle against feudal structures of domination and authority. In late modernity, by contrast, individualization is a product of the labor market and manifests itself in the acquisition, proffering, and application of a variety of work skills. This argument can be elaborated by looking at three dimensions of the labor market – education, mobility, and competition.

Education

Schooling means choosing and planning one's own educational life course. The educated person becomes the producer of his or her own labor situation, and in this way, of his or her social biography. As schooling increases in duration, traditional orientations, ways of thinking, and lifestyles are recast and displaced by universalistic forms of learning and teaching, as well as by universalistic forms of knowledge and language. Depending on its duration and contents, education makes possible at least a certain degree of self-discovery and reflection. The educated person incorporates reflexive knowledge of the conditions and prospects of modernity, and in this way becomes an agent of reflexive modernization.

This means, for instance, that hierarchical models of divisions of labor no longer function without friction. The content and meaning of the waste of human material resources and its social consequences are adopted. Education, furthermore, is connected with selection and therefore requires the individual's expectation of upward mobility; these expectations remain effective even in cases where upward mobility through education is an illusion, since education is little more than a protection against downward mobility (as to some extent happened during the period of expansion of educational opportunities). For it is after all only possible to pass through formal education by individually succeeding by way of assignments, examinations, and tests. Formal education in schools and universities, in turn, provides individual credentials leading to individualized career opportunities in the labor market.

Mobility

As soon as people enter the labor market, they experience mobility. They are removed from traditional patterns and arrangements, and unless they are prepared to suffer economic ruin, they are forced to take charge of their own life. The labor market, by way of occupational mobility, place of residence or employment, type of employment, as well as the changes in social location it initiates, reveals itself as the driving force behind the individualization of people's lives. They become relatively independent of inherited or newly formed ties (e.g. family, neighborhood, friendship, partnership). There is a *hidden contradiction between the mobility demands of the labor market and social bonds*. As Georg Simmel argued in the case of money, this means loosening local and constructing non-local networks. By becoming independent from traditional ties, people's lives take on an independent quality which, for the first time, makes possible the experience of a personal destiny (Kaelble 1983b; Goldthorpe 1980).

Competition

Competition rests upon the interchangeability of qualifications and thereby compels people to advertise the individuality and uniqueness of their work and of their own accomplishments. The growing pressure of competition leads to an individualization among equals, i.e. precisely in areas of interaction and conduct which are characterized by a shared background (similar education, similar experience, similar knowledge). Especially where such a shared background still exists, community is dissolved in the acid bath of competition. In this sense, competition undermines the equality of equals without, however, eliminating it. It causes the isolation of individuals within homogeneous social groups.

Education, mobility, and competition, however, are by no means independent of each other. Rather they supplement and reinforce each other.

Only by thus reinforcing each other do they cause the processes of individualization.

Other developments also play an important role here. First, there is the collective upward mobility and increasing standards of living and higher income in Germany during the last four decades. At the same time the distance between different income groups has persisted. Nevertheless this means a *democratization of formerly exclusive types of consumption and styles of living*, such as private cars, holiday travel and so on. The effects of individualization here can be illustrated with the example of the women's movement. Women *now earn their own money*, which means they are no longer dependent on their husbands' earnings and can construct their own lives inside or outside the family.

The second example is the *juridification of labor relations*. The differentiation of labor law as a special form of legislation leads to an individualization of interests which no longer depend upon highly aggregated interest groups (e.g. organizations and parties) for their recognition. Individuals who are affected are thus able to defend their rights (which they strongly defend) directly in the courts.

Individualization and Class Formation: Marx and Weber

The thrust toward individualization in the welfare state can be understood more precisely by examining Karl Marx's and Max Weber's theories of social inequality. It is quite possible to regard Marx as one of the most resolute theorists of 'individualization'. Marx often stressed that an unparalleled process of emancipation had been set in motion as a result of the development of industrial capitalism. In his view, emancipation from feudal relations was a precondition for the establishment of capitalist relations of production. But even *within* capitalism itself people are uprooted in successive waves and wrested loose from tradition, family, neighborhood, occupation, and culture.

Marx never followed up on this variant of a class society caught in the process of individualization. For him this capitalist process of isolation and 'uprooting' *had always been cushioned by the collective experience of immiseration and the resulting class struggle*. Marx thought that it was precisely the process of emancipation and uprooting and the deterioration of the living conditions of workers under capitalism that led to the transformation of the working class from a 'class in itself' into a 'class for itself'. He dismissed as irrelevant the question of how individual proletarians, as participants in a market of exchange, could ever form stable bonds of solidarity, given that capitalism systematically uprooted their lives. Marx always equated processes of individualization with the formation of classes. This still appears to be the basic position of many contemporary class theorists.

The thesis of the individualization of social inequality may be regarded as the exact mirror image of the Marxian position. Processes of individualization, as I have described them, can only become entrenched when material immiseration, as the condition for the formation of classes predicted by Marx, has been *overcome*. Trends toward individualization are dependent upon complex structural conditions, which have until now been realized in very few countries, and even then only during the most recent phase of the development of the welfare state.

I can now refine my argument and turn to Max Weber as the other important theorist of social inequality. On the one hand, as is well known, Max Weber recognized the great range of modern ways of life much more emphatically than Marx. On the other hand, he ignored the latent tendencies toward individualization within market society. Weber, in fact, argued that these could not succeed, but without sharing Marx's belief in class formation resulting from immiseration. Tendencies toward individualization were blocked, according to Weber, by the *continuity and the authority of traditions and subcultures based on status*. In industrial capitalism traditional 'status-bound' attitudes, Weber argues, have been combined with expertise and market opportunities into substantively differentiated 'social class positions'. Thus Weber's work already contained the basic arguments spelled out in detail by Marxist labor historians at the end of the 1960s (Thompson 1963; Giddens 1973). For these historians and sociologists the characteristic norms governing lifeworlds, value orientations and lifestyles during the expansion of industrial capitalism are less the product of 'class structure' and 'class formation' (as understood by Marx) than remnants of pre-capitalist and pre-industrial traditions. 'Capitalist culture' is consequently a less autochthonous creation than is often assumed. It is rather of pre-capitalist origins, modernized and assimilated by a system of industrial capitalism which recasts and consumes it. Even though different trends toward 'disenchantment' and the 'demystification' of traditional lifestyles do gain a footing, the dynamic process of 'individualization' is still understood by Weber as contained and buffered by status-based community organizations, themselves linked to social class positions maintained by the market. Most research on social inequalities still follows Max Weber in this regard.

Historical studies suggest that this indeed applies to developments in the early 1950s, but I do not believe that it still holds for post-war developments in Germany at least, or in other European countries like Sweden or Finland. At that point in time the unstable unity of shared life experiences mediated by the market and shaped by status, which Max Weber brought together in the concept of social class, began to break apart. Its different elements (such as material conditions dependent upon specific market opportunities, the effectiveness of tradition and of pre-capitalist lifestyles, the consciousness of communal bonds and of barriers to mobility, as well as networks of contact) have slowly disintegrated. They have been changed beyond recognition by the increasing standard of living and the increasing dependence on education as well as by an intensified mobility, competition and the juridification of labor relations.

The traditional internal differentiations and social environments, which were still real enough for industrial workers in imperial Germany and in the Weimar Republic, have been increasingly dissolved since the 1950s. At the same time, differences within the industrial labor force and between rural and urban populations have been leveled. Everywhere educational reform is accompanied by a dependence on education. More and more groups get caught up in the race for educational credentials. As a result there emerge new *internal* differentiations. While these may still respond to traditional differences between groups, the impact of education makes them fundamentally different from traditional ones. Here we can employ Basil Bernstein's (1971) distinction that the new generation must move from a 'restricted' to an 'elaborated' code of speech. In conjunction with novel patterns of upward and downward mobility and increasing local labor mobility as well, new hierarchies and differentiations develop which are internal to social classes. They presuppose the expansion of the service sector and the creation of new occupations. The influx of large numbers of guest workers in Germany is also a condition contributing to this formation; for they occupy the lowest rung on the social ladder. These new hierarchies do not readily fit into the established categories of research. Thus their significance for the population's outlook on life has not yet been noticed.

During the same period, traditional forms of settlement have frequently been replaced by new urban housing projects. These changes have also generated new forms of individualization. They affect patterns of interaction dependent upon housing and living arrangements. The modern metropolis as well as urban developments in the smaller towns replace traditional settlement patterns. People from a great variety of cultural backgrounds are mixed together and social relations in the neighborhood are much more loosely organized. Thus traditional forms of community beyond the family are beginning to disappear. Often, the members of the family choose their own separate relationships and live in networks of their own. This need not imply that social isolation increases or that relatively private family life prevails – although this may happen. But it does imply that already existing (ascriptively organized) neighborhoods are shattered, together with their limitations and their opportunities for social control. The newly formed social relationships and social networks now have to be individually chosen; social ties, too, are becoming *reflexive*, so that they have to be established, maintained, and constantly renewed by individuals.

This may mean, to choose an extreme example, the absence of interaction, i.e. that social isolation and loneliness may become the major pattern of relationships, as often happens with elderly people. It may also mean, however, that *self-selected and self-created hierarchies and forms of stratification* may develop in relationships with acquaintances, neighbors, and friends. These relationships are no longer primarily dependent upon 'physical' proximity. Whether they transcend the local sphere or not, they are formed on the basis of the interests, ambitions, and commitments of individuals who regard themselves as organizers of their own circles of contacts and relationships. As a consequence, new residential patterns may develop, consisting of a rediscovery of neighborhoods and of communal and cooperative living arrangements. There is room for experimenting with lifestyles and social relations (Badura 1981: 20–38). The ability to choose and maintain one's own social relations is not an ability everyone has by nature. It is, as sociologists of class know, a *learned* ability which *depends on special social and family backgrounds. The reflexive conduct of life, the planning of one's own biography and social relations, gives rise to a new inequality, the inequality of dealing with insecurity and reflexivity.*

Nevertheless, all this documents the emergence of new historical possibilities for individual self-formation and for a development of the private sphere under conditions of relative social security and of the declining authority of tradition. The complex new relationships can also manifest themselves politically, i.e. in the form of *political privatism.* By this I mean the expansion of social and legal limits imposed upon the private sphere; of unconventional and even publicly offensive forms of social experimentation which are quite consistent with new forms of personal freedom; and of challenges to conventional distinctions between acceptable and unacceptable behavior. Thus there emerge divisions between culture and counterculture, society and alternative groups. These new forms of cultural and social identity often have politically provocative effects. Their force has been regularly experienced during the past twenty years.

These and other developments permit the conclusion that the unstable association of community and market society which Max Weber had in mind when he spoke of social class has been partially transformed or even dissolved in the course of post-war developments. People at any rate no longer seem to understand or experience it. The new forms of living reveal dynamic possibilities for the reorganization of social relations, which cannot be adequately comprehended by following either Marx or Weber.

As a result, the following question becomes paramount: what actually does take place when in the course of historical development the identity of social classes rooted in the lifeworld melts away? When, on the one hand, the conditions and risks of wage labor become *generalized* and, on the other, *class loses its subcultural basis and is no longer experienced*? Is a class identity no longer shaped by status even conceivable? Can the inequalities persisting under conditions of individualization still be grasped by means of the concept of class or by means of even more general hierarchical models of social inequality? Perhaps all these hierarchical models categorically depend on traditional status dependency? But are there interpretations which can replace these models? It may, of course, also be the case that processes of individualization are embedded in contradictions which in turn produce new social groupings and conflicts. How then are processes of individualization transformed into their opposites? How can new forms of social identity be discovered and new ways of life be developed? Could the social perceptions of risk and the political dynamics of the risk society be or become one central axis of social conflict and identity beyond status or class? Or does the risk society, on the contrary, *lack* political counteraction *because* of individualization? One can imagine three consequences which are by no means mutually exclusive. Indeed, they may even overlap.

First, class does not disappear just because traditional ways of life fade away. Social classes are rather emancipated from regional and particularistic restrictions and limitations as a result. A new chapter in the history of classes is beginning, but we still need to comprehend its historical dynamics. It can in any case no longer be said without further qualification that this still is a history of the formation of class solidarities.

Second, in the course of the developments just described both the firm and the workplace lose their significance as loci of conflict and identity formation. New sources for the formation of social bonds and for the development of conflicts arise. They lie first in *ascribed* differences and inequalities of race, ethnicity, nationality, gender, age and so on; second, in new and changing differentiations which arise from reflexivity in the domain of private social relations and private ways of living and identity. Thus, new social lifestyles and group identities inside persistent social inequalities begin to emerge.

Third, the end of class society is not some big revolutionary bang. It consists of a relentlessly progressing and collectively experienced process of individualization and atomization in post-traditional societies. Paradoxically, these are societies in which people become increasingly less self-sufficient (see Chapter 7). At the same time, risks, risk perception and risk management in all sectors of society become a new source of conflict and social formation (see Part III).

Toward an Individualized Society of Employees

There are a great many different attempts to develop new social formations, but however strong the convulsions triggered by them may be, they are invariably qualified by the fact that they, too, are exposed to ever new thrusts toward individualization. The motor of individualization is going at full blast, and it is not at all clear how new and lasting social arrangements, comparable in depth of penetration to social classes, can even be created. Quite to the contrary, especially in the immediate future it is very likely that, as a way of coping with unemployment and economic crises, social and technological innovations will be set in motion which will open up new opportunities for individualization processes, in particular in regard to a greater flexibility in labor market relations and in regard to regulations governing working hours. But this also applies to the new forms of communication. These technological and social revolutions, which either still lie ahead or are already in full swing, will unleash a profound individualization of lifestyles.

If this assessment is correct, a variant of social structure which neither Marx nor Weber foresaw will gain in importance. Class society will pale into insignificance beside an *individualized society of employees*. Both the typical characteristics as well as the dangers of such a society are now becoming increasingly clear. In contrast to class society, which is defined essentially in terms of tradition and culture, a society of employees must be defined *in terms of labor law and by means of socio-political categories*. The result is a peculiar stage of transition, in which traditional and sharpening inequalities coincide with certain elements of a no longer traditional, individualized post-class society (which bears no resemblance to Marx's vision of a classless society). This transitional society is distinguished by a variety of typical structures and changes.

First, processes of individualization *deprive class distinctions of their social identity*. Social groups lose their distinctive traits, both in terms of their self-understanding and in relation to other groups. They also lose their independent identities and the chance to become a formative political force. As a result of this development, the idea of social mobility (in the sense of individual movement between actual status classes), which until very late in this century constituted a social and political theme of considerable importance for social identity formation, pales into insignificance.

Second, inequalities by no means disappear. They merely become redefined in terms of an *individualization of social risks*. The result is that social problems are increasingly perceived in terms of psychological dispositions: as personal inadequacies, guilt feelings, anxieties, conflicts, and neuroses. There emerges, paradoxically, a *new immediacy of individual and society, a direct relation between crisis and sickness*. Social crises appear as individual crises, which are no longer (or are only very indirectly) perceived in terms of their rootedness in the social realm. This is one of the explanations for the current revival of interest in psychology [*Psychowelle*]. Individual achievement orientation similarly gains in importance. It can now be predicted that the full range of problems associated with the achievement society and its tendency toward (pseudo-)legitimations of social inequalities will emerge in the future.

Third, in attempting to cope with social problems, people are forced into political and social alliances. These, however, need no longer follow a single pattern, such as the class model. The isolation of privatized lives, shielded against all the other privatized lives, can be shattered by social and political events and developments of the most heterogeneous kind. Accordingly, *temporary* coalitions between *different groups* and *different camps* are formed and dissolved, depending on the *particular issue* at stake and on the *particular situation*. In this way, risks and risk conflicts, as far as they are personally experienced, are becoming an important issue as well. It is possible to cheerfully embrace seemingly contradictory causes, for example, to join forces with local residents in protests against noise pollution by air traffic, to belong to the Metalworkers' Union, and yet – in the face of impending economic crisis – to vote conservative. Such coalitions represent *pragmatic alliances in the individual struggle for existence and occur on the various battlefields of society*. A peculiar multiplication of areas of conflict can be observed. The individualized society prepares the ground for new and *multi-faceted conflicts*, ideologies, and alliances, which go beyond the scope of all hitherto existing schematizations. These alliances are generally focused on single issues, are by no means heterogeneous, and are oriented toward specific situations and personalities. The resulting so-called structure is susceptible to the latest social fashions (in issues and conflicts) which, pushed by the mass media, rule the public consciousness just as the spring, autumn, and winter fashion shows do.

Fourth, permanent conflicts tend to arise along the lines of *ascribed characteristics*, which now as much as ever are undeniably connected with discriminations. *Race, skin color, gender, ethnicity, age, homosexuality, physical disabilities* – these are the major ascribed characteristics. Under the conditions of advanced individualization, such quasi-natural social inequalities lead to the development of quite *specific organizing effects*. These attempt to gain political muscle by focusing upon the inescapability and permanence of such inequalities as well as upon their incompatibility with the achievement principle, their tangibility, and the fact that – as a result of their direct visibility – they make possible independent social and individual identifications. At the same time, individual fate is increasingly determined in a new way by economic trends and by historical necessity, as it were, for example by economic crisis or boom, restricted admission to universities and to the professions, the size of age cohorts, etc.

Will it be possible to choose as a point of departure the claims and the promises of the process of individualization now under way together with its impulse toward social emancipation, thereby in a new way – beyond status and class – uniting individuals and groups as self-conscious subjects of their own personal social and political affairs? Or will the last bastions of social and political action be swept away as a result of that very process? Would the individualized society then not fall, torn apart by conflicts and displaying symptoms of sickness, into the kind of political apathy that precludes virtually nothing, not even new and insidious forms of a modernized barbarism?

Notes

1 The text of this chapter is not identical with Chapter 3 of the German edition; rather, it is based upon Beck (1983; 1984). It first appeared as pp. 340–53 in Meja et al. (1987): translation by Volker Meja and Gerd Schroeder.

2 I am referring here to the peculiarities of the development of the class structure in

Germany, which differs from the developments in Great Britain or France, for example. In Britain, class membership is still very apparent in everyday life and remains the object of conscious identification. It is evident in speech (i.e. accents, expressions, vocabulary), in the sharp class divisions between residential areas ('housing class'), in types of education, in clothing, and in everything that can be included under the concept of 'lifestyle'. See Gordon Smith (1982) and the following three essays in Wehler (1979): Eric J. Hobsbawm, 'Soziale Ungleichheit und Klassenstruktur in England: Die Arbeiterklasse'; Sidney Pollard, 'Soziale Ungleichheit und Klassenstruktur in England: Mittel- und Oberklasse'; Heinz-Gerhard Haupt, 'Soziale Ungleichheit und Klassenstruktur in Frankreich seit Mitte des 19. Jahrhunderts'. See also Pierre Bourdieu (1979).

4

'I AM I': GENDERED SPACE AND CONFLICT INSIDE AND OUTSIDE THE FAMILY

The linguistic barometers are indicating stormy weather: 'The *war* over the family' (Berger and Berger 1983), 'The *battle* of the sexes' (Ehrenreich 1983), or the '*terror* of intimacy' (Sennett 1976). More and more frequently, authors take recourse to not very peaceful vocabulary in order to characterize the state of affairs between the sexes. If one takes language for reality one would have to believe that love and intimacy had turned into their opposites. Certainly, these are linguistic exaggerations in the competition for public attention. They also indicate, however, the deep insecurity and hurt with which men and women confront each other in the everyday reality of marriage and family (or what is left of them).

If it were only a matter of marriage and family! But to determine the relationships between the sexes solely by what they appear to be – relations between the sexes involving the topics of sexuality, affection, marriage, parenthood and so on – is to fail to recognize that besides that, they are also everything else at the same time: work, profession, inequality, politics, and economics. It is this unbalanced mixture of everything, no matter how disparate, which makes the issue so difficult. Anyone who would talk about the family must also discuss work and money, and anyone who would talk about marriage must also talk about training, professions and mobility, and specifically about *un*equal distributions despite by now (largely) *equal* educational prerequisites.

Has this omni-dimensionality of inequality between men and women actually begun to change in Western countries over the past decade or two? The data speak a double language. On the one hand, epochal changes have occurred – especially in the areas of sexuality, law and education. On the whole, however, other than in sexuality, these changes exist more in *consciousness* and on *paper*. They contrast, on the other hand, with a *constancy in behavior and conditions* of men and women (in particular in the labor market, but also in the realm of social security). This has the seemingly paradoxical effect that the increased equality brings the continuing and intensifying inequalities even more clearly into consciousness.[1]

This historically created mixture of new consciousness and old conditions is explosive in a double sense. Through more equal educational opportunities and an increased awareness of their position, young women have built up expectations of more equality and partnership in professional and family life which encounter *contrary* developments in the labor market and in male behavior. Conversely, men have practiced a *rhetoric of equality*, without matching their words with deeds. On both sides the ice of illusion has grown thin; with the equalization of the prerequisites (in education and the law) the positions of men and women become *more* unequal, *more* conscious, and *less* legitimated. The contradictions between female expectation of equality and the reality of inequality, and between male slogans of mutual responsibility and the retention of the old role assignments, are sharpening and will determine the future development in the thoroughly contradictory variety of their expressions in politics and in private. Thus we are situated at the very *beginning* of a liberation from the 'feudally' ascribed roles for the sexes – with all the associated antagonisms, opportunities and contradictions. Consciousness has rushed ahead of conditions. It remains unlikely that anyone can turn back the clock of consciousness. There is much to be said for the *prognosis of a long conflict*; the opposition of the sexes will determine the coming years.

These themes and conflicts between men and women are not *only* what they appear to be: themes and conflicts between men and women. In them *also* a social structure is crumbling in the private sphere. What appears as a private 'relationship conflict' has a general socio-theoretical side which will be developed here in three theses.

(1) The ascription of the gender characters is the *basis* of the industrial society, and not some traditional relic that could easily be dispensed with. Without the separation of male and female roles there would be no traditional nuclear family. Without the nuclear family, there would be no bourgeois society with its typical pattern of work and life. The image of the bourgeois industrial society is based on an incomplete, or more precisely, a *divided* commercialization of human labor power. Total industrialization, total commercialization *and* families in the traditional forms and roles are mutually exclusive. On the one hand, wage labor presupposes housework, production mediated through the market presumes the forms and ascribed roles of the nuclear family. In that respect, industrial society is dependent upon the unequal positions of men and women. On the other hand, these inequalities contradict the principles of modernity, and become problematic and conflictual in the continuity of reflexive modernization. Thus however, in the course of the *actual* equalization of men and women, the foundations of the family (marriage, sexuality, parenthood, etc.) are called into question. That means that in the modernization phase since the Second World War, the *advancement* and the *dissolution* of industrial society *coincide*. This is exactly the process of reflexive modernization. The universalism of the market fails to recognize even its own, self-delineated taboo zones and weakens the ties of women to their industrially produced 'status fate' of compulsory housework and support by a husband. With that, the biographical harmonization of reproduction and production as well as the division of labor within the family become fragile, gaps in social protection for women become visible, and so on. In the conflicts breaking out today

between men and women, therefore, what must be settled are the *personalized contradictions of an industrial society* that has also destroyed the foundations of their ability to live together through its reflexive modernization and individualization.

(2) The dynamic of individualization, which removed people from class cultures, does not stop at the gates of the family, either. People are being removed from the constraints of gender, from its quasi-feudal attributes and givens, or shaken to the very depths of their souls, and the agent is a force they do not understand themselves, though they are its most inward embodiment, no matter how strangely it befalls them. The law that comes over them is called *I am I*, and then, I am a woman. I am I, and then, I am a man. Worlds gape in this distance between 'I' and the *expected* woman, I and the *expected* man. Here the process of individualization in the relations of the sexes has quite contradictory consequences. On the one hand, men and women are *released* from traditional forms and ascribed roles in the search for a 'life of their own'. On the other hand, in the prevailing diluted social relationships, people are *driven into* bonding in the search for happiness in a partnership. The need for a shared inner life, as expressed in the ideal of marriage and bonding, is not a primeval need. It *grows* with the losses that individualization brings as the obverse of its opportunities. As a consequence the direct route from marriage and the family usually leads, sooner or later, back to them – and vice versa. What lies beyond the frustration and desire of the sexes is, over and over again, the frustration and desire of the sexes, their opposition, dependence, togetherness, indifference, isolation, sharing – or all of these at once.

(3) In *all* forms of male–female cohabitation (before, during and after marriage), the *conflicts of the century* break through. Here they always show their private, personal face. But the family is *only the setting, not the cause* of the events. One can change the stage. The play being performed remains the same. The involvement of the sexes in its stratification of work, parenthood, profession, politics, development and self-realization in and against the other has begun to waver. In marital (and extramarital) relationships, conflicts are initiated by the opening up of *possibilities to choose* (for instance, diverging professional mobility of the spouses, division of housework and child care, type of contraception and sexuality). In making decisions, people become aware of the different and contradictory consequences and risks for men and women, and thus of the *contrasts in their conditions*. Deciding on the responsibility for children also depends on the professional careers of the parents and thus on their present and future economic dependence and independence with all the consequences for men and women that are in turn connected with that. These possibilities to make decisions have a personal *and* an institutional side. That is, a lack of institutional solutions (e.g. lack of day care and flexible work times, insufficient social protection) aggravates conflicts in private relationships, and conversely, institutional provisions ease the

private 'squabbles' of the sexes. Accordingly, private *and* political strategies for solutions must be seen as connected.

The three basic theses – the 'feudal character' of industrial society, the individualization tendencies in female and male life contexts, and the recognition of conflict situations through the opportunities for and constraints on choice – will now be developed and elucidated in succession.

Industrial Society is a Modern Feudal Society

The peculiarities of the antagonisms in the life conditions of men and women can be determined theoretically by differentiating them from class conditions. The class antagonisms ignited on the material immiseration of large parts of the working population. They were fought out in public. The antagonisms that emerge with the detraditionalization of the family erupted mainly in private relationships, and they are fought out in the kitchen, the bedroom and the nursery. Their verbal accompaniment and symptoms are the everlasting discussions of relationships or the silent opposition in a marriage, the flight to solitude and back, the loss of trust in the partner one suddenly no longer understands, the pain of divorce, the idolization of children, the struggle for a bit of life to call one's own, to be wrested away from the partner and still shared with him/her, the search for oppression in the trivialities of everyday life, an oppression which one *is* oneself. Call it what you will, 'trench war of the sexes', 'retreat into the subjective', 'the age of narcissism'. This is exactly the way a *social form* – the feudal inner structure of industrial society – implodes into the private sphere.

The class antagonisms that arise with the industrial system are in a way 'inherently modern', grounded in the industrial mode of production itself. The antagonisms between the sexes *neither* bow to the pattern of modern class antagonisms *nor* are a mere relic of tradition. They are a third entity. Just as much as the antagonisms between labor and capital, they are the *product* and the *foundation* of the industrial system, in the sense that wage labor *presupposes* housework, and that the spheres and forms of production and the family are separated and *created* in the nineteenth century. At the same time the resulting conditions of men and women are based on *ascriptions* by birth. In that respect, they are that strange hybrid, *modern estates*. With them, an *industrial society* hierarchy of status is established in modernity. They derive their explosive power and their logic of conflict from the *contradiction* between modernity and counter-modernity *within* industrial society. Correspondingly, the ascribed roles and antagonisms of gender status erupt like class antagonisms not in early modernity, but in *late* industrial modernity, that is, at the point where the social classes have already become detraditionalized and modernity no longer hesitates at the gates of the family, marriage, parenthood and housework.

In the nineteenth century the triumph of industrialism accompanied the shaping of the forms of the nuclear family, which today are in turn becoming detraditionalized. Production and family work are subjected to contrary organizational principles (Rerrich 1986). If the rules and power of the *market* apply to the former, in the latter the *unpaid* performance of everyday work is taken for granted. The *contractual nature* of relationships contrasts with the collective *communality* of marriage and the family. *Individual competition and mobility*, which are required for the realm of production, run up against the contrary demand in the family: *sacrifice* for the other and absorption in the collective communal project of the family. In the shape of familial reproduction and market-dependent production, then, two epochs with contrary organizational principles and value systems – modernity and modern counter-modernity – are welded together in the industrial society, two epochs that complement, condition, and contradict each other.

The life conditions that are created and imposed by the separation of family and production are just as epochally different. There is thus not only a system of inequality that has its basis in production, differences in pay, professions, the position with respect to the means of production, and so forth. There is also a system of inequality located *transversely* to it, which comprises the epochal differences between the 'family situation' in its relative equality, and the variety of production situations. Production work is mediated through the labor market and performed in return for money. Taking it on makes people – no matter how tightly they are bound to dependent work – into *self*-providers. They become the targets of mobility processes, related plans, and the like. Unpaid family work is imposed as a natural dowry through marriage. By nature, taking it on means *dependence* for support. Those who take it on – and we know who they are – run a household with 'second-hand' money and remain dependent on marriage as a link to self-support. The distribution of these jobs – and here lies the feudal foundation of industrial society – remains outside of decision. They are *ascribed* by birth and gender. In principle, one's *fate is already present in the cradle even in industrial society*: lifelong housework or making a living in conformity with the labor market. These feudal 'gender fates' are attenuated, canceled, aggravated or concealed by the love which is also devoted to them. Love is blind. Since love can appear as an escape from its self-created distress, no matter how great that might be, the inequality which it represents cannot be real. It is real, however, and that makes love seem stale and cold.

What appears and is lamented as 'terror of intimacy' are – in terms of social theory and social history – the *contradictions of a modernity bisected by the plan of industrial society*, which has always withheld the indivisible principles of modernity – individual freedom and equality beyond the barriers of birth – from one gender by birth and ascribed them to the other. Industrial society *never* was or can be possible solely as industrial society, but is always only half industrial and half *feudal*. This feudal side is not a relic of tradition, but the *foundation* and *product* of industrial society, built into the institutional plan of work and life.

In the welfare state modernization after the Second World War, a double process takes place: on the one side the requirement for a market-dependent standardized biography is extended to the female life context. Here nothing that is new in principle is occurring, only the application of the principles of developed market societies over and above the gender line. On the other, totally new camps within the family and between men and women in general are created in this way, indeed the feudal foundations of industrial society are being abolished. This is a specific feature of *reflexive modernization*. The *extension* of industrial society beyond its gender-specific division carries out in equal measure the *dissolution* of its family morals, its gender fates, its taboos on marriage, parenthood and sexuality, even the reunification of housework and industrial work.

The status-based hierarchy in industrial society is a building put together from many elements: division of the spheres of labor in production and the family and the contrasting organization of the two, the ascription of the corresponding life conditions by birth, the concealment of the overall conditions through promises of affection and a remedy for loneliness offered by love, marriage and parenthood. Considered retrospectively, this structure had to be constructed, that is, pushed through against resistance.

So people have tended to view modernization too one-sidedly. It actually has a double face. Parallel to the emergence of industrial society in the nineteenth century, the *modern* feudal gender order was constructed. In this sense modernization was accompanied in the nineteenth century by *counter*-modernization. The temporal differences and antagonisms between production and the family were established, justified and transfigured into eternal truths. An alliance of male-inspired philosophy, religion and science ties the whole thing up – for good measure – with the 'essence' of the woman and the 'essence' of the man.

Modernization, then, not only dissolves the feudal conditions of agrarian society but also creates new feudal conditions, and in its reflexive phase dissolves these. The same thing – modernization – has *opposite* consequences under the different overall conditions of the nineteenth and the twentieth centuries. Then the consequences were the *division* of housework and wage labor, today they are the struggle for new forms of *reunification*; then the tying down of women through *marital support*, today their rush into the labor market; there the *establishment* of the stereotypical male and female roles, here the *liberation* of men and women from the feudal dictates of gender.

These are symptoms of how modernity is encroaching today on the counter-modernity it installed in industrial society. The relations of the sexes, which are welded to the separation of production and reproduction and held together with everything the compact tradition of the nuclear family can offer in concentrated communality, role assignments and emotionality, are breaking apart. Suddenly everything becomes uncertain, including the ways of living together, who does what, how and where, or the views of sexuality and love and their connection to marriage and the family. The institution of parenthood splits up into a clash between motherhood and fatherhood, and children with their naturally intense bonding ability become the only partners who do not leave. A general process of struggle and experimentation with 'forms of reunifying' work and life, housework and wage labor is beginning. In short, the private sphere is becoming reflexive and political and this radiates into other areas.

But this only indicates the direction of the development. The salient point of these reflections lies in the following: the problemata of the *established* market society cannot be overcome within the social life forms and institutional structures of the divided market society. Where men *and* women have to and want to lead an economically independent existence, this can occur *neither* in the traditional role assignments of the nuclear family, *nor* in the institutional structures of professional work, social laws, city planning, schools, and so on, which *presuppose* precisely the traditional image of the nuclear family with its gender status foundations.

The 'central conflicts', which discharge themselves in personal guilt feelings and disappointments within the relations of the sexes, also have a basis in the fact that an attempt is still being made to practice the liberation from gender stereotypes (almost) *solely* through the private confrontation of men and women, *within* the framework of the nuclear family, while keeping the institutional structures *constant*. This is tantamount to the attempt to accomplish a change in society with social structures *in* the family remaining the same. What remains is an *exchange of inequalities*. The *liberation* of women from housework and marital support is to be forced by the regression of men into this 'modern feudal existence' which is exactly what women reject for themselves. Historically, that is like an attempt to make the nobility the serfs of the peasants. But men are no more willing than women to follow the call 'back to the kitchen!' (women ought to know that better than anyone else!). But this is only one feature. What remains central is that *the equalization of men and women cannot be created in institutional structures that presuppose their inequality*. We cannot force the new, 'round' person into the 'square' hole required by the labor market, the employment system, city planning, the social security system and so on. If this is attempted, no one ought to be surprised that the private relationship of the sexes becomes the scene for conflicts that can only be inadequately solved by the tug-of-war of 'role swapping' or 'mixed roles' for men and women.

Liberation from Male and Female Roles?

The perspective just sketched out contrasts oddly with the empirical data. They, after all, document impressively the counter-trend to a *renewal* of the gender status hierarchy. In what sense is it at all permissible to speak of a 'liberation' at all? Are women and men freed equally from the dictates of their 'gender fate?' Which conditions bring this about, which work against it?

Essential turning points in the past decades – as the data referred to above attest – have freed women somewhat from the traditional traits ascribed by femininity. Five central conditions are apparent although by no means causally related to one another.

First of all, the biographical structure, the succession of life phases has been shifted by the *increasing of life expectancy*. As has been shown in particular by Arthur E. Imhof in his studies of social history, this has led to a '*demographic* liberation of women'. While in earlier centuries the lifespan of a woman – in statistical terms – was just sufficient to produce and raise the socially 'desirable' number of surviving children, these 'maternal duties' come to an end today at about the age of forty-five. The 'existence-for-children' has become a *passing* life phase for women today. It is succeeded on average by *three decades* of an 'empty nest' – beyond the traditional focus of women's lives. 'Today, in the Federal Republic alone, over five million women in their "best years" are living in post-parental relationships . . . often . . . without any concrete meaningful activity' (Imhof 1981: 181).

Second, modernization, especially in the phase after the Second World War, has *restructured housework*. On the one hand, the *social isolation* of housework is by no means an inherent structural feature as such, but the result of historical developments, to wit the detraditionalization of the lifeworlds. In the wake of individualization processes, the nuclear family sharpens its demarcations, and an 'insular existence' is formed, which autonomizes itself with respect to the remaining commitments (class cultures, neighborhoods, acquaintances). Only in that way does an existence as a housewife become the isolated worker existence *par excellence*. On the other hand, *processes of technical automation* extend into housework. A variety of appliances, machines and consumer goods unburden and empty work in the family. It becomes the invisible and never ending 'left-over work' between industrial production, paid services and technically perfected domestic furnishing of private households. Taken together, isolation and automation bring about a '*de*skilling of housework' (Offe 1984), which also directs women towards work outside the home in search of a 'fulfilled' life.

Third, if it remains true that motherhood is still the strongest tie to the traditional female role, it is difficult to overestimate the importance of *contraceptive and family planning measures*, as well as the *legal possibility of terminating pregnancies* in removing women from the traditional demands. Children and thus motherhood (with all its consequences) no longer constitute a 'natural fate', but, at least in principle, are *wanted* children and *intentional* motherhood. Of course, the data also show that motherhood *without* economic dependence on the husband and responsibility for child care remains a *dream* for many. But the younger generation of women, unlike their mothers, can (co)determine whether, when and how many children to have. At the same time, female sexuality is released from the 'fate of motherhood' and can also be consciously discovered and developed *against* male norms.

Fourth, the growing number of divorces points to the *fragility of marital and family support*. Women are often just 'a husband away from' poverty (Ehrenreich 1983). Almost 70 percent of single mothers must make do with less than DM 1200 per month [1985]. They and female pensioners are the most frequent clients of relief agencies. In this sense too, women are 'freed', i.e. *cut off* from lifelong support by a husband. The statistically documented rush of women into the labor market also shows that many women have understood this historical lesson and seen the consequences.

Fifth, the equalization of educational opportunity, which is among other things also the expression of a strong *career* motivation among young women, tends to work in the same direction.

All these taken together – demographic liberation, deskilling of housework, contraception, divorce, participation in education and occupations – express the degree of *liberation of women from the dictates of their modern, female status fate, which can no longer be altered.* Hence the individualization spiral – labor market, education, mobility, career planning – affects the family with doubled or trebled impact. The family becomes a continuous juggling act with divergent multiple ambitions involving careers and their requirements for mobility, educational constraints, conflicting obligations to children and the monotony of housework.

But these conditions leading towards individualization face others which reconnect women to traditional role assignments. The really *established* labor market society, which would make an independent economic living available to *all* men and women, would multiply the already scandalous unemployment figures. This means that under the conditions of mass unemployment and displacement from the labor market, women are freed *from* marital support, but not free *to* lead an autonomous life through work outside the home. This also means, however, that they continue to be largely *dependent* upon an economic protection from their husbands which *no longer* exists. This intermediate status between 'freedom from' and 'freedom to' in the context of real wage laborer behavior is also further strengthened by their reconnection to *motherhood*. As long as women bear children, nurse them, feel responsible for them, and see them as an essential part of their lives, children remain wished-for 'obstacles' in the occupational competition, as well as temptations to a conscious decision *against* economic autonomy and a career.

In this way, the lives of women are pulled back and forth by this contradiction between liberation from and reconnection to the old ascribed roles. This is also reflected in their consciousness and behavior. They flee from housework to a career and back again, and attempt in different phases of their lives to hold together the diverging conditions of their life 'somehow' through contradictory decisions. The contradictions of the environment amplify their own; for instance, they have to put up with being asked by a divorce court judge why they have neglected their career planning. In family policy they are asked why they have not fulfilled their maternal duties. They are accused of spoiling their husbands' already difficult professional lives with their career ambitions. Divorce law and divorce reality, the lack of social protections, the closed doors of the labor market and the main burden of family work characterize some of the *contradictions* which the individualization process has brought into the female life context.

Men's situations are quite different. While women have to loosen their old ascribed roles of an 'existence for others' and have to search for a new social identity, for reasons of economic security *among others*, for men, making a living *independently* and the *old* role identity *coincide*. In the stereotypical male gender role as 'career man', economic individualization *and* masculine role behavior are joined together. Support by a spouse (the wife) is unknown to men historically, and the 'freedom to' work for a living is taken for granted. The background work that belongs to it traditionally falls upon women. The joys and duties of fatherhood could always be enjoyed *in small doses* as a recreational activity. Fatherhood held no obstacle to practicing a career; on the contrary it was a compulsion to do so. In other words, all the factors that *dislodge* women from their traditional role are *missing* on the male side. In the context of male life, fatherhood *and* career, economic independence *and* familial life are not contradictions that have to be fought for and held together against the conditions in the family and society; instead their compatibility with the traditional male role is prescribed and protected. But this means that individualization (in the sense of making a living through the mediation of the market) *strengthens* masculine role behavior.

If men also turn against the dictates of their gender role, they do so on other grounds. Contradictions are also present in the career fixation of the male role, for instance, sacrificing oneself for something one has neither the leisure, the needs nor the abilities to enjoy, aggressive competition for nothing, exhaustion for professional and organizational goals with which one cannot identify but must anyway, the resulting 'indifference' that really is nothing of the kind, and so on. Nevertheless, essential impulses for liberation from the masculine role are not inherent, but are *externally induced* (through changes in women), and in a double sense. On the one hand, men are freed by the greater participation of women in the labor force from the yoke of being *sole* supporter of the family. That, however, loosens the constraints to subordinate oneself in a career to the will and purposes of others *for* the wife and the children. As a consequence, a different type of commitment to the career *and* the family becomes possible. On the other hand, 'family harmony' is becoming fragile. The female-determined side of male existence is getting out of balance. At the same time men get an inkling of their dependency in everyday matters and their emotional reliance on women. In both areas, essential impulses are found to loosen identification with the dictates of the male role and to try new modes of life.

The conflicts cause the antagonisms between men and women to stand out more sharply. Two 'catalyzing elements' are central: *children* and *economic security*. In both cases conflicts on these themes can be kept hidden during marriage, but they emerge openly in case of divorce. Characteristically, the distribution of burdens and opportunities changes in the transition from the traditional to the two-earner model of marriage. In the marital support model, to put it schematically, the woman is left after divorce *with* children and *without* an income, the man by contrast *with* an income and *without* children. In the two-earner model, little seems to have changed at first glance, other than that the woman has an income *and* she has the children (following prevalent law practice). But to the degree that the economic inequality between men and women is decreased – whether through professional activity of the woman, the support regulations of divorce law, or old-age assistance – *fathers become aware of their disadvantage*, partially naturally and partially legally. The woman has *possession* of the child as a product of her womb, which we all know does belong to her, biologically and legally. The property relations between ovum and sperm become differentiated. The father in the child always remains dependent on the mother and her discretion. This is also true for all questions of terminating a pregnancy. To the extent that the alienation from male *and* female roles progresses, the pendulum tends to swing back. The men who free themselves from the 'fate' of a career and turn to their children come home to an empty nest. This is clearly illustrated by the increasing number of cases (especially in the USA), in which fathers kidnap children not awarded to them in divorce proceedings.

But individualization, which separates the conditions of men and women, conversely also pushes them back to bonding. *As the traditions become progressively diluted*, the promises of relationships grow. Everything that has been lost is suddenly being sought in the other. First God departed (or we displaced him). The word 'belief', which once meant 'having experienced', has taken on the rather shabby tones of 'against our better judgment'. As God disappears, so does the possibility of going to a priest, and thus the guilt grows, and can no longer be thrown off. As the distinctions between right and wrong become blurred, guilt does not grow less significant under keen questioning but only less distinct and less distinguishable. The culture of social class, which at least knew how to interpret built-up suffering, has evaporated from life into a cloud of speeches and statistics. Neighborhoods, grown up with memories and interaction, have melted away due to mobility. Acquaintanceships can be made, but they revolve around their own central point. One can also join clubs. The palette of contacts grows larger, broader and more colorful. But their multiplicity makes them more fleeting, more easily dominated by façades. In the proclaimed interest in each other, any thought of something more is immediately refused. Even intimacies can be exchanged like this, fleetingly, almost like handshakes.

All this might keep things moving and open up 'possibilities', and yet the variety of relationships probably cannot replace the identity-forming power of a stable primary relationship. As studies show, *both* are necessary: a variety of relationships and lasting intimacy. Happily married housewives suffer from contact problems and social isolation. Divorced men who have formed groups to air their problems, cannot overcome the emerging loneliness even by being included in networks.

In the idealizations of modern love the trajectory of modernity is reflected once again. The exaltation is the opposite of the losses modernity leaves behind. Not God, not priests, not class, not neighbors, well at least You. And the size of the You is the inverted emptiness that otherwise prevails.

That also means that it is less material foundation and love than the fear of being alone that holds marriages and the family together. What threatens or is feared beyond marriage and the family is perhaps the most stable foundation of marriage, despite all the crises and conflicts: loneliness.

In all of this, there is first of all a fundamental relativization of the controversy on the family. The bourgeois nuclear family, in whose forms the coexistence of the sexes has been standardized in the highly industrialized democracies of the West, has been sanctified or cursed; people have seen one crisis following the other, or they have seen the family rising again from the nimbus of crisis ascribed to it. All this remains bound to the verdict of the *false alternative*. Anyone who burdens the family with all the good or all the evil is not reaching far enough. The family is only the surface on which the historical conflict situations *between men and women become visible*. In the family, or beyond it, the sexes always encounter each other and thus so do the accumulated contradictions between them.

In what sense can one speak of a *liberation relative to the family*? With the extension of the dynamic of individualization into the family, forms of living together begin to change *radically*. The relationship between family and individual biography loosens. The lifelong standard family, which sublates the parental biographies of men and women summarized in it, becomes a limiting case, and the rule becomes a movement back and forth among various familial and *non*-familial forms of living together, specific to the particular phase of life in question. The family commitment of biography becomes perforated along the time axis between phases of life, *and thus canceled*. Among the family relationships which are becoming interchangeable, the autonomy of the male and female *individual biography* separates inside and outside the family. Each person lives through several family lives as well as non-familial forms of life, depending on the life phase, and *for that very reason* lives more and more his/her *own biography.* Thus it is only in a *longitudinal section* of the biography, and not in a given moment or in family statistics, that the individualization of the family is seen, that is the reversal of priorities between individual biography and family (in and beyond the family). Empirically, the degree of liberation from the family consequently results from the *biographical synopsis* of the data on divorce *and* remarriage, as well as pre-, inter- and extramarital forms of living together, which, taken individually and related to the pro or con of the family, remain contradictory. Placed between the extremes of family or no family, a growing number of people begin to 'decide' on a third way: a contradictory, *pluralistic overall biography in transition.* This biographical pluralism of forms of life, i.e. the alternation between families, mixed with and interrupted by other forms of living together or alone, is becoming the (paradoxical) 'norm' for the cooperation and opposition of men and women under conditions of individualization.

Considered over their entire life, the majority of people have thus entered a painful and fearful *historically prescribed test phase of their forms of living together.* They have begun a *reflexive way of loosening and coordinating* male and female biographies, whose outcome cannot be predicted at all today. But all the suffered 'mistakes' cannot deter anyone from renewed 'attempts'.

Becoming Conscious of Inequalities: Chances for and Constraints on Choice

Differences and antagonisms in the situations of men and women did not just come into existence yesterday. And yet until the sixties they were accepted as 'self-evident' by the overwhelming majority of women. For two decades attention to them has been growing and there have been political efforts targeted at obtaining equal rights for women. With the first successes the consciousness of the inequalities is *heightened.* The *actual* inequalities, their conditions and causes must be distinguished from the *awareness* of them. The antagonisms between men and women have two sides, which can vary quite independently of one another, the objectivity of the situations *and* their delegitimation and the awareness of this. If one compares the long period of acceptance of inequality to the short period when it has been problematized and simultaneously sees that the removal of some inequalities has only really opened people's eyes to them, one should not underestimate the independent significance of awareness. We shall now inquire into the conditions for this awareness.

As modernization proceeds, the decisions and constraints to decide multiply in all fields of social action. With a bit of exaggeration, one could say: 'anything goes'. Who does the dishes and when, who changes the screaming baby's diaper, who takes care of the shopping and pushes the vacuum cleaner around the house is becoming just as unclear as who brings home the bacon, who decides whether to move, and why the nocturnal pleasures in bed must be enjoyed only with the daily companion duly appointed and wed by the registrar's office. Marriage can be subtracted from sexuality, and that in turn from parenthood; parenthood can be multiplied by divorce; and the whole thing can be divided by living together or apart, and raised to a higher power by the possibility of multiple residences and the ever-present potentiality of taking back decisions. This mathematical operation yields a rather large, though fluctuating, sum on the right side of the equation, and gives some idea of the variety of direct and multiply nested shadow existences that are more and more often concealed today behind the unchanged and so upright words 'marriage' and 'family'.

In all biographical dimensions, *opportunities* for and *constraints* on choice open up, as if forced upon us. A whole apparatus of planning and agreements becomes necessary, which in principle is revocable and dependent on legitimation in its assignment of unequal burdens. In discussion and agreements, in mistakes and conflicts related to these choices, the differing risks and consequences for men and women become clearer. Transforming givens into decisions has a double meaning if considered systematically. The *option of not deciding is tending to become impossible*. First, the opportunity to decide acquires a compulsive character which one cannot readily retreat behind. It is necessary to go through the mills of the private relationship, the problems and thus the balancing of the differing consequences. But this also means, secondly, that the decisions being thought through become *consciousness raisers of the emerging inequalities as well as the conflicts and efforts at solution they ignite*.

This already begins with the rather conventional decision on mobility. On the one hand, the labor market demands mobility without regard to personal circumstances. Marriage and the family require the opposite. Thought through to its ultimate consequence, the market model of modernity implies a society *without* families and children. Everyone must be independent, free for the demands of the market in order to guarantee his/her economic existence. The market subject is ultimately the single individual, 'unhindered' by a relationship, marriage or family. Correspondingly, the ultimate market society is a *childless* society – unless the children grow up with mobile, single, fathers and mothers.

This contradiction between the requirements of a relationship and those of the labor market could only remain hidden so long as it was taken for granted that marriage meant renunciation of a career for women, responsibility for the children and 'comobility' according to the professional destiny of the husband. The contradiction bursts open where *both* spouses must or want to be free to earn a living as a salary earner. *Institutional* solutions to or ameliorations of this contradiction are quite conceivable (for instance, a minimum income for all citizens, or social protections not linked to professional work; the removal of all impediments to the joint employment of married couples; corresponding 'acceptability criteria', etc.). These, however, are neither present nor in any way contemplated. Accordingly the couple must search for *private* solutions, which under the options available to them amount to an internal distribution of *risks*. The question is: who will *give up* economic independence and security, the very things that are the unquestioned prerequisites for leading a life in modern society? Anyone who moves with a spouse, after all, must (usually) accept considerable professional disadvantages, if *she* is not in fact thrown completely off her career path. The level of conflict rises accordingly. Marriage, family and relationships become places where the personalized contradictions of a thoroughly modernized market society are compensated, but no longer completely.

The decisive question of professional mobility is joined by other, equally vital ones: the timing, number and support of children, the ever-present issue of dividing everyday chores equally, the 'one-sidedness' of contraceptive methods, the nightmarish issue of terminating a pregnancy, differences in type and frequency of sexual urges, not forgetting the irritation of an attitude that senses sexism even in margarine advertisements. In all these conflict-igniting central issues of how men and women live together, the *dissociation of positions* becomes conscious: the *timing* of parenthood encounters quite different presuppositions and impediments in the male than in the female life context, and so on.

If marriage is then finally conducted 'subject to recall' – 'suitable for divorce', so to speak (as the marriage counseling books flooding the market demand through contractual agreements covering everything from splitting property to extramarital sexuality) – then the split which was to be avoided is simply anticipated, and the unequal consequences of all the decisions and regulations emerge more and more openly. If one thinks of the new technical possibilities and the breakdown of taboos – the possibilities of shaping children's psyches as demonstrated by psychology and pedagogy, the possibilities of intervening in the gestation process, not to mention the science fiction realities of human genetics – then what is besetting the family divides the positions once united in it, piece by piece: woman against man, mother against child, child against father. The traditional unity of the family breaks apart in the face of decisions demanded of it. It is not that people bring many of these problems into the family, as they may believe and accuse themselves. Almost all the issues of conflict also have an institutional side (the children issue, for instance, is essentially based on the institutionally well protected impossibility of uniting caring for children with professional commitment). But this insight of course, does not support the children! In this way, everything that strikes the family from outside – the labor market, the employment system or the law – is distorted and foreshortened with a certain inevitability into the personal sphere. In the family (and in all its alternatives) there arises the systematically conditioned delusion that it contains the strings and the levers required to change the newly evident central fate of the inequality of the sexes within the concrete relationship.

Even the core of the family, the sanctuary of parenthood, is beginning to disintegrate into its components, the positions of motherhood and fatherhood. In Germany today, compared with the United States and Sweden, 'only' every tenth child is growing up under the care of single men and women. The number of single-parent families is rising as the number of two-parent families diminishes. Being a single mother is no longer just a consequence of 'abandonment', but rather an option that is chosen. Given the conflicts with fathers (who in truth are needed merely *to father* and no longer for anything else), lone parenthood is seen by many women as the only way to the child now desired more than ever.

The relationship and quality of the commitment to the child varies along with the intrafamilial individualization process, as Elisabeth Beck-Gernsheim (1988) and Maria Rerrich (1986) show. On the one hand, the child is viewed as an *impediment* in the individualization process. It costs money and work, is unpredictable, ties one up and throws carefully drawn up daily plans and life plans into a hopeless confusion. As soon as it appears the child develops and perfects its 'dictatorship of neediness' and forces its biological rhythm of life on its parents through the naked power of its vocal cords and the warmth of its smile. And, on the other hand, that very thing makes it irreplaceable.

The child is the source of the last *remaining, irrevocable, unexchangeable primary relationship*. Partners come and go. The child stays. Everything that is desired, but not realizable in the relationship, is directed to the child. With the increasing fragility of the relationships between the sexes the child acquires a monopoly on practical companionship, on an expression of feelings in a biological give and take that otherwise is becoming increasingly uncommon and doubtful. Here an anachronistic social experience is celebrated and cultivated which has become improbable *and* longed for precisely because of the individualization process. The excessive affection for children, the 'staging of childhood' which is granted to them – the poor, overloved creatures – and the nasty struggle for the children during and after divorce are some symptoms of this. The child becomes the *final alternative to loneliness* that can be built up against the vanishing possibilities of love. It is the *private type of re-enchantment*, which arises with, and derives its meaning from, disenchantment. The number of births is declining, but the importance of the child is *rising*. Usually one child is all. The expense makes any more than that hardly affordable. But those who believe that the (economic) costs deter people from bringing children into the world, are simply falling into their own entrapment in cost–benefit thinking.

The bit of the Middle Ages that industrial society has not just preserved but produced, is melting away. People are being freed from the feudal bonds of gender, which have been transfigured into nature. It is important to recognize this in its historic dimensions, *because* this socio-historical change takes place as a private, personal conflict. Psychology (and psychotherapy), which trace the suffering now being referred to them *en masse* back to the individual history of early childhood socialization, are becoming *short-circuited*. Where conflicts confront people from the forms of living that are dictated to them, where they lose an example of how to live, their ills can no longer be traced back to mistakes and decisions of their individual biographical history. Under the conditions of a liberation from the modern feudal gender fates of men and women, sexuality, marriage, eroticism, and parenthood have a great deal to do with inequality, career, the labor market, politics, the family and the forms of living embedded in them that have lost their relevance for the future. Psychology has yet to undertake this historization and socio-historical revision of its forms of thinking, necessary if it is not to run aground on the appearance of individuality from which it profits by displacing the causes for problems into the very people who have them.

Scenarios for Future Development

Fundamental conflicts are building up. But how they will be 'overcome' – publicly and privately – is largely an open question. Conclusions on the *consciousness and behavior* of men and women cannot be drawn from the aforementioned *objective* factors of liberation. This depends essentially on the political development and the institutional possibilities of support and compensation – as well as on the individual constellations and the possibilities of personal arrangements which are present in familial and intimate relationships. The historically emerging scope of possibility will be delineated here by three (by no means mutually exclusive) variants: *return to the family* in its traditional form; *equalization* according to the male model; and experimentation with new forms of living *beyond male and female roles*.

Back to the Nuclear Family

In the question of the future of 'the' family, people often start from false premises. The known form of the nuclear family is confronted with some vague notion of 'lack of families' or it is imputed that another type of family is replacing the nuclear family. It is much more likely – if the analysis sketched out above is correct – not that one type of family will displace the other, but that a *broad spectrum of variations* on familial and extrafamilial forms of living together will arise and continue to exist side by side. Characteristically, many of these – single life, living together before and during marriage, living in communes, various parenthoods over one or two divorces, etc. – will be integrated as different phases into *one* overall biography.

But even this differentiation and pluralization of forms of living as a consequence of modernization is viewed and denounced by many as a threat to the cultural values and foundations of life in the modern world. To many the escape from marriage and family is *excessive individualism*, which must be opposed institutionally by targeted counter-measures to support the family. It is of course women in particular who desire to win a 'life of their own' beyond their ascribed roles in housework and marital support, and their private and political efforts encounter threats, skepticism and resistance. The measures to save 'the' family are thus oriented to the standard norm of domesticity – the husband as bread-winner, the wife who cooks and two or three children – a norm which only came into existence along with industrial society in the early nineteenth century. Despite all the demonstrated tendencies to individualization and liberation there are also conditions and developments which lend emphasis to the demand 'back to the kitchen!'.

The overwhelming majority of women are far removed from an economically independent, professionally secured biography. This is reflected even in the figures for job participation of women. In Germany only *just over half* (51.7 percent) of all women between the ages of fifteen and sixty-five were working in 1988, that is employed outside the home or officially registered as unemployed, although the rate was increasing (1983: 50.7 percent). Of all the men in the same age period, more than *four-fifths* were working. Put another way this means that a large portion of women remain dependent on support from marriage and their husbands. *The continuing mass unemployment, and the limited and more likely shrinking capacities of the labor market in general, conserve and restabilize the traditional roles and responsibilities of men and women.* This tendency of liberation *from* wage labor *to* marital support is supported by the wish of many women for children. Both stabilizers of the female role – unemployment and desire for children – could be especially effective where educational deficits of young women continue to exist or arise anew in vocational education; this could lead to a *polarization of biographical patterns* within the younger generation of women along the lines of the educational hierarchy.

But anyone who sees the salvation of the family behind the closed doors of the labor market is overlooking that men and women are supposed to and want to live together under these conditions. It remains completely unclear at the present how the young women will cope with the disappointment of their decisively expressed vocational wishes, and the related dependency on their husbands. It is equally unclear whether a correspondingly large number of young men are ready (and even able on the basis of their own professional situation) to reassume the yoke of the bread-winner role. In any case, the erupting discrepancies between women's expectations of equality and the reality of inequality in occupations and the family are shifted off to the private realm inside and outside the family. It is not difficult to predict that this will amount to an externally induced *amplification of conflicts in private relationships*. At the end of the day, the barriers of the labor market will only *appear* to stabilize the nuclear family; in reality they will fill the corridors of the divorce courts or the waiting rooms of marriage counselors and psychotherapists.

At the same time, the new poverty of women is pre-programmed in this way. Anyone who would force women out of the labor market and back to the kitchen sink in the face of rising divorce figures, must at least know that he or she *is reserving the holes in the social safety net* for a large part of society.

This points to fundamental deficiencies in the theory and practice of all attempts to restore the old relationships between men and women in professions and the family. First of all, they contradict legally established principles of modern, democratically constituted societies, according to which unequal positions in society are not ascribed by birth but are obtained by achievement and participation in work, which is open to everyone. Second, the changes within the family and between the sexes are foreshortened to a private problem, and the connection to social and cultural modernizations is ignored.

This is reflected not least in the often promoted suggestions as to how the disintegrating familial harmony is to be cemented back together. Some believe particular 'family education courses' could provide a remedy. Others view a professionalization of the choice of spouse as the central therapy. If only we had sufficient marriage counseling agencies and therapeutic facilities, still others believe, the problems would capitulate. From pornography to legalized abortion to feminism, everything is blamed for the 'crisis of the family', and the appropriate counter-measures are demanded. Here, perplexity and helplessness are fathers of the explanation. The historical development and the social contexts from which the conflicts grow remain totally outside the field of view.

Modernization, however, to borrow a comparison from Max Weber, is not a carriage one can step out of at the next corner, if one does not like it. Anyone who would really restore the nuclear family in the forms of the fifties, must turn back the clock of modernization. That means displacing women from the labor market not just covertly – through subsidies of motherhood, for instance, or by polishing up the image of housekeeping – but openly, and not just from the labor market, but from education as well. The wage differential between men and women would have to be increased; even equal legal rights would have to be reversed. It would have to be checked whether the evil did not begin with universal suffrage; mobility, the market, new media and information technologies would have to be limited or forbidden. In short the indivisible principles of modernity would have to be *divided*, ascribed – naturally – to one gender and reserved – naturally – for the other, and for all time.

Equality of Men and Women

As an alternative, the demand is raised for *equality* for women in all areas of society. The universal principles of modernity are to be vindicated against and established against its patriarchal division – in housework, in parliaments and governments, in factories, in management, and so on. In the discussions of the women's movement, the demand for equality is usually connected with a claim to *change* the 'masculine world of work'. The struggle is for economic security, influence, codetermination for women, but also in order to bring other, 'feminine' orientations into social life. The object of discussion here will be a – usually unseen – consequence of a certain interpretation. If equality is interpreted and operated in the sense of the establishment of the labor market society for everyone, then implicitly the *fully mobile society of singles* would be created along with it.

If thought through to its conclusion, the basic figure of *fully developed* modernity is the *single person*. In the requirements of the market, the requirements of family, marriage, parenthood or partnership are ignored. Those who demand mobility in the labor market in this sense without regard to private interests are pursuing the dissolution of the family – precisely in their capacity as apostles of the market. This contradiction between the labor market and marriage (or relationship in general) could remain concealed so long as marriage was synonymous for women with family responsibility and renunciation of a profession or mobility. It erupts today to the degree that the separation of family *and* professional work is placed within the discretion of the (married) couple. With this interpretation of the demand for equality in conformity with the market, the spiral of individualization tends more and more to seize control of the relationships between men and women. That this is not just a thought experiment is shown by the rapidly rising numbers of single-person households and single mothers and fathers in Germany and other countries. It also becomes clear from the type of life that is demanded of people under these conditions.

In the life that basically must be or ought to be led alone, despite all the social orientation and variety of any individual, precautions are necessary to protect this way of living against its built-in hazards. Circles of contact must be built up and maintained for the most varied occasions. This requires much readiness by people to help bear the burdens of others. An intensification of the friendship network remains indispensable, and it is also the pleasure offered by the single life. Even the well chosen ephemera have their attractions. All of this presumes as secure a professional position as possible – as an income source, self-confirmation and social experience. This must be correspondingly maintained and asserted. The 'cosmos of personal life' which comes into existence in this way is fashioned and balanced with respect to the ego as center, with its sensitivities, possibilities, weaknesses and strengths.

But to the extent this individualized mode of existence succeeds, the danger grows that it might become an insurmountable obstacle to the kind of relationship (marriage, family) which still is basically desired. In the single life, the longing for the other grows just as much as the impossibility of integrating that person into the architecture of a life that now really is 'one's own'. That life was fulfilled with the non-presence of the other. Now, there is no space left for him or her. Everything breathes the resistance to loneliness: the variety of relationships, the rights one grants them, living habits, control of one's schedule, the ways of retreating to cope with the agonizing pains behind the façade. The delicate and carefully adjusted balance of all this is endangered by the desired partnership. The designs of independence become the prison bars of loneliness. The circle of individualization closes. The 'life of one's own' must be better protected, the walls that help cause the pains they protect against must be raised even higher.

The form of existence of the single person is not a deviant case along the path of modernity. It is the archetype of the *fully developed* labor market society. The negation of social ties that takes effect in the logic of the market begins in its most advanced stage to dissolve the prerequisites for lasting companionship. It is thus a case of paradoxical sociation, in which the high degree of sociality that breaks through is no longer manifested. As presented here, this reflection has for now only an 'ideal-typical character'. As the data show, however, it certainly fits an increasing segment of reality. Furthermore: *it is probably the unseen and unwanted consequence to which the demand for equality of the sexes leads under the current institutional conditions*. It is the perfect right of anyone – like large parts of the women's movement – to extend further the traditions under which modernity started, and to assert and pursue the equality of men and women in conformity to the market. One ought to see, however, that the end of this road is in all probability not harmony with equal rights, but *isolation* in courses and situations that run counter and apart from each other, for which there are already a number of signs beneath the surface of the way people live together.

Beyond Male and Female Roles

Both of the above extreme variants misunderstand the basic state of affairs that occupies the center here. The emerging contradictions between family and labor market are *not* solved in the first model by preserving the family, or in the second by generalizing the labor market. It remains unrecognized that the inequality between men and women is not a superficial problem that can be *corrected within* the structures and forms of the family and the professional sphere. Rather, these epochal inequalities are built into the basic plan of industrial society, its relations between production and reproduction, and between familial and wage labor. In those relations the contradictions emerge between modernity and counter-modernity *within* industrial society. Accordingly, they cannot be eliminated by favoring 'freedom of choice' between the family and a profession. *The equality of men and women cannot be accomplished through the institutional structures that are connected by design to inequality*. Only to the extent that the entire institutional structure of developed industrial society is thought through and changed to reflect the vital requirements of families and relationships, can a new type of equality *beyond* male and female roles be achieved step by step. The pseudo-alternatives of *refamilialization* or *total* power of the market will be contrasted here to the third way of *limiting and cushioning market relationships*, in connection with the deliberate enablement of social forms of life. In the following we are essentially concerned with the outline of the basic concept.

The principle can be understood as an exact mirror image of the theoretical interpretation sketched out here. With the individualization of the family, one could say, the separation between production and reproduction is performed again in a second historical step *inside* the family. The contradictions that emerge from that can accordingly only be overcome if *institutional possibilities for the reunification of work and life* are offered or made possible at the level of the separation already achieved, and in all components of the diverging market biographies.

Let us begin with the *mobility* required by the labor market. For one thing, it would be conceivable to cushion the individualizing effects of mobility itself. So far it has been a matter of course that occupational mobility is *individual* mobility. The family, and thus the wife, move with the husband. The alternative that emerges – the wife's abandonment of her career (with all its long-term consequences) or a 'split family' (as a first step on the way to divorce) – is left to the married couple as a personal problem. In contrast to that, cooperative types of mobility should be attempted and institutionalized, on the principle: if you want him or her, you have got to find a career opportunity for his or her spouse. The employment office would have to organize job counseling and referral *for families*. Enterprises (and the government) would be required not only to invoke 'family values', but also to help secure them through cooperative employment models (perhaps encompassing several organizations). In parallel, one would also have to investigate whether existing mobility constraints in certain areas (in the part-time academic job market, for instance) could not be reduced.

Of course, in view of a stable mass unemployment of over two million [in Germany], the demand for a reduced universal mobility seems even more unrealistic than it already is. Similar effects can perhaps be achieved from quite different starting points, for instance by generally loosening the *connection between participation in the labor market and making a living*. Perhaps social assistance could be increased in the direction of a minimum income for all citizens, perhaps the problems of protecting people in ill health and old age might be decoupled from wage labor, and so on. This loosening of the screws in the labor market has a tradition (welfare state guarantees, reduction of the working week and so on). Considering the tightening effect being expressed in mass unemployment – the rush of women into the labor market simultaneously with the reduction of the volume of labor through its increasing productivity (see Chapter 6) – it will be on the agenda in any case.

But even a labor market dynamism that was strangled in a 'pro-family' manner would be only one side of the solution. The social coexistence of people would have to be made possible once again. The nuclear family with its diluted social relationships represents an enormous intensification of labor. Many things which could be accomplished (more) easily by several families together become an excessive long-term burden if one faces them alone. The best examples of this are the tasks and concerns of parenthood. But living and cooperating groups encompassing multiple families are usually excluded by *housing situations* alone. Professional mobility and the trend to single life have already literally been cast in concrete. Apartments are becoming smaller. They continue to be designed for the mobility of individual families. The plans of apartments, houses and residential quarters exclude the possibility of several families moving in together. And this is only one example. It is not just apartments, houses and residential quarters that prescribe individualization and prevent social living. There are hardly any limits to fantasies for concrete changes. Child-raising, for instance, could be eased not only by the possibility of neighborly help, but also by the legal recognition of a new specialty – 'day mothers' – or through a school system that would not have already made parental tutoring a part of the 'hidden curriculum', and so forth.

There is certainly something to be said about the realizability and financibility of this 'utopia'. That is not our concern here, however. Here we were centrally concerned with a theoretical argument, specifically with breaking up the false alternative between family conservatism and market conformity. To be sure, this or other institutional reforms are only meant to create and protect a realm of *possibility*. Men and women themselves will have to invent and test out new forms of living together *beyond* feudally ascribed roles.[2]

Thus the much maligned 'refuges of privacy and inwardness' acquire a central importance. Only at first glance does it appear that the social movements of the seventies declined into 'subjective self-reflection'. As near and as far as anyone can see, hard labor is being performed in the everyday reality of relationships and commitments inside and outside marriage and the family, under the burden of ways of life that are unfit for the future. In their totality, changes are coming into being here which we must disabuse ourselves of considering as private phenomena. Biography, which is becoming a reflexive project, does somehow have even revolutionary potentials. What is being patched together in this is the sensitive practice of all sorts of communal life, an attempt at renovating the relationship between the sexes, despite the experience of setbacks, and a reawakening solidarity based on *shared* and *admitted* oppression. The regressions in the progress result from a number of factors, but certainly also from the weight of the opposing institutional burdens. Much of what men and women reproach each other with today is not their personal responsibility. If this view could make headway, much would be gained, perhaps even the political energies necessary for the changes.

Notes

1 For empirical evidence on this very general dictum, see Beck and Beck-Gernsheim (1990). There the arguments have been developed further.

2 Rainer Maria Rilke, who knew a lot about the mistakes that are becoming general here, had already expressed hope at the turn of the century (1904): 'Girls and women, in their new personal development, will only temporarily remain imitators of masculine features and defects, and repeaters of their careers. After the insecurity of such transitions it will be seen that women only passed through the breadth and variety of that (often ridiculous) disguise in order to free their inmost essence from the distorting influences of the other sex . . . This humanity of the woman, born in pain and degradation, will appear when she has shed the conventions of mere femininity in the transformations of her external situation, and men who do not yet feel it coming, will be surprised and struck by it. Some day (for which reliable signs are already shining and speaking today, especially in the Nordic countries), some day there will exist a type of girl and woman, whose name will not signify simply the opposite of the masculine, but something of its own, something that does not suggest any supplement and limitation, but only existence and life – the female person. Much against the will of men at first, this progress will fundamentally change the experience of love, now full of aberration, will reshape it into a relationship meant from person to person and no longer from man to woman. And this more human love (which will manifest itself gently and with infinite consideration and will be good and clear in committing and letting go), will resemble the one that we are preparing with such effort and struggle, the love that consists of two lonelinesses protecting, limiting and greeting each other' (Rilke 1980: 79f.).

5

INDIVIDUALIZATION, INSTITUTIONALIZATION AND STANDARDIZATION: LIFE SITUATIONS AND BIOGRAPHICAL PATTERNS

'Individualization' – an overly significant concept, ambiguous, perhaps even an abomination, but one that does refer to something important. So far, people have attempted to approach it from the side of what is important, from reality. In the process, the tangle of meanings in this word has been pushed aside, to some degree. Now a few conceptual and theoretical clarifications will be added by way of a two-step argument. First, a general, analytical, ahistorical *model of individualization* will be sketched out. Much of the classical discussion from Marx via Weber to Durkheim and Simmel can be seen here, and perhaps a few of the central misunderstandings can be located. Second, this 'model' will be supplemented and clarified beyond the previous discussions in relation to post-war conditions. In so doing the individualization theory will be condensed down into the central thesis: what has manifested itself over the past two decades in Germany (and perhaps in other industrial states as well) can no longer be understood within the framework of existing conceptualizations. Instead (if I may be forgiven for the monstrous word) it must be conceived of as the beginning of a *new mode of societalization,* a kind of 'metamorphosis' or 'categorical shift' in the relation between the individual and society.[1]

The Analytical Dimensions of Individualization

'Individualization' is neither a phenomenon nor an invention of the second half of the twentieth century. Corresponding 'individualized' lifestyles and life situations are found in the Renaissance (Burckhardt), in the courtly culture of the Middle Ages (Elias), in the inward asceticism of Protestantism (Weber), in the emancipation of the peasants from feudal bondage (Marx), and during the nineteenth and early twentieth centuries in the loosening of intergenerational family ties (Imhof), as well as in mobility processes – the flight from the countryside and the explosive growth of cities (Lederer, Kocka), etc. In this general sense 'individualization' refers to certain subjective-biographical aspects of the civilization process (in the sense of Elias 1969). Modernization does not just lead to the formation of a centralized state power, to concentrations of capital and to an ever more tightly woven web of divisions of labor and market relationships, to mobility and mass consumption, and so on. It also leads, and here we have arrived at the general model, to a triple 'individualization': disembedding, *removal* from historically prescribed social forms and commitments in the sense of traditional contexts of dominance and support (the 'liberating dimension'); the *loss of traditional security* with respect to practical knowledge, faith and guiding norms (the 'disenchantment dimension'); and – here the meaning of the word is virtually turned into its opposite – re-embedding, a *new type of social commitment* (the 'control' or 'reintegration dimension').

These three factors – removal (or liberation), loss of stability and reintegration – are in themselves an infinite reservoir for misunderstandings. They constitute a general, *ahistorical model of individualization*. It seems essential to me, however, to differentiate this conceptually with a second dimension: specifically, according to (*objective*) *life situation* and (*subjective*) *consciousness* (identity, personalization). In that case the following six-field table results:

Individualization

	Life situation: objective	Consciousness/ identity: subjective
Liberation		
Loss of stability		
Reintegration		

A major misunderstanding connected with the word 'individualization' derives from equating it with the upper right-hand field. Many people associate 'individualization' with individuation (= personalization = uniqueness = emancipation). That may be true. But perhaps the opposite is also true. *So far, very little or nothing at all has been said about the entire right-hand side.* This would amount to a book all by itself. In essence the discussions have limited themselves to the left-hand, objective side. That is to say: individualization was understood as a sociological category, located in the tradition of research into biographies and life situations. That tradition assumed it was quite capable of distinguishing between what happens to people and how they deal with it in their behavior and consciousness.[2] In contrast to those inquiries, which are primarily concerned with consciousness, identity, socialization and emancipation, the main question of this chapter is: *how can individualization be understood as a change of life situations and biographical patterns?* What pattern of life situations, what types of biography prevail under the conditions of a developed labor market?

Individualization Reconsidered

How can this general model be made more concrete? That is, what are the social forms and assurances of support from which people are cut loose? What are the conditions and media which advance this process? To what new forms of control and societalization do they lead?

Two focal points of liberation [*Freisetzung*; in this context 'liberation' will be applied to this ambiguous phenomenon; liberation in the usual sense will be rendered by 'emancipation' (tr.)] have been worked out so far, and two others are beginning to come into view for the future (and are the theme of the next chapter). First we were concerned with the *removal from status-based classes*, which can be traced right back to the beginning of this century, but is now acquiring a new quality. These liberations relate to social and cultural class commitments *in the sphere of reproduction*. They do of course accompany changes in the sphere of production, such as a general elevation of the educational level and disposable income, the juridification of labor relations, changes in social composition with the retention of fundamental social relations of inequality. This can be described in the changes of family structures, housing conditions, geographical distributions, neighborhood relations, leisure time behavior, club memberships and so on. Projected onto the entire social structure, this 'dissolution of the proletarian milieu' (Mooser 1983) is revealed by the endemic difficulties in interpreting models from class and stratification research in an empirically meaningful way in view of tendencies towards differentiation and pluralization. These difficulties have led, on the one hand, to a *methodically concealed conventionalism in the determination of stratification boundaries* (see Bolte 1983 for the first example), and on the other, to a *retreat into the ahistorical apriority of the class antagonism*.

A second focal point for liberation lies in the changes in the *situation of women*. Women have been cut loose from marital support – the material cornerstone of the traditional housewife's existence. Thus, the entire structure of familial ties and support comes under pressure for individualization. The type of the *negotiated provisional family* emerges.[3]

Along with class cultures and the familial relationship structure there are two other focal points for liberation. They no longer start from the sphere of reproduction but rather from the production sphere, and occur as liberations relative to professions and the firm. We are referring especially to the *flexibilization of working hours* and the *decentralization of the work site* (of which electronic home work is an extreme case). In this way *new types of flexible, pluralized underemployment* arise (see Chapter 6). These bring about problems of support (for welfare law) and at the same time create new types of life situations and biographical developmental patterns.

So much for the summary of the argument to this point. Now to the more productive question: which *mode of reintegration and control* is connected with these emerging individual situations? First of all, I offer three theses.

(1) An essential peculiarity of individualization lies in its *consequences*. It is no longer compensated for by any *conscience collective* or by a social reference unit in the sphere of cultural life. To put it very schematically, it is no longer social classes that take the place of status groups, or the family as a stable frame of reference that takes the place of social class commitments. *The individual himself or herself becomes the reproduction unit for the social in the lifeworld.* Or put another way, the family collapses as the 'penultimate' synthesis of life situations between the generations and the sexes, and individuals inside and outside the family become the agents of their livelihood mediated by the market, as well as of their biographical planning and organization.

(2) This differentiation of socio-biographical situations is accompanied at the same time by a high degree of *standardization*. Or more precisely, *the very same media which bring about an individualization also bring about a standardization.* This applies to the market, money, law, mobility, education and so on, each in its own way. The individual situations that come into existence are thoroughly *dependent on the labor market*. They are, so to speak, the extension of market dependency into every corner of (earning a) living, they are its late result in the welfare state phase. They arise in the *fully established* market and labor market society, which barely remembers traditional possibilities of support any longer, if at all. Georg Simmel (1958a) has already demonstrated graphically how money both individualizes *and* standardizes. This holds true not only for money-dependent mass consumption and 'dismissals [*Freisetzungen*] in the labor market', but also for the removal from and reconnection to market society through training, juridification, scientization, and so forth.

(3) But the simultaneity of individualization and standardization does not yet adequately encompass the newly arising individual situations. For they display a *novel character*. They *span the separated areas of the private sphere and the various areas of the public sphere.* They are no longer merely private situations, but also always institutional. They have the contradictory double face of *institutionally dependent individual situations*. The apparent outside of the institutions becomes the inside of the individual biography. This design of life situations spanning institutional boundaries results from their institutional dependency (in the broadest sense). The liberated individuals become dependent on the labor market and *because of that*, dependent on education, consumption, welfare state regulations and support, traffic planning, consumer supplies, and on possibilities and fashions in medical, psychological and pedagogical

counseling and care. This all points to the *institution-dependent control structure* of individual situations. Individualization becomes the *most advanced* form of societalization dependent on the market, law, education and so on.

The Institutionalization of Biographical Patterns

Class differences and family connections are not really annulled in the course of individualization processes. Rather, they recede into the background relative to the newly emerging 'center' of the biographical life plan. Biographies too, are becoming *reflexive*. People with the same income level, or put in the old-fashioned way, within the same 'class', can or even must choose between different lifestyles, subcultures, social ties and identities. From knowing one's 'class' position one can no longer determine one's personal outlook, relations, family position, social and political ideas or identity. At the same time, new dependencies arise. These point to *inherent contradictions in the individualization process*. In advanced modernity individualization takes place under the general conditions of a societalizing process that makes individual autonomizations increasingly impossible. The individual is indeed removed from traditional commitments and support relationships, but exchanges them for the constraints of existence in the labor market and as a consumer, with the standardizations and controls they contain. The place of *traditional* ties and social forms (social class, nuclear family) is taken by *secondary* agencies and institutions, which stamp the biography of the individual and make that person dependent upon fashions, social policy, economic cycles and markets, contrary to the image of individual control which establishes itself in consciousness.

Thus it is precisely individualized private existence which becomes more and more obviously and emphatically dependent on situations and conditions that completely escape its reach. Parallel to that, risk conflicts arise which by their origin and design resist any individual treatment. As is known, these include more or less everything controversial under discussion politically and socially: from the so-called 'holes in the social safety net', to the negotiation of wages and working conditions, to fending off bureaucratic high-handedness, providing educational opportunities, solving traffic problems, protecting against environmental destruction, and so forth. Individualization thus takes effect precisely under general social conditions which allow an individual autonomous private existence even less than before.

Status-influenced, class cultural or familial biographical rhythms overlap with or are replaced by *institutional biographical patterns*: entry into and exit from the educational system, entry into and exit from work, or determinations of the retirement age based on social policy. And all of this exists in a longitudinal section of biography (childhood, adolescence, adulthood, retirement and old age) as well as in the daily rhythm and economy of time (harmonizing family, educational and career lives). The area of overlap is especially clear in the case of the 'standard biography' for women. While men remain essentially untouched by family events in their biographies, women lead a contradictory double life shaped equally by family and by organizations. For them the family rhythm *still* applies, and in the majority of cases the rhythm of education and career *already* do as well, which results in conflictual crises and continuing incompatible demands.

Individualization means market dependency in all dimensions of living. The forms of existence that arise are the isolated *mass market*, not conscious of itself, and *mass consumption* of generically designed housing, furnishings, articles of daily use, as well as opinions, habits, attitudes and lifestyles launched and adopted through the mass media. In other words, individualization delivers people over to an *external control and standardization* that was unknown in the enclaves of familial and feudal subcultures.

These ways in which institutions shape biographies mean that regulations in the educational system (e.g. educational schedules), in occupational life (e.g. work periods on a daily basis and in the overall biography) and in the system of social protection *are directly intermeshed with phases in the biographies of people*. Institutional determinations and interventions are (implicitly) also determinations of and interventions in human biographies. By raising the minimum age for day-care centers, for instance, it is made difficult or impossible for women to fulfill both their maternal and their occupational obligations (which also means: women are driven out of the labor market). In lowering the retirement age, the length of 'social old age' is increased for an entire generation (with all the associated opportunities and problems). Simultaneously a redistribution of labor participation to the following younger generations is accomplished. Individualization thus means precisely *institutionalization*, institutional shaping and, hence *the ability to structure* biographies and life situations *politically*. The actual shaping usually occurs 'unseen', as a 'latent side effect' of decisions explicitly related to intra-organizational matters (educational system, labor market, work, etc.). A rather anecdotal example – television – may illustrate this connection.

Television isolates *and* standardizes. On the one hand, it removes people from traditionally shaped and bounded contexts of conversation, experience and life. At the same time, however, everyone is in a similar position: they all consume institutionally produced television programs, from Honolulu to Moscow and Singapore. The individualization – more precisely, the removal from traditional life contexts – is accompanied by a uniformity and standardization of forms of living. Everyone sits isolated even in the family and gapes at the set. Thus arises the social image of an isolated mass audience – or, to put it more bluntly, the standardized collective existence of isolated mass hermits (Anders 1980).

This occurs simultaneously *transculturally* and *transnationally*. We could say people meet every evening around the world at the *village green of television* and consume the news. In this sense, individual situations can no longer even be determined to be institutionally dependent on nation states. They are part of a globally standardized media network. More than that: institutional and national boundaries are in a certain sense no longer valid. Through the media we lead a kind of *spatial and temporal double life*. We are at one and the same time here and somewhere else; we are alone, by ourselves, and yet we are listening to the same concert of the New York Philharmonic; or, while we eat dinner here in isolation, we are also participating observers of terrible scenes from the civil war over there in Lebanon. These sorts of emerging life situations seem to display an *individual and institutional schizophrenia* in their 'bilocality'. There are quite asymmetrical opportunities, however, of seeing through this. Transparency is quite limited if you are inside, but much better for those outside and *au-dessus de la mêlée*. Boundaries between interior and exterior, further, exist and do not exist at the same time.

New types of opportunities for control and influence are also connected with this. Considering the viewing habits of broad parts of the public (which cause withdrawal symptoms if ignored) television programs arrange *in one stroke* both the daily and the weekly schedule of the family.

The private sphere is not what it appears to be: a sphere separated from the environment. It is the *outside turned inside and made private, of conditions and decisions* made elsewhere, in the television networks, the educational system, in firms, or the labor market, or in the transportation system, with general disregard of their private, biographical consequences. Anyone who does not see this misunderstands an essential and basic characteristic of social ways of living in the phase of advanced modernity, the overlapping and networking of the emerging individualized privacy with the seemingly separate areas and production sectors of education, consumption, transportation, production, the labor market, and so on.

As this institutional dependency grows, so does the *susceptibility to crises* of the emerging individual situations. The institutional dependency does not exist in general, but in certain priorities. The key to a livelihood lies in the labor market. Suitability for the labor market demands education. Anyone who is denied access to either of these faces social and material oblivion. Without the proper training the situation is every bit as devastating as with training but without corresponding jobs. Only under these conditions do those rejected by the vocational training system fall into the social abyss. The provision or denial of apprenticeships thus becomes a question of whether young people will enter society or drop out of it. At the same time, economic or demographic 'ups and downs' can cause *entire generations* to drift *into the margins of society*. That is to say, institutionally dependent individual situations bring about generation-specific disadvantages or privileges in the corresponding *peer group situations* along economic and labor market cycles. These however always manifest themselves as insufficient care or support performance by governmental institutions, which hence come under pressure to prevent the institutionally pre-programmed dearth of opportunities for entire generations, periods of life or age groups, or compensate for that lack with legal regulations and welfare state redistribution of income.

Institutions act in legally determined *categories of standard biographies, to which reality conforms less and less.* The backbone of the standard biography is the standard work relation. Thus the system of social protection is geared to participation in wage labor. At the same time, there is a constantly growing number of people who cannot manage to enter the employment system, or can do so only with great difficulty, despite all their good intentions. Social insurance is based on standards of normality which are less and less likely to be fulfilled, considering constant mass unemployment, and to which the living conditions in the family and between men and women correspond less and less. The concept of *family bread-winner* has been displaced by a family in which the roles of earner and provider, care-giver and child-rearer are shared and alternated, depending on phases and decisions. The place of the 'intact' family has been taken by the broadest variety of 'broken homes'. The growing group of single fathers faces the discrimination of a divorce law committed to the maternal monopoly of child-raising, and so on.

A society developing away from the axes of lifestyle in industrial society – social classes, nuclear family, sex roles, and career – faces a system of human service, administrative and political institutions that are now increasingly taking on *a kind of representative function for the fading industrial period.* They intervene normatively with pedagogic and disciplinary actions in ways of life 'deviating' from the official standards of normality. They become the invokers and advocates of former certainties which only apply now to a diminishing part of the population. In this way *the contrasts between institutionally planned and socially valid normality* intensify, and the edifice of industrial society threatens to slip into normative legalism.

Through institutional dependency the individualized society simultaneously becomes vulnerable to all sorts of conflicts, commitments and coalitions *across* traditional (class) boundaries. The antagonism of the two sides in the labor market recedes as a definite contrast, and the center is occupied by the varied forms in which repressed sociality makes itself felt in private life. It may be incidents such as the planned highway in the vicinity of one's own back yard, the worsening school situation for children, or the atomic waste storage dump being built nearby which cause aspects of a 'collective fate' to penetrate into consciousness.

What is decisive, however, is *how* the institutionally shaped collective fate appears in the life context of people in individualized society, how it is perceived and how it is dealt with. To express this metaphysically, one could say that the concave mirror of class consciousness shatters without disintegrating, and that each fragment produces its own total perspective, although the mirror's surface with its myriad of tiny cracks and fissures is unable to produce a unified image. As people are removed from social ties and privatized through recurrent surges of individualization, a double effect occurs. On the one hand, forms of perception become private, and at the same time – conceiving of this along the time axis – they become *ahistorical*. Children no longer even know their parents' life context, much less that of their grandparents. That is to say, the temporal horizons of perception narrow more and more, until finally in the limiting case *history* shrinks *to the* (*eternal*) *present*, and everything revolves around the axis of one's personal ego and personal life. On the other hand, those areas where commonly organized action can affect personal life steadily diminish, and the constraints increase to shape one's own biography, and in precisely those areas where it is once again the product of new institutional conditions.

Individualization in this sense means that each person's biography is removed from given determinations and placed in his or her own hands, open and dependent on decisions. The proportion of life opportunities which are fundamentally closed to decision-making is decreasing and the proportion of the biography which is open and must be constructed personally is increasing. Individualization of life situations and processes thus means that biographies become *self-reflexive*; socially prescribed biography is transformed into biography that is self-produced and continues to be produced. Decisions on education, profession, job, place of residence, spouse, number of children and so forth, with all the secondary decisions implied, no longer can be, they must be made. Even where the word 'decisions' is too grandiose, because neither consciousness nor alternatives are present, the individual will have to 'pay for' the consequences of decisions not taken. This means that through institutional and biographical prescriptions, *construction kits of biographical combination possibilities* come into being. In the transition from 'standard to elective biography' (Ley 1984), the conflictual and historically unprecedented type of the *do-it-yourself biography* separates out (Gross 1985). The either–or of rich versus underprivileged life or of conflict situations is relativized by accumulations of problems specific to certain phases in life (for instance, for young adults the convergence of decisions on marriage, children and the spouses' careers), which require special private and institutional planning.

In the individualized society the individual must therefore learn, on pain of permanent disadvantage, to conceive of himself or herself as the center of action, as the planning office with respect to his/her own biography, abilities, orientations, relationships and so on. Under those conditions of a reflexive biography, 'society' *must* be individually manipulated as a 'variable'. Certainly, the scarcity of educational opportunities is a problem that affects everyone, but what does that mean for the forging of my own fate, which nobody else can do for me? What can

I do, what must I do, in order to be able to study medicine even with mediocre grades? This is how the social determinants that impact one's own life must be conceived of as 'environmental variables' that can be moderated, subverted or nullified for one's personal life space by 'creative measures' suited to one's own sphere of action and corresponding to the 'internal differentiations' of possible contacts and activities.

What is demanded is a *vigorous model of action in everyday life*, which puts the ego at its center, allots and opens up opportunities for action to it, and permits it in this manner to work through the emerging possibilities of decision and arrangement with respect to one's own biography in a meaningful way. Beneath the superficial intellectual shadow-boxing, this means that in order for one to survive, an *ego-centered world view must be developed*, which turns the relation of ego and world on its head, so to speak, conceiving of and making them useful for the purpose of shaping an individual biography.

As a consequence the floodgates are opened wide for the subjectivization and individualization of risks and contradictions produced by institutions and society. The institutional conditions that determine individuals are no longer just events and conditions that happen to them, but *also consequences of the decisions they themselves have made*, which they must view and treat as such. This is also favored by the fact that there is a surreptitious change in the character of the typical actions that throw individuals off the track. What assails them was formerly considered a 'blow of fate' sent by God or nature, e.g. war, natural catastrophes, death of a spouse, in short an event for which they bore no responsibility. Today, however, it is much more likely events that are considered 'personal failure', from not passing an examination to unemployment or divorce. One even has to choose one's social identity and group membership, in this way managing one's own self, changing its *image*. In the individualized society, risks do not just increase quantitatively; qualitatively new types of personal risk arise, the risk of the chosen and changed personal identity. And what is an additional burden, new forms of 'guilt ascription' come into being. Sooner or later, these constraints to a personal and reflexive handling, planning and production of biography will produce new demands on education, care-giving, therapy and politics.

In conclusion let us point out a final, apparently contradictory basic trait: individualized biographies, reconnected on one side to self-formation, are opened on the other hand into the virtually infinite. *Everything which appears separated in the perspective of systems theory, becomes an integral component of the individual biography*: family *and* wage labor, education *and* employment, administration *and* the transportation system, consumption, pedagogy, and so on. Subsystem boundaries apply to subsystems, not to people in institutionally dependent individual situations. Or, expressing it in Habermasian terms, individual situations lie *across* the distinction between system and lifeworld. The subsystem boundaries pass through individual situations which are, so to speak, the biographical side of that which is separated by system boundaries. Considered in this way, we are concerned with individualized institutional situations, whose connections and fractures (neglected on the level of the system) continually produce frictions, disharmonies and contradictions within and among individual biographies.

Under these conditions, how one lives becomes the *biographical solution of systemic contradictions* (as for instance between education and employment, or the legally presumed and the actual standard biography).[4] Against Luhmann (1985): biography is the *sum of subsystem rationalities*, and by no means their environment. It is not only that buying coffee in the shop on the corner may perhaps become complicit in the exploitation of the plantation workers in South America. And not only that given the omnipresence of pesticides a basic course in (alternative) chemistry is becoming a prerequisite for survival. Nor only that pedagogy and medicine, social law and traffic planning presume active 'thinking individuals', as they put it so nicely, who are supposed to find their way in this jungle of transitory finalities with the help of their own clear vision. All these and all the other experts dump their contradictions and conflicts at the feet of the individual and leave him or her with the well intentioned invitation to judge all of this critically on the basis of his or her own notions. With detraditionalization and the creation of global media networks, the biography is increasingly removed from its direct spheres of contact and opened up across the boundaries of countries and experts for a *long-distance morality* which puts the individual in the position of potentially having to take a continual stand. At the same moment as he or she sinks into insignificance, he or she is elevated to the apparent throne of a world-shaper. While governments (still) operate within the structure of nation states, biography is already being opened to the world society. Furthermore, world society becomes a *part* of biography, although this continual excessive demand can only be tolerated through the opposite reaction of not listening, simplifying, and apathy.

Notes

1 Kohli and Robert (1984) must have something similar in mind when they speak of 'individuality as a (historically new) form of societalization'.

2 The right side is in essence the central theme of cultural criticism – 'the end of the individual' – for instance, in the work of Adorno (1982) and Landmann (1971). In a different way, the corresponding inquiries have been the object of socialization theory and research (as summarized in the work of Geulen 1977). My impression is that more recent reflections by Luhmann (1985) also belong here. Compare also the summary in Nunner-Winkler (1985).

3 The fact that this state of affairs applies not just to parents, but also to *children and youth*, has been shown by the Shell Youth Study. Following up on that, this has also been demonstrated more recently, and with a more thorough theoretical basis, by Rosenmayr (1985), Hornstein (1985) and Baethge (1985). On the special problems of young female adolescents and workers, see in particular Diezinger and Bilden (1982).

4 A consequence for research practice is that biographical research which only follows in

the footsteps of family or stratification research is becoming problematic. Anyone who would investigate the standardization and (implicit) political configurability of individual situations, must also know something about education, employment conditions, industrial labor, mass consumption, social laws, the transport system, and urban planning. Biographical research in this sense – at least in the requirements imposed on it – would be something like interdisciplinary social research from the perspective of the subject, a type of research which lies *across* the layout of specialized sociology.

6

DESTANDARDIZATION OF LABOR

The importance that work has acquired in industrial society has no parallels in history. In the city-states of ancient Greece, slaves were assigned the labor necessary for subsistence, which was absorbed in the monotony of satisfying everyday needs and left no traces beyond assuring a living. The free citizens devoted themselves to political activity and cultural creation. Even in the Middle Ages, when work was still hand-work, the division of labor had a different meaning. For the aristocracy, work was ignoble. It was something for the lower ranks. The surest sign of a collapsing world appeared when the masculine offspring of a respected noble house had to practice a 'commoner's profession', i.e. descend into the depths of medicine or law. If one had informed those times of recent divinations of the decline or even the disappearance of wage labor, they would not have understood the message or the excitement about it.

The meaning of work for people's lives in industrial society is not based in the work itself, at least not fundamentally. Certainly it originates in the fact that the expenditure of labor force is the basis of earning of living, especially for the individualized way of life. But even this only explains a part of the shocks set off by the news of the decline of labor society. Wage labor and an occupation have become the *axis of living* in the industrial age. Together with the family this axis forms the bipolar coordinate system in which life in this epoch is situated. This can be illustrated in an ideal-typical longitudinal section of an intact industrial world. Already in childhood, while still completely tied to the family, the child experiences the occupation as the key to the world through his or her father. Later, education remains related through all stages to the missing 'other' of the occupation. Adult existence is held completely under the sway of wage labor, not merely because of the demands work itself makes on time, but also because of the time spent outside work, beforehand and afterwards, in pondering over it and planning for it. Even 'old age' is defined by non-occupation. Old age begins where the world of work discharges people – no matter if they feel old or not.

Nowhere, perhaps, is the meaning of wage labor for people's lives in the industrial world so clear as in the situation where two strangers meet and ask each other, 'what are you?' They do not answer with their hobby, 'pigeon fancier', or with their religious identity, 'Catholic', or with reference to ideals of beauty, 'well, you can see I'm a redhead with a full bosom', but with all the certainty in the world with their occupation: 'skilled worker for Siemens'. If we know our interlocutor's occupation then we think we know *him* or *her*. The occupation serves as a mutual identification pattern, with the help of which we can assess personal needs and abilities as well as economic and social position. Strange, to equate the person with the occupation he or she has. In society, where life is strung along the thread of the occupation, the latter does indeed contain certain key information: income, status, linguistic abilities, possible interests, social contacts, and so on.[1]

As late as the mid sixties, Helmut Schelsky (1942) still spoke in this sense of family and occupation as the two great forms of security that had remained for people in modernity. They provide their lives with 'inner stability'. In their occupations individuals are provided with access to contexts of social activity. Perhaps it can even be said that the 'holder of an occupation' is able to pass through the needle's eye of his job and become a 'coshaper of the world' on a small scale. In that respect, the occupation (like the family as well) guarantees *fundamental social experiences*. The occupation is a social reality that can be experienced in participation, at first hand, so to speak.[2]

Leaving aside for a moment the question of whether this image accurately reflects the situation in the sixties, it is in many cases no longer valid today or in the probable future. Just like the family on the other side, *the occupation has lost many of its former assurances and protective functions*. Along with their occupations, people lose an inner backbone of life that originated in the industrial epoch. The problems and demands of wage labor radiate through the entire society. Even outside of work, industrial society is a *wage labor society through and through* in the plan of its life, in its joys and sorrows, in its concept of achievement, in its justification of inequality, in its social welfare laws, in its balance of power and in its politics and culture. If it is facing a systemic transformation of wage labor then it is facing a social transformation.

From the System of Standardized Full Employment to the System of Flexible and Pluralized Underemployment

The topic of mass unemployment in the Western industrial states is still being discussed in terms of the old issues and concepts. In almost all political and economic camps, the hope still prevails that there will be a return towards full employment in the nineties as a result of a consistent stimulation of the economy. That we are standing at the start of a *counter*-industrial rationalization process, during the course of which the *principles* of the previously existing employment system will be at stake, and not just restratifications in the structure of occupations and qualifications – this is a possibility that has not so far been considered systematically, either theoretically or politically.

Despite all the controversy, the experts are united on at least one point: even with economic growth rates of 2 to 4 percent, high unemployment above the two-million person limit *will not be eliminated before the nineties* [in Germany]. Only then will the steeply growing potential of 'gainfully employed persons' diminish with the advent of the baby-bust generation, and concurrently the demand for jobs will fall below the level at the start of the eighties. There are many unknown quantities involved in this juggling of figures: the continually growing labor participation of women over the years, for instance; or how much in the end the rapidly growing utilization of information technologies and robotic production will be able to compensate with an increase in sales for the jobs such technologies destroy; finally to what extent there might be a wholesale conversion of full-time jobs into the broadest spectrum of part-time positions, so that all the previous calculations, which essentially measured the volume of wage labor in terms of full-time positions, might not pass away with the time on which they depend.

The uncertainties surrounding such calculations must not delude us about their great political significance. For this assessment of the development predicts a long dry spell until well into the nineties, but after those 'lean' years, 'fat' years in the labor market can be expected once again, with the decisive consequence that in this way a *non-policy of hibernation* is advocated (directly or indirectly). According to this version, which takes the pressure off the policy-makers, all that is needed are 'transitional measures' to mollify the situation for the 'affected generations'. Not only is there no need to experiment with the basic course in economic, educational and labor market policies, but ultimately, it would be impermissible to do so.

This interpretation, which has largely prevailed in recent years, in both scholarship and politics, rises and falls with the premise which will be systematically called into question here: the *continuity* of the traditional employment system and its supporting pillars – firm, job, career, wage labor, etc. That interpretation excludes the reflexive modernization of the employment system, the possibility of its *constitutional reform* through the surges of modernization in information technology, as well as in social policy and law. The possibility of such a *systemic transformation* of wage labor is to be thought through in what follows.

I proceed from the assumption, following dear old Popper, that an empirical test, even of an antithesis, is only possible if there is a theoretical *alternative*. We are thus concerned in the following with a set of hypotheses – no more and no less – which have yet to be critically discussed and empirically tested, but whose central function is to break up the prevailing (and so politically momentous) *theoretical monism* of continuity thinking. Only through the resultant competition between continuity and rupture in interpretations of the development of employment can an empirical testing of *both* perspectives be possible in the future. In this sense, what might be meant by the reflexive modernization of wage labor will first be illustrated (see also Chapter 8). Then it must be clarified in detail *by what means*, *how* and *with what consequences* this systemic change can be advanced and possibly put through, what resistances it will encounter, what risks it produces, and so on.

In the extrapolations of the development of unemployment up to the year 2000, but also in people's educational and career planning, as well as in political thought and action, the basic features of the current occupational system are presumed to remain constant. Entering into that assessment are the following assumptions, which are becoming questionable in current waves of modernization and automation.

The employment system, which arose in the past century from fierce social and political conflicts and crises, is based on high degrees of *standardization* in all its essential dimensions: the labor *contract*, the work *site* and the *working hours*. In its legal conditions, employment of labor follows standard contracts, which are sometimes negotiated collectively in general terms for entire industrial segments and employment groups. We have come to take it completely for granted that work is performed in spatial concentration into (large) business organizations. Until well into the 1970s 'lifelong full-time work' was the temporal organizational standard for planning and utilizing labor power in the plant, as well as in biographical life contexts. In principle, this system permits clear delineations between work and non-work, which can be determined spatially and temporally, but it also comprises mutually exclusive social and legal statuses of employment and non-employment. In the current and coming waves of automation, this *system of standardized full employment* is beginning to soften and fray at the margins into flexibilizations of its three supporting pillars: labor law, work site and working hours. Thus the *boundaries between work and non-work* are becoming *fluid*. Flexible, pluralized forms of underemployment are spreading.

By now it must have dawned in even the remotest corner that the norm of lifelong full-time work is being broken up by various forms of flexibilization of working hours. It is less well known that this would characterize the *spatial* concentration of wage labor. The various functions of a firm can already be linked electronically, at least in specific areas (administration, typing pool, management, services), and thus can be organized *decentrally*, 'geographically diffused' so to speak, or even 'independent of geography'. This spatial deconcentration of wage labor can occur in many different forms, from the relaxation of attendance rules, to geographically diffuse renetworkings of divisions and teams, to the outsourcing of subordinate functions through partial or complete electronic home work. But all are connected with the same consequence. The connection between social labor and production processes is loosened, the certainty that direct cooperation means 'working together at the same place' is undermined. In that process the employment system changes its appearance in a decisive way. The place of the *visible* character of work, concentrated in factory halls and tall buildings, is taken by an invisible organization of the firm. The observable symptom of such a transition from the old to the new employment system would be the gradual *abandonment* of large-scale work buildings, which, like the dinosaurs of the industrial age, would more and more serve only to remind us of a dying epoch. Ultimately, nothing essentially new would take place there. This would only reflect a displacement of the invisibility of the interlocking of capital onto the level of the substantive organization of work. Incidentally, this would provide management with similar gains in the possibilities for concealed organization and reconstituted networking.

It goes without saying that these temporal and spatial flexibilizations of wage labor need not proceed uniformly and in parallel for all subordinate areas of the employment system. It is to be assumed that pluralizations of working hours and work site advance independently of one another or in sequence. Nor can it be known today where the flexibilization will permanently or temporarily encounter an objective and/or political limit, nor what functional areas (and thus, occupational groups, sectors and divisions) will be excluded from it. It can already be stated, however, that the flexibilization of working hours, the transformation of full-time into the broadest variety of part-time jobs, cannot occur *neutrally with respect to income.* That is, the division of working hours (which after all does not serve the purpose of more employment but rather the generalization of *under*employment, the reduction of unemployment) is accompanied by an *unfavorable* redistribution of income, social protection, career opportunities and status in the organization, in the sense of a collective decline (across differentiations of specialty, occupation and hierarchy). In this sense, working hours policy is always *redistribution policy* as well, and creates new social insecurities and inequalities. Here lies the basis of trade union resistance in recent years and the active haste of many firms to push forward. This is true even though flexible forms of underemployment meet increasing interest among (young) men and women, in fact are virtually demanded by them in order to balance wage labor and family work, work and life, more equitably. As will be shown later, working people's gains in sovereignty over their work can be combined with a *privatization of the physical and mental health risks of work* through *spatial flexibilization of wage labor.* Norms for the protection of laborers resist public enforcement in decentralized labor forms, and the costs for violation or compliance are shifted off onto the workers themselves (just as, incidentally, the businesses save the costs of the centralized organization of wage labor, from building expenses to the maintenance of the stock of electronic equipment).

If one considers these consequences of the destandardization of working hours and work locations in their totality, then one can say that a transition is occurring in industrial society from a uniform system of lifelong full-time work organized in a single industrial location, with the radical alternative of unemployment, to a *risk-fraught system of flexible, pluralized, decentralized underemployment, which, however, will possibly no longer raise the problem of unemployment in the sense of being completely without a paid job.* In this system, unemployment in the guise of various forms of underemployment is 'integrated' into the employment system, but in exchange for a *generalization of employment insecurity* that was not known in the 'old' uniform full-employment system of industrial society. As in the nineteenth century, this development also is *fundamentally reminiscent of the two heads of Janus*. Progress and immiseration interpenetrate each other in a new way. Gains in productivity by the firms accompany control problems. The workers exchange a bit of freedom from work for new types of constraints and material insecurity. Unemployment disappears, but then reappears in new types of generalized risky underemployment. This all means that an ambiguous, contradictory development is set in motion in which advantages and drawbacks are indissolubly intermeshed, a development whose far-reaching consequences and risks are not calculable for political consciousness and action either. That is precisely what is signified when one speaks of a *risk society* system of underemployment.

After a long period of accustomization, it has come to be taken for granted in industrial society that wage labor is to be performed *outside the home*. This separation of domestic and wage labor is reversed once again in the risk society by relaxations of attendance regulations, electronic networking of decentralized work sites and so on. The far-reaching social consequences can only be guessed at. They might include: an easing of the daily commuter traffic, therefore reduced strain on the natural and human environment; the possible deurbanization of cities; limitations of everyday local mobility which can in a sense be electronically delegated and thus even increased despite spatial immobility; and so on.

The fundamental categories until now – firm, career, wage labor – no longer capture the emerging reality of the labor organization becoming increasingly invisible. They fit the emerging system of underemployment about as well as the labor concepts of feudal society applied to the labor relations of industrial society. This does not mean that with this development wage labor is being sublated in a positive sense; rather, on the contrary, the emerging flexible and plural forms of underemployment are at once *more thoroughly* than ever forms of wage labor while also *no longer* wage labor at all. That only means, however, that by looking through the spectacles of industrial society concepts we strain our eyes trying to make out the emerging labor reality.

One can also sketch out the perspective being developed here as that those aspects which have thus far been opposed antithetically – formal and informal labor, employment and unemployment – will be *merged* in the future into a new system of flexible, plural, risky forms of underemployment. This integration of unemployment through a pluralization of wage labor relations will not completely displace the familiar system of employment, but will overlap or, better, undermine it, and considering the shrinking overall volume of wage labor, will place it under continual pressure to adapt. This development can also be described as a *bifurcation of the labor market along lines of normative standardization* (with respect to time, space and social welfare laws). In this way a new division of the labor market is created between a uniform standard industrial society labor market and a flexible, plural risk society market for underemployment, where the second market is quantitatively expanding and increasingly dominating the first. Why? So far, we have only made a theoretical distinction and sketched a typology. Now we must justify the assessment that the modernization of the employment system through technology has already gone off in this direction.

All labor policy, whether governmental or within a firm, has been subject since at least the eighties to the law of *redistributing the systematically produced lack of work*. If people had previously assumed that an economic recovery would also lead to a reduction of unemployment, it has become clear in the last few years that those two are mutually independent variables. Many enterprises – almost all the large ones among German industry – have *increased* their turnover during the past few years, and simultaneously *eliminated* personnel. This is made possible by the broad introduction of microelectronics combined with a reorganization of the remaining labor. Numerically controlled machine tools, the electronic 'automation slaves of the modern era', are first of all taking over large parts of the work in the production area (the automobile, chemical and machine tool industries), but computers are also diluting the work in administrations and offices. The extent and the explosive power of this development become clear if one looks at the increase in productivity between 1977 and 1984. While productivity growth per hour worked in manufacturing and mining was 2.7 percent in 1977, it rose by 1979 to 4.7 percent and declined thereafter in a zigzag pattern to 1.5 percent. Not until the final quarter of 1983 did it suddenly rise steeply, and then it rose by an (estimated) 10.8 percent in 1984. That means *a considerable increase in productivity in slightly more than one year*! (*Der Spiegel* 1984, no. 21: 22ff.). This development finds its parallels in the numbers of industrial robots utilized, which was only 1255 in 1980, but rose to 3500 in 1982 and had already increased by 1984 to 6600 (*Süddeutsche Zeitung* February 8, 1985: 23). And here we are only dealing with the first wave of a development whose end cannot even be envisaged.

In the prevailing employment system of full-time jobs, unemployment is distributed according to the unambiguous, black and white pattern of employment or unemployment. In the current crisis situation, the hidden asset of working hours policy is being discovered and propagated as a *deus ex machina* for the organization and its advantages and disadvantages explored. It soon becomes obvious that the latitude for *standardized* reductions of the working week with retention of full pay is extraordinarily limited.[3] This is true for the working week, as the result of the struggle for the thirty-five hour week has made clear. It applies equally well, however, to the lowering of the retirement age or the lengthening of compulsory education – both of them overall reductions of the volume of wage labor that fall outside the competence of collective bargaining. Under the conditions of the standardized full-employment system – this conclusion is beginning to take shape – the reduction of wage labor necessarily leads to the exclusion of the unemployed. There is a corresponding growth in the pressure for a flexibilization of working hour conditions in employment. This has many advocates, including governmental institutions under pressure to act in view of the 'political scandal' of mass unemployment; women and younger employees, who hope for a better harmonization of familial and wage labor or more 'autonomy over time'; and corporations, which discover unsuspected sources of productivity in the organizational utilization of working hours. This *grand coalition* of the state, large parts of employee society and organizational management confronts the *resistance* of the trade unions (and the traditional social democratic workers' party), who see the foundations of the traditional employment system and their own positions of power slipping away.

In this apparent impasse, businesses are discovering *part-time work and underemployment as productive forces* or, more generally, the destandardization of the normal ways for utilizing labor and the organizational possibilities they contain for increasing productivity on the basis of microelectronics.[4] Of course, this occurs in a contradictory, non-uniform and disconnected way.

To the surprise of observers in industrial sociology, 'in the central industrial sectors a fundamental transformation [is occurring] before our very eyes in the utilization of the remaining labor force, which would be apprehended too narrowly and too one-sidedly under the cliché of the crisis of Taylorism. It is certainly possible to speak of a paradigm shift in the plants of the core sector' (Kern and Schumann 1984: 149). The displacement and reorganization of human labor under the conditions of Tayloristic forms of work occur in the exact *converse* of the originally valid 'management philosophy'. The restrictive partial activities can be completely or mostly assumed by production robots in the current or coming automations, and the resulting new tasks of supervision, direction and maintenance can be comprised in a few highly skilled specialized positions. The principle of division or, better, destruction of labor is replaced by the counter-principle of *the consolidation of partial tasks on a higher level of skill and specialized sovereignty*. Large numbers of unskilled or semi-skilled workers are replaced by a small number of 'professionalized automation workers'. Expansion of the scope for organizational flexibility and drastic reductions of personnel are made possible in this phase of plant automation by the consolidation and increased specialization of the remaining labor.

At first this essentially only fits the situation in the production spheres of the core industrial sectors. At roughly the same time, the *transformation of full-time to a variety of part-time work relations* is being pushed forward, especially in the service sector (retail trade, department stores, hotel and restaurant trade). After an initial period of resistance, the productivity benefits in this for the enterprises are becoming discernible. They lie essentially in the fact that on the one hand businesses are able to arrange the number of working hours flexibly with respect to orders received. In this way, portions of the entrepreneurial risk can be shifted onto the employees as flexible underemployment in view of the inhibiting threshold represented by open unemployment. On the other hand, the employers are allowed in this way to decouple production time from work time and therefore utilize the production arrangement longer, more intensively and more tightly. Finally, part-time work and underemployment generally broaden the scope of action for businesses in personnel policy, by making it easier to push through work changes, by compensating more rapidly for the devaluation of skills due to new technological requirements, and by generally weakening the power of the personnel through diversification.

In this sense one could say that Taylor's 'philosophy of dismemberment' is transferred here from the substantive aspects of labor to the temporal and contractual relations of employment. The starting points for this new 'Taylorism of employment relations' are no longer situated in the combination of labor and machine, but in the temporal limitation, legal (non-)protection, and contractual pluralization of the employment of labor. And the possibilities for a flexible arrangement of working hours on the basis of microelectronics are far from exhausted. The centerpieces of this organizational 'time puzzle' are flexitime (which already applies to over six million workers in Germany as of the first half of 1985) and various forms of part-time employment (job-sharing on a weekly or monthly basis and so on), of which at this time more than two million employees, mostly women, avail themselves.

Alongside these possibilities for rationalizations of work time, businesses are beginning initial experiments on the *outsourcing* of subordinate functions as a productivity reserve. This development has its origin in the reorganization of secretarial and administrative tasks. But this is a fundamental possibility in this phase of the development of productive forces, which could certainly be applied to other functional areas after a successful test phase. Central to it is the potential of microelectronics to reduce, or eliminate altogether, by means of information technology the requirements for direct cooperation between functional areas related to each other within the division of labor. In this sense the employment of telecommunications and the appropriate storage media permit a widespread *temporal and spatial decoupling* of labor and production processes and thus new types of *decentralized* work as well, of which the much discussed 'electronic cottage industry' represents only *one* extreme case. Here too, what is special lies in the fact that the development of the productive forces coincides with the reorganization of the traditional centralized paradigm of labor organization. The increase of productivity, and the testing and implementation of new forms of non-professional and non-shop-based organization of human labor, continue to be two sides of the same coin.

There is hardly any (reliable) information or data available on the extent to which contractually *unprotected* or *unorganized* forms of employment have already spread in Germany (or other Western states). In terms of its extent and its sector- and type-specific distribution this portion of the labor market is a 'blank spot' on the research map. According to Carola Müller's (1982) data on *legal work on temporary contract*, some 43,000 temporary employees were registered in 1981. *Illegal temporary work* is estimated to be six to nine times higher in incidence. It spreads mostly through pseudo-contracts for work and service, utilizing foreign workers, especially in the metal fabricating and construction industries. She also cites figures on *negligible employment* (less than twenty hours per week precludes unemployment benefits, and less than fifteen also eliminates health and old age insurance; in both forms roughly 1.24 million persons, mostly women, were employed in 1979), *seasonal employment* (full employment of limited duration) and *capacity-oriented variable work times* [*Kapovaz*]. The last is a temporally limited labor contract without set working hours in which the worker must be ready on call; because of its overwhelming advantages for business it is obviously being practiced increasingly, especially in the retail trade. One must also mention 'contracts for production and service', 'freelance work', illicit work and so on (Müller 1982: 183–200).

As always, the explosiveness of the situation lies in the development of productive forces. But the productive forces no longer break apart the relations of ownership, as Marx had conjectured. Thinking in Marxist terms, the revolutionary potential of the productive forces threatens instead to 'backfire'. *It will break apart the relations of the labor contract and the labor market*, the forms for the offering and utilization of labor power in industrial society, and in this way will create completely new types of *disequilibria of power* between the parties in the labor market and their interest organizations. In view of the interests invested in the prevailing system of wage labor and their political and organizational power, it is not difficult to predict that this systemic transformation of industrial society will encounter considerable resistance and will possibly be extended over a long period. For that reason, it is not possible today to make prognoses as to which parts of the labor system of industrial society will be affected by this reflexive modernization and which will be spared. Nevertheless, the new system of flexible pluralized underemployment and decentralized forms of work can appeal to its higher productivity, which has so far always been decisive. The 'historical superiority' of the new labor system lies in the possibility of removing the intensifying scarcity of work from its politically threatening manifestation as *open* unemployment, redistributing it and even transforming it into a development of productive forces. From the perspective of the employees, the risks accompanying the forms of underemployment compete with the partial freedom and sovereignty gained in being able to arrange their own lives.

Many will be of the opinion that an essential contribution to the overcoming of unemployment can be achieved by transforming full-time into part-time jobs. The opposite might well occur. Increasing individualization forces people into the labor market. With the creation of possibilities for flexible, plural underemployment and temporary employment, the *remaining dams of the truncated labor market society burst*. The obstacles that still block participation – the incompatibility of membership of the labor force with family or studies – are removed, and the women and young people waiting as 'hidden reserves' can rush into the market for flexible underemployment. With the creation of suitable supplies, the demand could *increase disproportionately*; an avalanche of demand could be set free, which would make scrap paper of all the previous estimates.

In the outline sketched here, we are concerned with a theory of the *self-revolutionizing* of the system of industrial society in its most advanced phase of development. The rationalization process no longer runs strictly *within* the industrial forms and course of wage labor, but increasingly, it runs *against* them. Not only are the quantitative distributions in presupposed categories of labor forces and jobs redistributed by the unleashed dynamism of innovation; their social forms and organizational principles themselves are *recast*. In this theory of reflexive modernization, the continuity and rupture of social development are interwoven in a certain way and condition each other: the rupture from the known industrial standardized system to a future system of pluralized, flexible decentralized underemployment occurs under an unchanged logic of profit-oriented rationalization. The parallels to the distribution of mass unemployment specific to life phases suggest that just as life phases of unemployment have already become components of the standard biographies for large parts of the population, now underemployment as the synthesis of full employment and unemployment is being 'integrated' into the employment system. To this biographical 'normalization' corresponds an institutional one – with an open ending. The political reactions remain essential. *Without* an extension of the social protection system a future of poverty threatens. *With* the creation of a legally guaranteed minimum income for everyone, a bit of freedom can be wrested from the development.

Notes

1 For extensive discussion of this, see Beck et al. (1980).
2 'Continuity of life and continuity of occupation are very closely connected for us, while we are more readily willing to change our social or regional environment. One can change residences, even countries and societies with relative ease today, without becoming "uprooted", if one can preserve one's occupational opportunities and achievements during the change' (Schelsky 1942: 32).
3 This integration of non-work (short of unemployment) into the employment system can assume many forms. The best known are as follows: raising the average age of initial employment; lowering the retirement or pension age; establishing part-time work; reducing the lifetime, daily or weekly working hours; increasing the average vacation, holiday

and break periods; increasing the frequency of work interruptions for participation in additional training courses throughout the course of working life. All these indicators point to a *shrinking* of the wage labor society in this century (and, to varying degrees, in all Western industrial societies). In Germany the daily, weekly, yearly and lifelong hours worked have diminished noticeably over the past one hundred years. In 1880 the working week was 65 hours, and before the First World War it still amounted to 55 hours; in the 1920s it was officially reduced to 48 hours. After the mid fifties it remained 47 hours, with six working days and an average yearly vacation period of roughly 2 weeks. Currently, in contrast, the average vacation period is some 6 weeks and the work week is 40 hours over 5 days. Lifelong work times are diminishing in parallel, through increasingly frequent early retirement; for many employees, working life already ends at age 57 to 60. Simultaneously, young people enter the employment system later and later. While in the fifties an average male worker had 2.9 non-working hours per working hour per year, that ratio had risen to 4.1:1 by 1980. Continuing education measures and the time devoted to them have also been explosively developed in plants over the past few decades, so that it is quite possible to speak of a reintegration of training and education into the system of work and employment.

4 This discovery of the reduction of the wage labor system through changes in working hours as an organizational productive force, however, has a longer tradition. In this sense, Martin Sklar (1968) moves the first signs of an erosion of the labor society in the USA back to before World War I. Of course, statistically testable developmental trends were not interpreted in this way for a long time, since they were considered reversible. In essence, three basic facts stood out. First, the number of production workers in the factories and the level of goods production expanded overall until 1919, while the number of workers *declined* from 1919 to 1929, although productivity increased by 65 percent at the same time. Second, while work participation within the economy as a whole, measured in person-years, rose from 28.3 million in 1890 to 42.5 million in 1910, the increase from 1910 to 1920 fell to only 1 million and finally shrank to zero growth in the 1920s. Sklar's interpretation of these statistically documentable developments and relationships is that new productive forces began to display their effects at the start of the twenties. In this way it was possible to push the increase of productivity forward *independently* of an expansion of labor participation (measured in work time). To that extent, one finds here the first symptoms of an erosion of the 'old' industrial system and the origin of a 'new' labor system. Three central management innovations sponsored the development of productive forces in the twenties. First, Taylorism was broadly implemented in the factories after two decades of resistance; second, electricity with its new possibilities spread across the entire production system; third, new organizational techniques were applied in order to balance out centralization and the decentralization of geographically very remote enterprises. Already in this early phase, the productivity increases discovered and utilized were opened up by the rationalization of information, technology, and organizational management. See also Hirschhorn (1979).

PART III

Reflexive Modernization: on the Generalization of Science and Politics

PART II

Human Choice &
... Science and Ethics

In the preceding two parts, the guiding theoretical idea of a *reflexive modernization of industrial society* was worked out aloig two lines of argument: first on the basis of the logic of risk distribution (Part I), then on the basis of the individualization theorem (Part II). How are these two strands of argumentation to be related to one another and to the fundamental concept? *of risk*

(1) The process of individualization is conceptualized theoretically as the product of reflexivity, in which the process of modernization as protected by the welfare state *detraditionalizes* the ways of living built into industrial society. The 'tradition' of industrial society itself replaces pre-modernity. Just as the forms of living and working in feudal agrarian society were dissolved at the turn of the nineteenth century, the same thing is happening today to those of developed industrial society: social classes and stratification, the nuclear family with the embedded 'standard biographies' of men and women, the standardizations of labor, and so on. Thus a nineteenth century myth is demystified, one that has continued to dominate thought and action in science, politics and everyday life to this day – the legend that industrial society is a modern society in its plan of work and life.

On the contrary, it is becoming clear that the project of modernity, which first achieved recognition in the form of industrial society, was also *truncated institutionally* in that form. In essential principles – the 'normality' of making a living through the mediation of the labor market, for instance – the *perfection* of industrial society also means its *sublation*. The generalization of the labor market society protected by the welfare state dissolves the social foundations of class society as well as of the nuclear family. The shock that strikes people here is a double one. They are *set free* from the *apparently naturally ordained* ways of life and certainties of industrial society, and this end of 'post-history' coincides with the *loss* of historical consciousness in their forms of thinking, living and working. Traditional forms of coping with anxiety and insecurity in socio-moral milieus, families, marriage and male–female roles are failing. To the same degree, coping with anxiety and insecurity is demanded of the individuals themselves. Sooner or later, new demands on social institutions in education, counseling, therapy and politics will arise from the associated social and cultural shocks and upsets.

(2) The reflexivity of the modernization process can also be illustrated through the example of the relation between wealth production and risk production. Not until the modernization process detraditionalizes its foundations in industrial society does the *monism* with which thinking using the terms of industrial society subordinates risk distribution to the logic of wealth distribution become fragile. It is not dealing with risks which differentiates the risk society from the industrial society; nor is it merely the increased quality and extent of the risks produced by automation and new technologies. The central point is, rather, that the structural social conditions are radically transformed in the wake of reflexive

modernization; as the risks of modernization are scientized, their latency is eliminated. The triumphant procession of the industrial system causes the boundaries between nature and society to become blurred. Accordingly, destructions of nature can no longer be shifted off onto the 'environment' either, but as they are universalized by industry, they become social, political, economic and cultural contradictions inherent in the system. Risks of modernization that have lost their latency and become globalized as a result of the system can no longer be dealt with implicitly under the assumption of conformity to the structures of inequality based on the model of industrial society. They develop instead a dynamism of conflict which withdraws from industrial society's pattern of production and reproduction, classes, parties and subsystems.

The distinction between risk and industrial society therefore not only coincides with the distinction between the 'logics' of the production and distribution of wealth and risk production, but also results from the fact that the *primary relationship becomes reversed*. The concept of the industrial society supposes the *dominance* of the 'logic of wealth' and asserts the compatibility of risk distribution with it, while the concept of risk society asserts the *in*compatibility of distributions of wealth and risk, and the *competition* of their 'logics'.

In Part III, these arguments will be developed further in two directions. In all conceptions of industrial society, the *specializability* of scientific knowledge and political action is assumed, that is to say, it is assumed they can be delineated and monopolized. This is expressed not least in the social systems and institutions planned for these two systems – the 'system of science' and the 'political system'. In contrast to that, the following perspective will be developed here: reflexive modernization which encounters the conditions of a *highly developed* democracy and an *established* scientization, leads to characteristic *unbindings* [*Entgrenzungen*] of science and politics. Monopolies on knowledge and political action are becoming differentiated, moving away from their prescribed places and in a certain, changed manner becoming more generally available. Thus it is suddenly no longer clear whether it is *still* family policy, or *already* human genetic science which has the primary authority for deciding how people live together *outside* democratic consent and voting. This means that in addition to the features already developed, the risks emerging today are distinguished firstly (Chapter 8) from all the earlier ones by their *society-changing scope*, and secondly by their particular *scientific constitution* (Chapter 7).

7

SCIENCE BEYOND TRUTH AND ENLIGHTENMENT?

If we were previously concerned with *externally* caused dangers (from the gods or nature), the historically novel quality of today's risks derives from *internal decision*. They depend on a simultaneously *scientific and social construction. Science is one of the causes, the medium of definition and the source of solutions* to risks, and by virtue of that very fact it opens new markets of scientization for itself. In the reciprocal interplay between risks it has helped to cause and define, and the public critique of those same risks, techno-scientific development becomes *contradictory*. This perspective can be illustrated and elaborated by way of four theses.

(1) Corresponding to the distinction between modernization of tradition and reflexive modernization of industrial society, two constellations can be differentiated in the relationship of scientific practice and the public sphere: *primary* and *reflexive* scientization. At first, science is applied to a 'given' world of nature, people and society. In the reflexive phase, the sciences are confronted with their own products, defects, and secondary problems, that is to say, they encounter a *second creation in civilization*. The developmental logic of the first phase relies on a *truncated* scientization, in which the claims of scientific rationality to knowledge and enlightenment are still spared from the application of scientific skepticism to themselves. The second phase is based on a *complete* scientization, which also extends scientific skepticism to the inherent foundations and external consequences of science itself. In that way both its *claim to truth* and *its claim to enlightenment* are *demystified*. The transition from one constellation to another takes place within the *continuity* of scientization, but precisely because of that, *changed* internal and external relationships of scientific work come into being.

Primary scientization gains its dynamism from the contrast of tradition and modernity, of lay people and experts. Only under the conditions of this demarcation can the *skepticism* in the internal relations of science be generalized at the same time as the application of scientific results is advanced in an *authoritarian* fashion in external relations. This constellation of an unbroken faith in science and progress is a characteristic of modernization in industrial society into the first half of the twentieth century (although certainty diminishes). In this phase, science faces a practice and a public sphere whose resistance it can sweep aside, supported by its success, with promises of liberation from constraints not yet understood. The situation changes fundamentally to the extent that the *reflexive* constellation gains importance (and symptoms of this can be traced back to the beginning of the twentieth century, with the development of cognitive sociology, ideology critique, fallibilism in the theory of science, the critique of experts, and so on).

When they go into practice, the sciences are now being confronted with their own objectivized past and present – with themselves as product and producer of reality and of problems which they are to analyze and overcome. In that way, they are targeted not only as a source of solutions to problems, but also as a *cause of problems*. In practice and in the public sphere, the sciences increasingly face not just the balance of their defeats, but also that of their victories, that is to say, the reflection of their unkept promises. The reasons for this are varied. As success grows it seems that the risks of scientific development increase disproportionately faster; when put into practice, solutions and promises of liberation have emphatically revealed their negative sides as well, and these have in turn become the objects of scientific analyses. And, paradoxically enough, in the scientifically partitioned and professionally administered world, the future perspectives and possibility for expansion of science are also linked to the critique of science.

The *expansion* of science presupposes and conducts a *critique* of science and the existing practice of experts in a period when science concentrates on science, and therefore scientific civilization is subjecting itself to a publicly transmitted criticism that shakes its foundations and its own self-conception. It reveals a degree of insecurity with respect to its foundations and outcomes which is exceeded only by the potential for risks and developmental perspectives it uncovers. In this way, a process of demystification of the sciences is started, in the course of which the structure of science, practice and the public sphere will be subjected to a fundamental transformation.

(2) As a consequence, a momentous *demonopolization of scientific knowledge claims* comes about: science becomes more and more *necessary*, but at the same time, *less and less sufficient* for the socially binding definition of truth. This loss of function is no accident. Nor is it imposed on the sciences from outside. It arises instead as a consequence of the *triumph* and differentiation of scientific validity claims; it is a *product of the reflexivity* of techno-scientific development under the conditions of risk society. On the one hand, as it encounters itself in both its internal and its external relations, science begins to extend the methodological power of its skepticism to its own foundations and practical results. Accordingly, the claim to knowledge and enlightenment is systematically scaled back in the face of the *successfully* advanced fallibilism. The access to reality and truth which was imputed to science at first is replaced by decisions, rules and conventions which could just as well have turned out differently. Demystification spreads to the demystifier and in so doing changes the conditions of demystification.

On the other hand, as science becomes more differentiated, the flood of conditional, uncertain and detached detailed results increases and becomes impossible to survey. This *hyper-complexity* of hypothetical knowledge can no longer be mastered by mechanical testing rules. Even substitute criteria such as reputation, type and place of publication, institutional basis also fail. Accordingly, as scientization proceeds, the systematically produced uncertainty spreads to external relations, and conversely turns the target groups and appliers of scientific results in politics, business and the public into *active coproducers* in the social process of knowledge definition. The 'objects' of scientization also become *subjects* of it, in the sense that they can and must actively manipulate the heterogeneous supply of scientific interpretations. And this not only means choices between contradictory highly specialized validity claims; the latter can also be played off against one another and must in any case be recombined into an image suitable for action. For the target groups and appliers of science, reflexive scientization thus opens up *new possibilities of influence and development* in the processes of production *and* application of scientific results. This is a development of great ambivalence. It contains the opportunity to emancipate social practice *from* science *through* science; on the other hand it *immunizes* socially prevailing ideologies and interested standpoints against enlightened scientific claims, and throws the door open to a feudalization of scientific knowledge practice through economic and political interests and 'new dogmas'.

(3) The new *taboos of unchangeability* which arise contrary to the triumph of scientific knowledge claims are becoming the touchstone for the independence of scientific research. The further scientization proceeds and the more clearly risk situations and conflicts enter public conscience, the greater becomes the pressure to act, and the more techno-scientific society threatens to metamorphose into a scientifically produced 'taboo society'. More and more sectors, agencies and conditions, which are all changeable in principle, are being systematically excluded from this expectation of change through the construction of 'objective constraints', 'system constraints' and 'auto-dynamisms'. The sciences can no longer remain in their traditional Enlightenment position of taboo *breakers*; they must also adopt the contrary role of taboo *constructors*. Accordingly, the social function of the sciences wavers between opening and closing opportunities for action, and these contradictory outside expectations stir up conflicts and divisions within the profession.

(4) Even the *foundations of scientific rationality* are not spared from the generalized demands for change. What was made by people can also be changed by people. It is precisely reflexive scientization which makes the self-imposed taboos of scientific rationality visible and questionable. The suspicion is that 'objective constraints', 'latent side effects', which stand for the 'auto-dynamism' of the techno-scientific development, are themselves *manufactured* and thus are in principle *solvable*. The project of modernity, Enlightenment, is unfinished. Its actual rigidification in the industrial understanding of science and technology can be broken open by

a revival of reason and converted into a dynamic theory of scientific rationality which digests historical experience and in that way develops itself further in a way that is capable of learning.

Of decisive importance for the issue of whether science will contribute in that way to the self-limitation and self-control of its practical risks is not whether it reaches beyond its own range of influence and makes a bid for a (political) voice in the application of its results. The essential thing is, rather, *what type of science is conducted with regard to the measurability of its allegedly immeasurable side effects.* Of decisive importance in this manner is whether the *overspecialization* that produces side effects on its own and thus seems to confirm their inevitability will endure, or whether the power for *specialization in the context* will be discovered anew and developed; whether the ability to learn to deal with practical consequences will be won back, or whether by ignoring the practical consequences *irreversible situations* will be created that are based on the *imputation of infallibility* and hence make learning from practical mistakes impossible from the start. It is important as to what extent in dealing with risks of modernization the treatment of the *symptoms* can be replaced by genuine removal of the *causes*, and to what extent *practical taboos* on risks can be scientifically depicted or broken up through the variables and causes considered. That is to say, what matters is whether risks and threats are methodically and objectively interpreted and scientifically displayed, or whether they are downplayed and concealed.

Primary and Reflexive Scientization

The starting phase of *primary* scientization, in which lay people were driven out of their 'hunting grounds' and pushed back into 'reservations' like Indians, concluded long ago, and with it the whole myth of superiority and the gradient of power that characterized the relation of science, practice and the public sphere was created. The developmental logic of that period (which is, after all, a central theme of classical sociology) can be observed today only in marginal areas of modernization, if at all.[1] Its place has been taken almost everywhere by the conflicts and relationships of reflexive scientization. Scientific civilization has entered a stage in which it no longer merely scientizes nature, people and society, but increasingly itself, its own products, effects and mistakes. Science is no longer concerned with 'liberation' from *pre-existing* dependencies, but with the definition and distribution of errors and risks which are *produced by itself.*

Different conditions and processes, different media and agents are characteristic of reflexive modernization than were typical of error management processes in the phase of primary scientization. In the first wave, scientists of various disciplines could rely on the superiority – sometimes real, sometimes only apparent – of scientific rationality and methods of thought with respect to traditional knowledge bases, folk knowledge and lay practices. This superiority can hardly be attributed to a lesser degree of error in scientific work, but rather to the *way the treatment of mistakes and risks was socially organized in that phase.*

First of all, the scientific penetration of a world still untouched by science permits a clear demarcation between solutions of problems and causes of problems, where this boundary runs between the sciences on one side and their (actual and potential) 'objects' on the other. The application of science takes place with the attitude of a clear *objectification* of problems and errors. Wild, uncomprehended nature and the unbroken compulsions of tradition are 'to blame' for the sicknesses, crises and catastrophes from which people suffer.

This projection of the sources of problems and errors into the as yet unexplored no man's land of the sciences is obviously connected to the fact that the sciences did not as yet overlap significantly in the fields where they were applied. It is also connected with the fact the sciences' own theoretical and practical sources of error were organized in a systematic way. With good reasons one can proceed from the perspective that the history of sciences was always less a history of the acquisition of knowledge than one of mistakes and practical lapses. That is why scientific 'knowledge', 'explanations', and practical 'suggested solutions' contradict each other diametrically over time, at different places, in different schools of thought, cultures and so on. This need not imply any loss in the credibility of scientific rationality claims so long as the sciences can succeed in handling the mistakes, errors and criticism of their practical consequences essentially *within* science. In that way they maintain their monopoly claim to rationality against the non-specialized public sphere on the one hand, and on the other they prepare a forum for critical discussions within the discipline.

In this social structure it is even possible, conversely, to trace erupting problems, technical shortcomings and risks of scientization to previous insufficiencies in the *degree of development* of the scientific support system, which can then be converted into *new* plans and surges of technological development and thus ultimately into a consolidation of the scientific monopoly on rationality. This *transformation of mistakes and risks into opportunities for expansion and perspectives for the development of science and technology* generally tended in the first phase to immunize scientific development against the critique of modernity and civilization, and made it *ultra-stable,* so to speak. Actually, however, this stability is based on a truncation of methodological skepticism; inside the sciences (at least according to the pretension) the rules of *criticism* were generalized, while at the same time the scientific results were enforced towards the outside in an *authoritarian* manner.

Obviously, these conditions are also undermined to the extent that science directs its attention at science, in an interdisciplinary manner. Conversely, it is precisely the projection of mistakes and causes of problems that now must bring *science and technology* into view *as possible causes of problems and errors.* The risks that move to the center of attention in reflexive modernization destroy the pattern of intra-disciplinary transformation of mistakes into development opportunities. At the same time, they dissolve the model of primary scientization, broadly established in the late nineteenth century, with its harmonious power relationships between professions, business, politics and the public sphere.

The scientific discovery and research on modernization risks means that techno-scientific development – in an *inter*disciplinary mediation – becomes a problem for itself; here scientization is scientized *as a problem.* By virtue of that, all the problems and difficulties the sciences and professions have in dealings with each other will immediately burst forth. For here science is encountering science, and hence all the skepticism and contempt one science is capable of showing towards another. The often equally aggressive and impotent resistance of lay people is replaced by the opportunities sciences have for resistance: counter-criticism, methodological critique, as well as a clubbish 'obstructive behavior' in all the fields of professional competition for resources. In this sense, the consequences and risks of modernization can only be brought into view by passing through the *critique* (and counter-critique) of the scientific service systems from different sciences. The opportunities for reflexive scientization consequently seem to grow in direct proportion to the risks and the list of shortcomings of modernization, and in inverse proportion to the unbroken faith in progress of techno-scientific civilization. The gate through which risks can be scientifically opened up and treated is called the critique of science, critique of progress, critique of experts and critique of technology. Risks destroy the opportunities to work out mistakes internally, and force *new forms for the division of labor* within the relationship of science, scientific practice and the public sphere.

In this way, the revelation of the risks of previous modernization necessarily stirs up the hornets' nest of competitive relations between the scientific professions, and arouses all the impulses to resistance that a scientific profession will have built up over the generations with all of its powers (including its scientific ones) against 'expansionist encroachment' on its own 'pet problems' and on its carefully installed 'pipeline of research funding'. The social recognition and treatment of risks will run aground on the competitive problems that erupt here and the unresolvable conflicts between schools of thought, so long as the *public* sensibility with regard to certain problematic aspects of modernization does not grow, turn into criticism and perhaps even social movements, articulate itself and discharge itself as protests against science and technology. Modernization risks, then, can only be 'forced on' the sciences, 'dictated to them', from the *outside*, by way of public recognition. They are based *not* on *intra*scientific but on *overall social definitions and relationships.* Even within the sciences they can only develop their power through the motives in the background: the social agenda.

This in turn presumes a so far unknown power of the critique of science and culture, which is based at least in part on a *reception of alternative expertise*. With reflexive modernization, public risk consciousness and risk conflicts will lead to *forms of scientization of the protest against science*. The critique of progress and civilization that we are experiencing distinguishes itself from that of the past two hundred years. The themes of the critique are generalized; the critique is supported scientifically, at least in part, and now confronts science with the full definition-making power of science. In this way, a movement is set in motion, in the course of which the scientists will be forced more and more emphatically to display before the whole public their awkwardness, all their limitations and their 'birth defects', all of which have long been well known internally. Forms of 'alternative' and 'advocacy science' come into being that relate the entire 'hocus-pocus of science' to different principles and different interests – and therefore reach exactly the opposite conclusions. In short, *in the course of the scientization of protest against science, science forces itself to run its own gauntlet.* New public-oriented scientific experts emerge, the dubious aspects of the foundations of scientific argumentation are exposed with counter-scientific thoroughness, and many sciences are subjected through their applied practices to a 'politicization test' of a previously unknown extent.

In this way, science not only experiences a rapid diminution of its public credibility, but also opens *new fields of activity and application* for itself. For example, the natural and engineering sciences have taken up many of the public criticisms of themselves and been able to transform them into opportunities for expansion. These criticisms relate to the conceptual, instrumental and technical differentiation of 'still' or 'no longer' tolerable risks, health threats, labor stresses and so on. Here the self-contradiction that scientific development has got into in its reflexive phase becomes tangible: *the publicly transmitted criticism of the previous development becomes the motor of expansion.*

This is the developmental logic in which modernization risks are constituted through a tense interplay of science, scientific practice and the public sphere, and then played back into science, precipitating 'identity crises', new forms of work and organization, new bases for theories, new methodological developments and so on. The assimilation of errors and risk is thus connected to the circulation of overall societal discussions, so to speak, and occurs, among other things, in confrontation and amalgamation with social movements critical of science and modernization. Nevertheless, one should not be deceived here; through all the contradictions, a path of scientific *expansion* has been taken. Public discussion of modernization risks *is* the route for the transformation of mistakes into opportunities for expansion under the conditions of reflexive scientization.

This interpenetration of critique of civilization, interdisciplinary antagonisms and publicly effective protest movements can be clarified in *exerpt*

a particularly illustrative manner with the case of the <u>environmental</u> <u>movement</u>.[2] Conservation movements have existed since the beginning of industrialization. Yet the selective critique expressed by conservation organizations (which in addition involved neither large costs for nor a fundamental critique of industrialization) was never able to shake off the nimbus of hostility to progress and backwardness that surrounded it. This only changed when the social evidence of threats to nature through industrialization grew and at the same time scientific interpretations completely detached from the old ideas of conservation were offered and accepted. These explained the growing public discontent with the obviously destructive consequences of industrialization, supported it, freed it from concrete individual cases and occasions, generalized it and joined in a broad protest against industrialization and technification.

In the United States this took place essentially through critical *biological* research that concentrated on the destructive consequences of industrialization for natural biosystems, and sounded the 'alarm' in the truest sense of that word. That is to say, using scientific arguments and language understandable to the general public, researchers investigated the existing and impending consequences of industrialization for life on this earth and concentrated these into images of a looming destruction.[3] As these and other arguments were taken up by protest movements, the process began that was referred to above as the scientization of protest against certain forms of scientization.

The goals and themes of the environmental movement were gradually detached from concrete occasions and individual demands that are ultimately easy to meet (closing off a wooded area, protecting a certain species and the like) and brought into a general protest against the conditions and prerequisites of industrialization itself. The occasions for protest are no longer exclusively individual cases, visible threats that can be traced back to attributable offenses (oil spills, pollution of rivers by industrial waste and so forth). More and more, the center comes to be occupied by threats that are often neither visible nor tangible to the lay public, threats that sometimes will not even take their toll in the lifespan of the affected individuals, but only in the second generation of their offspring. They are in any case threats *that require the sensory organs of science – theories, experiments, measuring instruments – in order to become visible and interpretable as threats at all.*

Paradoxical as it might sound, in the scientized ecology movement the occasions for and the themes of protest have largely become independent of the agents of the protest, the affected lay people. In the limiting case the threats have even detached themselves from any possibility of perception, and are not only transmitted by science, but in the strict sense are *scientifically constituted.* This does not diminish the importance of 'lay protest', but it does show its dependence on 'counter-scientific' mediations. The diagnosis of the threats and the struggle against their causes is often possible only with the aid of the entire arsenal of scientific measurement, experimental and argumentative instruments. It requires considerable special knowledge, the readiness and ability to engage in unconventional analysis, as well as technical facilities and measurement instruments that are generally quite expensive.

This example is representative of many others. One can therefore state that science is involved in the origin and deepening of risk situations in civilization and a corresponding threefold crisis consciousness. Not only does the industrial utilization of scientific results create problems; science also provides the means – the categories and the cognitive equipment – to recognize and present the problems *as* problems at all, or just not to do so. Finally, science also provides the prerequisites for 'overcoming' the threats for which it is responsible itself. Thus – referring once again to the example of environmental problems – little remains today among the professionalized segments of the ecology movement of that abstinence from acting on nature that was previously propagated by the movement.

> Quite to the contrary, the relevant demands are founded on the newest and best results that physics, chemistry, biology, systems research and computer simulations have to offer. The concepts with which ecological systems research operates are highly modern and have the aim of comprehending nature not only as individual parts (and thereby running the risk of causing second- to nth-order damage and consequences due to the systematically produced ignorance) but as a totality . . . those eating muesli and carrying natural fiber bags are in reality the *precursors of a new modernity*, whose characteristic will be a much more perfected and efficient but above all more comprehensive scientization and technification of nature. (Weingart, 1984: 74)

It is precisely the awareness of its dependence on the object of its protests that produces so much bitterness and irrationality in the anti-science attitude.

The Demonopolization of Science

It is not their failure but their *success* that has *dethroned* the sciences. One could even say, the more successfully the sciences have operated in this century, that much faster and more thoroughly have their original validity claims been relativized. In this sense scientific development in the second half of this century is passing through a *rupture of its continuity*, and not only in its external relations (as has already been shown), but also in its internal relations (as will be shown here): in its view of itself, socially and theoretically, in its methodological foundations and its relation to application.

The model of primary scientization is based on the 'naiveté' that the methodical skepticism of the sciences can be institutionalized on the one hand, and yet be limited to the *objects* of science on the other. The foundations of scientific knowledge remain as exempt from skepticism as do all issues of the practical application of scientific results. What is subject to challenging questions and internal skepticism is *dogmatized* externally. Behind this is concealed not only the difference between 'action-free' research practice and the constraints to action of practice and politics, where as a condition of the system skepticism must be cut short and replaced by clear plans of action. This bisection of scientific rationality along the boundaries between the internal and the external corresponds in particular to the *market and professionalization interests* of scientific expert groups. The consumers of scientific services and knowledge pay not for admitted or uncovered errors, falsified hypotheses, or self-doubt, no matter how cleverly advanced, but for 'knowledge'. Only those who succeed in asserting knowledge claims in the market against competing professional and lay groups can ever earn the material and institutional prerequisites to indulge in the 'luxury of skepticism' (known as basic research) internally. What must be generalized from the point of view of rationality, must be turned into the opposite in the interest of prevailing in the market.

Dogmatizing and the art of doubting complement *and* contradict one another in the process of 'successful' scientization. While internal success is based on the *demolition* of the 'demigods in lab coats', external success, on the contrary, relies on the deliberate *construction*, adulation and dogged defense of the 'infallibility claims' of those same demigods against all the 'suspicions of irrational criticism'. Results that are always 'errors subject to recall' according to the conditions under which they were produced, must simultaneously be styled into 'knowledge' with eternal validity, which it would be the height of ignorance to ignore in practice.

In this sense, *modernity and counter-modernity have always been fused in a contradictory way* in the model of primary scientization. The indivisible principles of criticism were divided; their range of validity was truncated. The absoluteness of the knowledge claims that were advanced in external relations contrasts oddly with the generalization of doubt which is elevated to the norm internally. Everything that comes into contact with science is planned to be *changeable, except scientific rationality itself*. These limitations of the illimitable are no accident, rather they are *functionally necessary*. Only they provide science with its cognitive and social superiority *vis-à-vis* prevailing traditions and lay practices. Only in this way can critical knowledge claims and *efforts at professionalization* be (contradictorily) bound together.

This assessment has two consequences. Firstly, the process of scientization from the nineteenth century until now must *also* be understood as a *dogmatization*, as practice for the unquestioned validity claimed by the 'dogmas' of science. Secondly, the 'dogmas' of primary scientization are *unstable* in quite a different way than those dogmas (of religion or tradition) against which science prevailed: *they carry within themselves the standards for their own critique and abolition*. In this sense, scientific development undermines its own delimitations and foundations through the continuity of its successes. In the course of the *triumph* and generalization of the norms of scientific argument, a completely different situation arises. Science becomes *indispensable* and at the same time *devoid* of its original validity claims. In equal measure 'practical problems' are incited. Science's methodically pursued loss of security, in both its internal and external relations, brings about a *decline of its power*. The results are conflictual *equalization tendencies* in the gradient of rationality between experts and lay people (one good indicator of which among many, for instance, is the increase in 'medical malpractice' lawsuits). Furthermore, the usual concepts that reflect the power gradient *fail*: modernity and tradition, experts and lay people, or the production and the application of results. *This unbinding [Entgrenzung] of skepticism* under the conditions of reflexive scientization can be traced along the lines of (a) the *theory of science* and (b) the *practice of research*.

Fallibilism in the Theory of Science

This transition from primary to reflexive scientization is for its own part conducted *scientifically and institutionally*. The *agents of rupture* are the disciplines of the critical application of science to itself – the theory of science and the history of science, cognitive sociology and the sociology of science, psychology and empirical ethnology of science, and so on – which have been gnawing at the foundations of the self-dogmatization of scientific rationality with varying success since the beginning of the century.

On the one hand these disciplines are conducted professionally and institutionally, and specifically under the claims of the *still* valid model of primary scientization; on the other hand, they cancel out the conditions of their application, and in this sense they are already forebears of the self-critical variant of reflexive scientization. In this sense, 'alternative science' is no invention of the sixties or seventies. It has belonged rather to the program of science from the beginning. One of the first examples of 'alternative expertise' in this sense, with long-term effects up to the present, was the Marxian critique of 'bourgeois science'. It already contained the entire contradictory tension between faith in science in one's own case and the generalized ideology critique of existing science, which was subsequently presented in ever new variations – in the cognitive sociology of Mannheim, in the falsificationism of Popper or in Kuhn's historical critique of normativism in the theory of science. The systematic 'nest-fouling' that occurs here step by step is the consistent application to itself of fallibilism, which was at first only partially institutionalized. And this process of self-criticism did not proceed steadily, but in the consistent dissolution of repeated attempts to salvage the 'core rationality' of the scientific enterprise. This ultimately blasphemous process of 'conjectures and refutations' could be traced in many examples. Nowhere, however, is it practiced in such an exemplary fashion as in the course of the discussion of the theory of science in this century.

Ultimately, Popper had already used the same 'dagger' against foundation thought that is used against all his own 'attempts to give foundations' to the principle of falsification that he constructed to guard against charlatanism. All the 'remnants of foundations' in the falsification principle are gradually revealed and cleared away by consistent application to themselves, until the columns on which the falsification principle was to rest are destroyed. Feyerabend's famous phrase, 'anything goes', then only serves to summarize this situation worked out with so much scientific competence and scrupulous exactitude.[4]

Fallibilism in Research Practice

But one can say, and people do say in the practice of science: *so what*? What do we care about the self-evisceration of a theory of science that was nothing more than the 'philosophical fig-leaf' for a research practice that it did not care about? But after advocating the falsification principle, there must be some consequences in subsequently announcing its always existent superfluity. Nothing has happened. Nothing at all. In its progress, science has just *lost the truth* – as a schoolboy loses his milk money. In the past three decades science has changed from an activity *in the service* of truth to an activity *without* truth, but which has to make the most it can socially of the benefits of truth. Scientific practice has definitely followed scientific theory into conjecture, self-doubt and *convention*. Internally, science has retreated to making decisions. Externally the risks proliferate. Neither internally nor externally does science still enjoy the blessing of reason. It has become *in*dispensable to *and in*capable of truth.

This is neither coincidental nor accidental. Truth has taken the usual route of modernity. The scientific religion of controlling and proclaiming truth has been *secularized* in the course of reflexive scientization. The truth claim of science has not withstood penetrating self-examination, neither empirically, nor in the theory of science. On the one hand, science's claim to be able to explain things has retreated to the *hypothesis*, the conjecture subject to recall. *On the other hand* reality has sublimated into *data* that are *produced*. Thus 'facts' – the former centerpieces of reality – are nothing but answers to questions that could just as well have been asked differently, products of rules for gathering and omitting. A different computer, a different specialist, a different institute – a different 'reality'. It would be a miracle if it did not already exist, a miracle and not science. To provide another proof of the irrationality of (natural) scientific research practice would amount to mutilation of a corpse. Approaching a scientist with the question of truth is almost as embarrassing as asking a priest about God. Uttering the word 'truth' in scientific circles (like 'reality', by the way) signals ignorance, mediocrity, unreflected use of ambiguous, emotion-laden words from everyday language.

Certainly, the loss has an attractive side. Truth was a supernatural effort, an elevation to the near-divine. It was a close relative of dogma. If once one possessed it, had pronounced it, it was difficult to change and yet it changed continually. Science is becoming human. It is packed with errors and mistakes. Science can be conducted even without truth, perhaps even better, more honestly, with greater versatility, more audaciously and bravely. The opposite attracts, it always has opportunities as well. The scene is becoming colorful. If three scientists get together, fifteen opinions clash.

The Feudalization of Cognitive Practice

The recourse to scientific results for the socially binding definition of truth is becoming *more and more necessary*, but at the same time *less and less sufficient*. This disparity between necessary and sufficient conditions and the resulting gray area reflect science's loss of functionality in its most central occupation, the representative determination of knowledge. The target groups and users of scientific results – in politics and business, mass media and everyday life – become more dependent on scientific arguments *in general*, but at the same time more independent of *individual* findings and the judgment of science regarding the truth and reality of its statements.

The transfer of knowledge claims to external agencies is *based* on the *differentiation* of the sciences – that is the apparent paradox. It lies first of all in the hyper-complexity and variety of findings, which, even if they do not openly contradict each other, do not complement each other either, but generally assert different, even incomparable things, and thus virtually *force* the practitioner to make his own cognitive decisions. In addition to that is their self-proclaimed semi-arbitrariness, which is usually denied in concrete situations, but appears nevertheless in the discord of the many findings and in the methodological recourse to conventions and decisions. In return, the 'yes, but', the 'on the one hand, on the other hand' in which hypothetical science always operates, offers options of choice in the definition of knowledge.

The flood of findings, their contradictoriness and overspecialization, turn reception into participation, into an autonomous process of knowledge formation *with and against* science. Now one can say, that was always the case. The autonomy of politics or business with respect to science is as old as that relationship itself. In the process, however, two of the peculiarities mentioned here disappear under the table. This type of autonomy is *produced* by science. It arises in the *surplus* of science, which has simultaneously scaled back its own demands into the hypothetical, and offers an image of the self-relativizing pluralism of interpretations.

The consequences have a strong impact on the conditions of knowledge production. Science, having lost reality, faces the threat that others will dictate to it what truth is *supposed* to be. This is not only the case with the flourishing 'court science', by way of direct influence. The approximate nature, the indecisiveness, the accessibility to decision-making of the results make this possible. Selection criteria that escape scientific scrutiny achieve a new and perhaps decisive meaning in the hyper-complexity that must be mastered in any case. These include the compatibilities of basic political views, the interests of sponsors, the anticipation of political implications; in short, *political acceptance.*

In view of the overcomplexity it produces itself, science is threatened with an *implicit feudalization of its cognitive practice* on its way into methodological conventionalization. Correspondingly, a *new particularism* arises in external relations: groups of scientists, large and small, who isolate themselves from each other and group around implicit priorities of application. The central point is that this occurs not only subsequently, in practical contacts, but already in the research laboratory, in the offices of scientists, in the inner sanctum of their production of scientific results itself. The more unforeseeable the risks of techno-scientific production become and the more emphatically they determine public consciousness, the more intense becomes the pressure for action on political and economic agencies, and the more important it becomes for social agents to ensure access to 'science as a definition-making power', whether for minimization, distraction, redefinition, or for the dramatization or blocking of 'external interference in definition-making' through critique of methodology.

But the process also has other sides. A bit of enlightenment can also be brought into reality with it. People are freed from the 'patronizing' cognitive dictates of the experts (Illich 1979). More and more people are able to play the role of assessors of science. There is something irritating for scientists about the functional transformation of science which occurs in this generalization of scientific argumentation figures, as Wolfgang Bonß and Heinz Hartmann (1985) show:

> In this generalization, scientific arguments, recognized since the Enlightenment as the only authoritative agency of legitimation, seem to lose their aureole as rationally unassailable authorities, and to become socially available. From sociological perspectives this trend presents itself as the *result* of scientization processes. The fact that scientific statements are no longer sacrosanct, but can be disputed in everyday ordinary life, means nothing other than that systematic skepticism as the structure-bearing principle of scientific discourse is no longer a privilege of the latter. The difference between 'unenlightened mob' and 'enlightened citizens' or, in more modern terms, between lay people and experts, shrivels and transforms itself into competition between different experts. In practically all social subsystems the internalization of norms and values is replaced by reflection in the light of competing components of systematic knowledge. (16; see also Weingart 1983: 328)

In order to survive this interprofessional competition among experts, it is no longer sufficient to present 'tidy' tests of significance. At times one must appear personally *and* be convincing. Under conditions of reflexive scientization, *the production (or mobilization) of belief* becomes a central source for the social enforcement of validity claims.[5]

Where science used to be convincing *qua* science, today, in view of the contradictory babble of scientific tongues, the *faith* in science or the *faith* in alternative science (or *this* method, *this* approach, *this* orientation) becomes decisive. Perhaps it is only the 'extra' of presentation, personal persuasive power, contacts, access to the media or the like which will provide the 'individual finding' with the social attribute of 'knowledge'. Where faith (helps) decide on scientific arguments, it can soon resume dominance – of course, no longer *as* faith in its external form, but *as* science. In the emerging interregnum, where science is necessary for the production of knowledge, but no longer sufficient, the broadest variety of doctrines will accordingly re-establish themselves. That makes many things possible: fatalism, astrology, occultism, ego worship and ego sacrifice, paired and mixed with scientific detailed findings, radical criticism of science and faith in science. These *new alchemists* are oddly immune to the critique of science, since they found their 'truth' and their supporters not before science, but in interaction with it.

This immunity of science does not apply only to these extreme cases. Quite generally, ideologies and prejudices, now scientifically armed, are able to defend themselves anew against science. They take recourse to science itself in order to reject its claims. One just has to read *more*, including the alternative investigations. The objections are consumed *before* the results, with advance notice as it were. Keeping a couple of basic (methodological) objections on hand for all cases is enough to make this or that obstinate scientific news collapse in itself. Until the sixties, science could count on an uncontroversial public that believed in science, but today its efforts and progress are followed with mistrust. People suspect the unsaid, add in the side effects and expect the worst.

Techno-scientific civilization is swarming everywhere with *taboos of unalterability*. In this jungle, where the existence of things that result from actions is not permitted to be acknowledged, the scientist in search of a 'neutral' analysis of problems gets trapped in a new kind of *predicament*. Every analysis faces the decision of whether to research *around* the social tabooizations of action variables or to research *into* them. These decision-making possibilities affect the design of the investigation itself (even where they are dictated by the employer); they are therefore located in the most central realm of scientific practice in the type of inquiry, the selection of variables, the direction and scope of pursuing conjectures, the conceptual design, the methods of calculating 'risks', etc.

In contrast to the consequences of primary scientization, the consequences of these research decisions are inherently rather *estimable*. If the latter were *outside* industry and production in the (powerless) *latent* areas of society – the health of people and nature – determinations of risk today have a direct effect on the *central power zones* – business, politics, institutional control agencies. These certainly possess the 'institutionalized attentiveness' and the 'collective clout' to make audible any cost-intensive secondary effects on themselves. The 'invisibility' of risks is thus severely limited according to social situation. The same holds true for the 'secondary character' of the effects. The observation of development falls under the official competence of risk research (or an auxiliary division). The guidelines are known, as is the legal basis. Everyone knows roughly what concentrations of toxins and what exceeding of the allowable limits can be connected with what decisive (legal and economic) consequences.

But that means that risks are scientized; the assessability of secondary effects is transformed from an *external* to an *internal* problem, from a problem of *application* to one of *knowledge*. The external is gone. The consequences are internal. Contexts of origin and application push together. Thus the autonomy of research becomes *at the same time* a problem of knowledge *and* a problem of application. The possible violation of taboos becomes an inherent condition of good or bad research. This might still remain hidden in the gray zone of research decisions that could be made this way or that. From its institutional, scientific-theoretical and moral constitution, research must put itself in a position to accept and thoroughly investigate the political implications it has, if it is not willing to jump through all the hoops at the first crack of a whip.

At the same time it becomes recognizable here that the opportunities of scientific cognitive practice for influence and direction lie in its *scope for selection*, which has so far been excluded by the theory of science for reasons of validity and thus been subjected to no evaluation. According to the prevailing theories of hypothesis formation, the chain of causality can be projected in quite different directions, *without* colliding with any validity standards, so long as one's own conjectures are verified. In developed civilization, scientific cognitive practice becomes an *implicit, objectivized manipulation of latently political variables, hidden behind the pretense of elective decisions not subject to justification*. This does not mean that objectivization is excluded. Nor does it mean that the presumed causal relationships can be produced politically. Of course, causal and action analysis are intermeshed – quite independently of scientists' view of themselves. *The doubled, constructed reality of risk politicizes the objective analysis of its causes.* When science conducts research under these conditions in conformity with taboos from a misunderstood 'neutrality', then it contributes to the fact that the law of the unseen side effect still dominates the development of civilization.

On the Assessability of 'Side Effects'

We can no longer tolerate the fairy tale of the unforeseeability of consequences. The stork does not bring consequences – they are *made*. With and despite all the incalculability, they are made *in the sciences themselves*. This becomes visible when there is a systematic differentiation between the *calculability* of the actual external consequences and their inherent *assessability*.

According to the prevailing understanding, the incalculability of the secondary consequences of scientific work *necessarily* intensifies with the increasing differentiation of the sciences. Scientists actually are separated from the utilization of their work; they have no possibilities of influence at their disposal in that sphere; others are responsible. Consequently, scientists cannot be called to account for the actual consequences of the results they worked out from the analytic point of view. Even though people are beginning to speak a common language in many areas, the distances between theory and practice do not diminish but increase because of that fact, as do the possibilities for the application side to use the results according to their own interests.

This assessment rests on the concept of 'calculability' – a key concept in the classical theory of scientization, whose degree of significance and conditions of application are just beginning to become dubious today. The possibilities of estimating the secondary conditions only come into view when one sees that with *reflexive modernization the concept of calculable–incalculable itself changes*. Calculability no longer means only instrumentally rational controllability; nor does incalculability still mean the impossibility of an instrumental mastery. If that were so, then the 'incalculability of secondary effects' would still be preserved in today's organization of science; it would even grow, because the ends rationality is contextualized and the uncertainty grows.

If on the other hand one understands calculability in the sense of *estimability*, then this fits exactly the state of affairs that comes into being under conditions of reflexive modernization. In point of fact, the *actual* consequences remain *more* incalculable *than ever*. At the same time, however, secondary effects are robbed of their latency and thus become assessable in the following threefold sense. Knowledge of them is (in principle) available; nor is it possible any longer to make the classical excuses of uncontrollability, and to that extent one is under pressure to make a move because of the knowledge of *possible* effects. Decreasing 'calculability' is thus accompanied by increasing 'estimability', and what is more, the one is a *condition* of the other. The knowledge of secondary effects, by now a sufficiently differentiated branch of knowledge, is always (potentially) present. The broadest variety of consequences and recursive causal patterns must thus be weighed in their meaning for themselves and others. In this way, the *actual* consequences ultimately become more and more incalculable, *because* the possible effects become more and more estimable and their assessment takes place more and more in the research process and in interaction with its inherent taboo zones, and determine those zones in the course of results. But that also means that within research itself, implicit dealings with *expected* consequences gain a greater and greater importance. On the level of expectations (and expectations of expectations) secondary effects are anticipated, which in that way impact on the research process directly, although at the same time the ultimate consequences remain invisible. This is the *extremely effective lobotomy of the scientists.* The emphasis with which they insist on the absolute incalculability of the actual long-term consequences grows by the same extent as the expected consequences actually determine their work, the starting and stopping points of their questioning and explaining.

This only apparently contradictory double thesis of (a) the growing incalculability with (b) the simultaneous increasing estimability of what were 'secondary effects' will now be discussed. Only by opening up the entire argument can we see how far and in what sense this fatalism in techno-scientific civilization can be overcome.

The Autonomization of Application

In the phase of reflexive scientization the *places and participants* of knowledge production change. As was shown above, the target groups of the sciences in administration, politics, business and the public sphere become *coproducers* of socially valid 'knowledge' – in a conflictual collaboration and opposition. But with that, the *relations of the transfer* of scientific results to practice and politics become agitated. The 'fellow shareholders' of the liquidated 'knowledge capital' of science intervene in a new and self-assured way in the transfer of science into practice.

In the model of primary scientization the relationship of science and politics is conceived *deductively*. Results worked out scientifically – according to the model – are *enforced* in an *authoritarian* way from top to bottom. Wherever this encounters resistance, irrationalities must still hold sway, according to the self-understanding of the scientists, and these can be overcome by 'raising the level of rationality' among practitioners. This authoritarian model of deductivist application can no longer be maintained under the conditions of the reflexive self-doubt of the sciences. Application is absorbed more and more in processes of external knowledge production, that is, in sorting and selection, in casting doubt on and reorganizing interpretations offered and in deliberately enriching them with 'practical knowledge' (chances of adoption, informal power relationships and contacts and the like). Thus arises the *end of the scientifically directed, instrumentally rational control of practice.* Science and practice once again split up under the conditions of dependency on science. The application side begins to make itself more and more independent *of* science *through* science. In a certain way, one can say that we are experiencing at the moment how the level of rationality *inverts.*[6]

The *new autonomy* here of the target groups is based not on ignorance but on knowledge, not on underdevelopment but on differentiation and the hyper-complexity of possible scientific interpretations. It is – and this only seems to be paradoxical – *produced by science.* The *success* of the sciences makes demand more independent of supply. An important indicator for this trend to autonomization is first of all the specific *pluralization of the knowledge sources* and the *critical-methodological reflection* on it. As they become more differentiated (and not necessarily as a result of their deterioration or moral fleetness of foot), the sciences, including the natural sciences, are transformed into *self-service shops* for financially well endowed customers in need of arguments. The hypertrophic complexity of individual scientific findings puts opportunities in the hands of customers for selection within *and between* expert groups. It is not uncommon for political programs to be decided in advance simply by the choice of what expert representatives are included in the circle of advisers. Not only are practitioners and politicians able to choose between expert groups, but those groups can also be *played off against each other* within and between disciplines, and in this way the autonomy of the customers is increased. Precisely as a result of successful learning in contacts with the sciences, this will be happening in an increasingly less amateurish way. Instead, from the experts and the fundamental controversies they have fought out (or not fought out) one can learn how unwelcome results can be blocked *professionally* (by methodological criticism, for instance). Since the starting points for this are likely to increase as a result of the self-doubt of the sciences, the opportunities for defensive criticism presented to the practical side through reflexive scientization will grow.

Of course, the sciences in that case are less and less capable of satisfying the need *for security* among the customers under pressure to make decisions. With the generalization of fallibilism, the scientific side shifts its self-doubt over to the practical side and in addition forces upon it the alternative role of the *reduction of uncertainty necessary* for action. All of this – to stress it once again – occurs not as an expression of impotence or underdevelopment in the sciences but, quite to the contrary, as a product of their highly advanced differentiation, hyper-complexity, self-criticism and reflection.

On the Manufacture of Objective Constraints

Those who stop at this point in the argumentation, conceal the *participation* of science, its structural division of labor and its theoretical programmatics in the unpredictability of the practical consequences of science. Specifically, they would be proceeding from the assumption that the route of the sciences into the *generalization of uncertainty is unrevisable.* At the same time, science is considered to be *constant* in its historical prerequisites and forms. Science, however, has changed the world as hardly any other power has. Why should the changing of the world not also force science into changing itself? Where everything becomes changeable, science, which brought change into the world, can no longer use the immutability of its foundations and work forms as an excuse. The opportunities to change itself grow along with the autonomy of the practical side. The separation permits and forces a rethinking and redefinition of scientific knowledge in the canon of interpretation and application claims coming from the public sphere, politics and business. A number of questions arise: where are the starting points *within* scientific practice itself to lessen self-produced insecurity as the cognitive process continues and differentiates? Can the practical and theoretical sovereignty of science be refounded this way? How can the generalization of skepticism and the reduction of insecurity be reharmonized in their internal and external relations? Some exemplary reflections illustrating the general concept will be presented here.

The prevailing theoretical self-concept of science implies that the sciences cannot make value judgments with the authority of their rationality. They deliver so-called 'neutral' figures, information, or explanations which are to serve as the 'unbiased' basis for decisions on the broadest variety of interests. *Which* interests they select, however, on *whom* or *what* they project the causes, *how* they interpret the problems of society, *what sort* of potential solutions they bring into view – these are anything but neutral decisions. In other words: the sciences have developed their steering abilities *independently of* and *beyond* explicit value statements. Their possibilities of exerting practical influence lie in *how* they design scientific results. Thus the 'purely objective' interpretation of 'need' and 'risk' in the various fields of action provides a cloak behind which the directions of future developments are negotiated. What is considered 'need' and 'risk' is a central question in the decision between nuclear power plants, coal-based energy, energy conserving measures or alternative energy sources, just as it is in old-age insurance, social welfare insurance, the determination of poverty lines, and so on. And each of these problems contains implicit decisions on a *series* of related consequences which ultimately flow into the issue of a different form of social life. Value free or not, the determination and operationalization of consequences, hypothetical conjectures and the like are therefore levers with which fundamental decisions on the social future are carried out.

This means that the decisive factor for whether the sciences will contribute to the self-control and taming of their practical risks is not whether they reach out beyond their scope of influence and seek political consultation and cooperation in the application of their results. What is essential, rather, is *what kind of science is conducted with respect to the assessability of its allegedly immeasurable secondary consequences*. This does not mean that science should jump from one extreme to the other, and in a boundless exaggeration of its own powers should make itself the sole responsible party for what happens socially with scientific results. But it does imply that it should accept reports that come back on threats and risks as empirical challenges to its self-concept and for the reorganization of its work. In this sense what is essential to a reduction of external insecurity from within science is: (a) to what extent treatment of the *symptoms* can be replaced by elimination of the *causes*; (b) whether the *ability to learn from practice* will be preserved or created, or whether, by ignoring the practical consequences, *irreversible situations* will be created that are based on the imputation of *infallibility* and make learning impossible from the start; (c) whether the isolated view will be preserved or whether the power for *specialization in the context* will be rediscovered and developed.

Removing the Causes or Fighting against the Symptoms

In the course of secondary scientization, the constructions of objective constraints, with which the conditions and products of primary scientization were removed from the reach of action, are fused together into opportunities for change. The more objective constraints become, the more difficult it becomes to maintain the character of an objective constraint, and the production of them bursts forth on all sides. 'Technological or economic determinism', declared and thought through under considerations of technological control, can no longer maintain its determining power and remain sealed against legitimation demands and other possible arrangements. Determinism itself becomes configurable – at least in principle. Even self-produced objective constraints are transformed by the reflexive approach of the sciences into *constructed, manufactured* constraints, according to the same principle by which recognized causes of a cold, for instance, can be used to overcome or prevent it. Toxic substances and pollutant emissions, which were first considered 'latent' and then 'unavoidable' side effects, are gradually related under the observation of the scientists to the decision-making party concealed in them, and reconnected to the conditions of their controllability.

In this way, the veil of 'objective constraints' that had been drawn over all the conditions and agents of modernization and industrialization during primary scientization is systematically researched away in reflexive scientization. In the process, all the conditions become, first, *structurable,* and second, *dependent on legitimation.* The idea 'it could be different' increasingly comes to dominate, overtly or covertly, all fields of action as a threatening possibility in the background with its insistence on argument. And this happens even where science tries with all the defining power of its theories and methods to put up new barriers of unchangeability for risks produced. But then the central issue becomes, not only *what* is investigated, but also *how* it is investigated, that is, with what approach, scope of thought, end points and so on with respect to the increase or avoidance of industrialization risks.

Thus there are fundamentally *two options* confronting each other in dealing with civilizational risks: removing causes in primary industrialization, or the secondary industrialization of consequences and symptoms, which tends to expand markets. To this point, the *second* route has been taken almost everywhere. It is cost-intensive, leaves the causes obscure and permits the transformation of mistakes and problems into market booms. The learning process is systematically foreshortened and prevented. The self-origination of the threats of modernization is submerged under the selective consideration and treatment of symptoms. This can be illustrated with the example of the treatment of diseases of civilization, such as diabetes, cancer or heart disease. These illnesses could be fought where they originate: by reducing the stresses of work or the pollution of the environment, or through a healthy way of life and a nutritious diet. Or the symptoms can be alleviated through chemical preparations. The different schools of fighting illness do not of course exclude one another, but one cannot actually speak of a cure through the second method. Nonetheless, we have so far generally opted for the medical and chemical 'solution'.

In more and more areas, industry is beginning to profit from its secondary problems, ignoring its own role in their origin. This once again raises alternative decisions for science and its research: *either* it delivers the appropriate risk definitions and causal interpretations for this in its isolated specialization, *or* it breaks through this cost-intensive controlling of the symptoms and develops independent, theoretically sound alternative perspectives that demonstrate and illuminate the sources of problems and their elimination in industrial development itself. In the first case, science becomes the participant and the legitimating agency for continuing chains of 'objective constraints'; in the second case, it demonstrates starting points and ways to break these chains and thus gain a bit of sovereignty *within* modernization *over* modernization.

In this sense, the risk society is potentially also a *self*-critical society. Reference points and presuppositions of critique are always being produced there in the form of risks and threats. The critique of risks is not a normative critique of values. Precisely where traditions and hence values *have deteriorated*, risks come into being. The basis for critique is less the traditions of the past than the threats of the future. What is needed to recognize toxic substances in the air, the water and food, is not so much established values as, rather, expensive measuring instruments and methodological and theoretical knowledge.

Determinations of risk thus oddly straddle the distinction between objective and value dimensions. They do not assert moral standards openly, but in the form of a *quantitative, theoretical and causal implicit morality*. Correspondingly, in the investigation of risks with a generally conventional understanding of science, a kind of 'objectified causal morality' is being undertaken. Statements on risk are the moral statements of scientized society. All these things – reference points and object of critique, the possibilities of discovering and grounding – are themselves produced in the modernization process on a large and a small scale. In this sense, therefore, a detraditionalized *and self*-critical society also comes into being along with the risk society, at least potentially. The concept of risk is like a probe which permits us over and over again to investigate the entire construction plan, as well as every individual speck of cement in the structure of civilization for potentials of self-endangerment.

Infallibility or Ability to Learn

If side effects are no longer to be accepted, techno-scientific development must guarantee the ability to learn at every stage, at its pace and through the ways it advances. This presupposes that developments which create *irreversible situations* will be avoided. What is important, in contrast, is to reveal and work out those variants of techno-scientific development that leave room for mistakes and corrections. Technological research and policy must proceed from the 'theory' that has to this point proven most confirmed and most attractive: *that of the entrapment of human thought and action in mistakes and errors.* Where technological developments begin to contradict this one certainty – perhaps the ultimate one, and basically comforting at that – they encumber humanity with the unbearable burden of *infallibility.* As risks multiply, the pressure grows to pass oneself off as infallible and thereby deprive oneself of the ability to learn. The most self-evident thing, the admission of human failure, then coincides with causing *catastrophes* and must be avoided by all means. In this way, risk multiplications join forces with the imputation of infallibility and set loose pressures for the minimization of risks that correlate directly with the extent of threats. All this must be concealed by hook or by crook through the 'adherence to objective law' in one's own actions.

Thus we must investigate practical developments as to whether they contain a 'monstrosity of risk' that would rob people of their humanity and *condemn them to perfection* for all eternity. Techno-scientific development is beginning to be trapped more and more within a striking new contradiction: while the foundations of knowledge are being explored in the institutionalized self-skepticism of the sciences, the development of technology has been isolated against skepticism. Just as the risks and the pressure for action grow, absolutist claims to knowledge, infallibility and security, which have long since become untenable, are being renewed in technological development. Dogma flourishes under the pressure on the engineering sciences to take action. The unleashed and systematically fomented skepticism encounters the *anti-modernity* of scientific infallibility taboos in the development of technology. These harden as the risks increase. The 'safest' thing is ultimately the immeasurable; nuclear bombs and energy with their threats surpassing all concepts and imaginative abilities. It is necessary, therefore, to free *fallibilism* from its theoretic-empirical *enclosure*, to devalue technology as a possibility and to test possible variants of technological development for their 'humanity', that is their 'freedom from error'.

Nuclear energy in this sense is a highly dangerous game with the imputed 'infallibility' of technological development. It releases objective constraints from objective constraints, which are scarcely alterable and only capable of learning to a limited extent. It commits people for generations (in disposing of or storing atomic waste), for periods, that is, in which not even the unchanged meaning of the key words can be assured. It even casts shadows of immeasurable consequences over quite different areas. This applies to the social controls it requires, which have found expression in the phrase 'authoritarian nuclear state'. It applies equally well, however, to the long-term biological effects, which cannot be measured at all today. By contrast, decentralized forms of energy supply are possible which do not contain this 'auto-dynamism of objective constraints'. Developmental variants can thus close off the future *or* they can keep it open. Depending on which we choose, we make a *decision* for or against a trip into the unknown no man's land of unseen but measurable secondary consequences. Once the train has left the station it is difficult to stop it. Therefore, we must choose developmental variants that do not close off the future, but transform the modernization process itself into a *learning process*, in which the revisability of decisions makes possible the revocation of side effects discovered later.

Specialization in the Context

A further central condition for the production of latent side effects lies in the *specialization* of cognitive practice. More precisely, the higher the degree of specialization, the *greater* is the range, number and incalculability of the secondary consequences of techno-scientific action. Not only does the 'unseen' and 'secondary' character of the 'unseen secondary consequences' *arise* from specialization. The probability also increases that selective solutions will be conceived and implemented, whose intended main effects will be continually covered over by the unintended side effects. Overspecialized science thus becomes a 'shunting yard' for problems and the cost-intensive treatment of their symptoms. The chemical industry produces toxic wastes. What is to be done with them? The 'solution': dumps. Its consequence: the waste problem becomes a ground water problem. The chemical industry and others can profit from this through 'purification additives' to drinking water. If the drinking water with these additives impairs people's health, there are medicines available, whose 'latent side effects' can be intercepted *and* prolonged by an elaborate medical care system. In this way, *chains of problem solution and problem production* come into being – according to the degree of overspecialization – and these 'confirm' the 'fairy tale' of unseen secondary consequences all over again.

The genetic structure from which 'objective constraints' and 'auto-dynamism' arise is thus in essence the model of overspecialized cognitive practice in its narrow-mindedness, its understanding of methods and theory, its career ladders and so on. Division of labor pushed to the limit produces everything: the secondary consequences, their unpredictability, and the reality which makes this 'fate' appear inevitable. Overspecialization is an active model of social practice that concentrates the fatalism of consequences in a self-confirming circle.

A science that would break this 'fate' must (*learn to*) *specialize in the context* in new forms. The isolated analytical approach does not lose its justification, but it becomes *false* and a risk producer in practice when it becomes the guiding line for partial measures and a 'patchwork approach' that is seemingly founded scientifically. The center of a specialized context research could then be occupied, for instance, by *shunting yards* of problems (which are precisely typical of dealings with risks and environmental problems, but also appear to prevail in many areas of social welfare policy and of social and medical services), as well as by the tracking down of essential developmental alternatives and the *switch settings* they contain that will avoid or multiply insecurity.

Thus, in the relationship between food supply, agriculture, industry and science, variants of models of the division of labor are concealed, which by themselves can either produce or shorten chains of secondary problems. A central fork in the road is marked by the issue of whether the chemical way of working the soil and processing food will be pursued further, or whether there will be a return to ways of dealing with nature *that learn from nature itself*, for instance, how weeds can be combated and the power and fertility of the soil increased by the proper rotation of crops. If the chemical way is maintained, the center of research will be the manufacture of ever more effective 'biocides' and consequently also the study of the effects of such toxins, the determination of allowable levels, which in turn require research into their damage to health and therefore animal research (with the accompanying mistreatment), public protests, legal and police measures, etc. If the path of an ecologically conscious agriculture is chosen, it too will require support from research, but of a different sort. The latter would have to improve knowledge of crop cycles and the possibilities of using the soil without impoverishing it. At the same time, however, chains of consequences and objective constraints that draw wider and wider circles can be broken. In the connection between agriculture and nutrition there are *switch settings for alternative social futures* which would connect the realms of industry, research, politics and law through chains of risk-producing 'objective constraints' in one case, and would not do so in the other.

Plea for a Pedagogy of Scientific Rationality

The rationality and irrationality of science are questions never only of the present and the past, but also of the *possible future*. We can learn from our mistakes – which also means that an *alternative* science is always possible. Not only an alternative theory, but an alternative *theory of cognition*, an alternative relationship of theory *and* practice, and an alternative *practice* of this relationship. If it is correct that the present is nothing but a hypothesis that we have not yet surpassed, then today is the age of the counter-hypothesis. The 'touch stones' (or, better 'mountains') which such hypotheses must face are obvious: the project of modernity needs first aid. It threatens to choke on its own anomalies. Science in its present form is one of these.

We need a theory of the objective constraints of techno-scientific action that will place the *production* of objective constraints and 'unforeseeable side effects' of techno-scientific action at the center of attention. The lever for the avoidance and cancellation of the fatalism of consequences must also be found in the framework of action, in the self-conception of the sciences themselves. Not *according to* scientific practice, but *in it*, in what it considers noteworthy or not, how it asks questions and casts the 'nets' of its causal hypotheses, how it decides on the validity of its conjectures: that is where criteria must be discovered for how the unpredictability of consequences is produced *and* can be avoided. By changing its self-conception and political arrangement, we must, as it were, install *brakes and a steering wheel* into the 'non-steering' of the racing techno-scientific development that is setting explosive powers free. That this is possible was assumed more by illustration than proven by the foregoing considerations. At least the requirements on this conception are clear in outline: science must be conceived as (one) originator of the objective constraints from which the general uncertainty arises. It must break up that uncertainty through the practically effective change of its self-concept. The hope remains that reason, which was silenced in science, can be activated and mobilized against it. Science *can change itself* and revive enlightenment theoretically and practically through a critique of its historic self-conception.

A key reason for the solution of this demand comes from the question of whether and how it will prove possible to *institutionalize such a transformed practice of science* – whether of data production or of the 'theoretical gymnastics on semantic branches' (Mayntz 1980) – and to reconnect scientific work at the level of its methodological reflection and self-criticism to *reality* in a way yet to be laid out. Against the background of the arguments presented, this certainly means that the demonstration of theoretical connections is essential for the autonomous-critical and practical potential of the sciences. It also means, however, that the concept of empiricism must be rethought and redetermined, precisely from a theoretical and historical understanding. Given the level of scientifically produced insecurity we can no longer presume what empiricism 'is', but must plan this out theoretically. The conjecture is that only in a *theory of empiricism* can the speculative power of thought be related again to 'reality' and at the same time the complementary roles of theory and empiricism be outlined and marked out in their collaboration and opposition.

Social scientists can make a contribution to this. It would be up to them to encourage the emancipation of science from its self-inflicted fate of immaturity and blindness with respect to risks. Nowhere is there a recipe for this, and there is scarcely even any advice. In the case of the social sciences the guiding question at least is: how can social science and social experience be related to each other in such a way that the spectrum of unseen secondary consequences is reduced? And how can sociology – for all its fragmentation into individual fields of work – be made capable of producing a contribution to *scientific specialization in the context* (basically therefore its original goal)?

What is sought is a *pedagogy* of scientific rationality which will conceive of that rationality as changeable by discussion of self-produced threats. Different from the case of the theory of science, which presumes and attempts to reconstruct the rationality of science from its historical status quo, the knowledge claim of science becomes a *future project*, which can be neither refuted nor gained from the forms of the present alone. The proof of the irrationality of the prevailing practice of science no more means the end of science than the refutation of Newtonian mechanics meant the end of physics. The precondition for that proof is to transfer the substantive abilities for criticism and learning, which were traditional in research practice, to the foundations of knowledge and the application of it. At the same time, that would mean the elevation of the *actually latent* reflexivity of the modernization process into scientific consciousness. But where modernization encounters modernization, this word also changes its meaning. In the social and political application of modernization to itself, the interest in mastery that is spread in this way loses its technical grip and assumes the form of 'self-control' and 'self-limitation'. Amidst the tumult of contradictions and new doctrinal disputes, there will perhaps also arise the *opportunity* for practical self-domestication and self-alteration of the techno-scientific 'second nature', its forms of thought and work.

Notes

1 In the current wave of 'scientization of the family', for instance, as visible in the prominence of experts in family and marriage counseling; but even here, scientization encounters a field of practice that is professionally and scientifically pre-formed and influenced in multiple ways.

2 I rely here particularly on (I believe unpublished) discussions by Robert C. Mitchell (1979). See also, on the same subject, Novotny (1979), Weingart (1979) and Küppers et al. (1978).

3 I am thinking in particular of *Silent Spring* by Rachel Carson, which was published in 1962 and sold 100,000 copies in three months, as well as Barry Commoner's *Science and Survival* (1963).

4 The argumentation can be sketched in several steps. First, on closer inspection, empirical data are insufficient as a falsification agent of 'speculative' theory. The latter must be grounded. Grounding it in experience removes it from intersubjectivity. At the same time the *production* of data in the experiment (interview, observation, etc.) continues to be ignored. If the latter are included, then the boundary between theoretical and empirical statements, the point of the entire undertaking, is destroyed. How should the insistence on the search for falsifiers actually be understood? Let us assume an experiment does not satisfy the theoretical expectations. Has the theory then been *refuted* once and for all, or have inconsistencies between expectations and results simply been demonstrated, which

point to different decision possibilities and to that extent can be worked out or blocked in very different ways (by suspecting an error in the experiment, for instance, or by building up and developing the theory further along quite contrary lines; Lakatos 1974)? In the shift in the history of science initiated by Thomas S. Kuhn's influential essay (1970), the empirical basis is removed from reflection on the philosophy of science. In the process, however, the status of the theory of science as a theory without empiricism becomes problematic. Is the theory of science just a logistically qualified theory of norms, a supreme censure authority for 'good' science, hence the scientific equivalent of the religious Inquisition in the Middle Ages? Or does it fulfill its own demands on an empirically testable theory? Then its validity claims must be drastically scaled down in view of existing contradictory principles of knowledge production and fabrication. Ethnologically oriented research on science finally 'discovers' even in the putative birthplace of natural scientific rationality – the laboratory – that the prevailing practices resemble modern variants of rain dances and fertility rituals, which are oriented to the principles of career and social acceptance (Knorr-Cetina 1984).

5 This may be one of the reasons why, precisely as an oversupply of interpretations develops, personality characteristics and personal networks tend to increase in importance for the practical application and utilization of these interpretations.

6 In the following I am referring back to arguments that I presented together with Wolfgang Bonß (Beck and Bonß 1984) as part of the conference of the Deutsche Forschungsgemeinschaft on 'Application Aspects of Social-Scientific Results'. See also Bonß and Hartmann (1985).

8

OPENING UP THE POLITICAL

In contrast to all earlier epochs (including industrial society), the risk society is characterized essentially by a *lack*: the impossibility of an *external* attribution of hazards. In other words, risks depend on *decisions*; they are industrially produced and in this sense *politically reflexive*. While all earlier cultures and phases of social development confronted threats in various ways, society today is *confronted by itself* through its dealings with risks. Risks are the reflection of human actions and omissions, the expression of highly developed productive forces. That means that the sources of danger are no longer ignorance but *knowledge*; not a deficient but a perfected mastery over nature; not that which eludes the human grasp but the system of norms and objective constraints established with the industrial epoch. Modernity has even taken over the role of its counterpart – the tradition to be overcome, the natural constraint to be mastered. It has become the threat *and* the promise of emancipation from the threat that it creates itself. A central consequence connected thereto, which will occupy the center of this chapter, is that risks become the motor of the *self-politicization* of modernity in industrial society; furthermore, in the risk society, the *concept, place and media of politics* change.[1]

Politics and Sub-Politics

This assessment of a transformation of politics in the risk society will first be sketched out by way of *four theses*.

(1) The relationship between social transformation and political direction was originally conceived in the project of industrial society on the model of the 'divided citizen'. On the one hand, as a *citoyen*, the latter avails himself of his democratic rights in all arenas of political will formation, and on the other hand, as a *bourgeois*, he defends his private interests in the fields of work and business. Correspondingly, a differentiation occurs between a politico-economic and a techno-economic system. The axial principle of the political sphere is the participation of citizens in the institutions of representative democracy (parties, parliaments, etc.). Decision-making, and with it the exercise of political power, follow the maxims of legality and the principle that power and domination can only be carried out with the consent of the governed.

The actions of the *bourgeois* and the spheres of techno-economic pursuit of interests, by contrast, are considered *non*-politics. This design is based first on the equation of technical and *social* progress; then on the assumption that the direction of development and the results of technological transformation follow more or less inescapable techno-economic *objective constraints*. Technological innovations increase the individual and collective well-being. The negative effects (deskilling, risks of unemployment or transfer, threats to health and natural destruction) have always found justification in these rises of the standard of living. Even dissent over the 'social consequences' does not hinder the accomplishment of techno-economic innovation. That process remains in essence removed from political legitimation, particularly by comparison to democratic-administrative procedures and the long periods needed for implementation; indeed, it possesses a power of enforcement virtually immune to criticism. *Progress replaces voting.* Furthermore: progress becomes a substitute for questions, a type of consent in advance for goals and consequences that go unnamed and unknown.

In this sense the innovation process that is enforced by modernity against the predominance of tradition is *split in two democratically* through the project of industrial society. Only a part of the decision-making competencies that structure society are gathered together in the political system and subjected to the principles of parliamentary democracy. Another part is removed from the rules of public inspection and justification and delegated to the freedom of investment of enterprises and the freedom of research of science. Social changes in these contexts are *displaced* as latent side effects of scientific and techno-scientific decisions. People do something quite different: they assert themselves in the market, use the rules of profit-making, carry forth scientific and technical inquiry, and in so doing they turn over the conditions of everyday life.

With the globalization of the industrial society, then, two contrary processes for organizing social change interpenetrate one another: the establishment of political parliamentary democracy and the establishment of an unpolitical, non-democratic social change under the legitimating umbrella of 'progress' and 'rationalization'. The two behave towards each other like modernity and counter-modernity. On the one hand, the institutions of the political system – parliament, government, political parties – *functionally* presuppose in a manner *conditioned by the system* the production circle of industry, technology and business. On the other hand, this pre-programs the permanent change of all realms of social life under the justifying cloak of techno-economic progress, in contradistinction to the simplest rules of democracy – knowledge of the goals of social change, discussion, voting and consent.

(2) As we can say retrospectively, this demarcation of politics and non-politics in the process of modernization rested in the nineteenth and the first half of the twentieth century on at least two essential historical presuppositions that have become dubious since the seventies in all Western industrial states. These are: (a) the *social obviousness of inequalities in class society* which has given meaning and impetus to the

expansion of the welfare state; (b) a *level of development of the productive forces and of scientization* whose potentials for change neither exceed
the radius of possible political actions nor cancel the basis of the legitimation of the model of social change through progress. Both prerequisites
have become fragile over the past two decades in the course of reflexive
modernization. In establishing itself, the welfare state has sacrificed its
utopian energies. Simultaneously, its limits and drawbacks have entered
public consciousness. But whoever only laments and criticizes the ensuing
paralysis of the political overlooks the fact the *opposite* is also *true*.

Waves of current, announced or emerging changes pass through and
convulse society. In their scope and depth, they will probably overshadow
all the reform attempts of the last few decades. Thus, the political stand-
off is being undermined by *hectic changes* in the techno-economic system
that put human imagination to a test of courage. Science fiction is
increasingly becoming a memory of past times. The key words are well
known and have been sufficiently elaborated in this book, including the
continuing destruction of external and internal nature; the systemic
transformation of work; the fragility of status-based gender orders; the
loss of class traditions and the intensification of social inequalities; new
technologies balancing on the verge of catastrophe.

The impression of 'political' standoff is deceptive. It arises only because
the political is limited to what is *labeled* political, to the activities of the
political system. If one conceives it more broadly, then one sees that
society is caught in a whirlpool of change that richly deserves the title
'revolutionary' – quite apart from how one evaluates it. This social
transformation, however, occurs in the form of the *non*-political. In this
sense the discontent with politics not only is a discontent with politics
itself, but results from the misproportion between an authority to act
which plays political and is becoming powerless, and a broad-scale change
of society, closed off to social decision-making, that approaches unstop-
pably but quietly in the guise of the non-political. Correspondingly, the
concepts of the political and the non-political become blurred and require
a systematic revision.

(3) Both developments – the waning of welfare state interventionism
due to its success and the waves of large-scale technological innovation
with as yet unknown future hazards – add up in a double sense to an
unbinding of politics. On the one hand established and utilized rights limit
freedom of action *within* the political system and bring about new
demands for political participation *outside* the political system in the form
of a *new political culture* (citizens' initiative groups and social movements). In this sense, the loss of governmental powers of structuration
and enforcement is not the expression of a political failure, but the
product of *established* democracy and the welfare state, in which the
citizens are able to utilize all the media of public and legal control and
consultation for the protection of their interests and rights.

On the other hand, techno-economic development loses its character as non-politics in parallel to the increase in scope of its potentials for change and endangerment. Where the outlines of an alternative society are no longer seen in the debates of parliament or the decisions of the executive, but rather in the application of microelectronics, reactor technology and human genetics, the constructs which had heretofore politically neutral- ized the innovation process begin to break up. At the same time, techno- economic action continues to be shielded by its own constitution against parliamentary demands for legitimation. Techno-economic development thus falls between politics and non-politics. It becomes a third entity, acquiring the precarious hybrid status of a *sub-politics*, in which the scope of the social changes precipitated varies inversely with their legitimation. As risks grow, the places, conditions and media of their origin and inter- pretation are stripped of their techno-economic objective constraints. Legally responsible, governmental monitoring agencies and a risk-sensitive media publicity sphere begin to talk their way into and govern the 'intimate sphere' of plant management. The direction of development and the results of technological transformation become fit for discourse and subject to legitimation. Thus business and techno-scientific action acquire a *new political and moral dimension* that had previously seemed alien to techno-economic activity. If one wished, one might say that the devil of the economy must sprinkle himself with the holy water of public morality and put on a halo of concern for society and nature.

(4) In that way a movement is launched which runs counter to the accomplishment of the welfare state project in the first two-thirds of this century. Given that politics then acquired the power potentials of the 'interventionist state', now the potential for structuring society migrates from the political system into the sub-political system of scientific, technological and economic modernization. A precarious reversal of politics and non-politics occurs. *The political becomes non-political and the non-political political.* Paradoxically, this role reversal behind unchanged façades proceeds more emphatically the more unthinkingly the division of labor between political and non-political social change is adhered to. The promotion and protection of 'scientific progress' and of 'the freedom of science' become the greasy pole on which the primary responsibility for political arrangements slips from the democratic political system into the context of economic and techno-scientific non- politics, which is not democratically legitimated. A *revolution under the cloak of normality* occurs, which escapes from possibilities of interven- tion, but must all the same be justified and enforced against a public that is becoming critical.

This development is extraordinarily momentous and problematic. In the welfare state project, politics had been able to develop and maintain a *relative autonomy* against the techno-economic system for purposes of a political intervention in market events. Now, on the contrary, the political system is being threatened with *disempowerment* while its democratic constitution remains alive. The political institutions become the administrators of a development they neither have planned for nor are able to structure, but must nevertheless somehow justify.

On the other hand, decisions in science and business are charged with an effectively political content for which the agents possess no legitimation. Lacking a place to appear, the decisions that change society become tongue-tied and anonymous. In business they are tied into investment decisions which shunt their potential for social change off into the 'unseen side effect'. The empirical and analytical sciences that plan the innovations remain cut off by their self-understanding and institutional ties from the social consequences of their innovations and the consequences of those consequences. The unknowability of the consequences, their indefensibility is the developmental project of science. The structuring potential of modernity begins to creep back into the 'latent side effects', which on the one hand expand into risks threatening existence, and on the other lose their veil of latency. What we *do not* see and *do not* want is changing the world more and more obviously and threateningly.

The game with the roles of politics and non-politics reversed, while the façade remains unchanged, is becoming ghostlike. Politicians have to be told where the path devoid of plan and consciousness is leading – and told by those who *do not* know either and whose interests are directed at something quite different and therefore *also* attainable. Then, with the practiced gesture of fading trust in progress, they must present this journey into the unknown alternative country to the voters as their own invention, and if one considers it carefully, for one single reason: because from the beginning there was and remains no alternative. The necessity, the non-decidability of technological 'progress' becomes the bolt securing the process to its democratic (non-)legitimation. The 'anarchy' (Arendt 1981) of the (no longer) unseen side effect takes over power in the developed stage of Western democracy.

The Political System's Loss of Function

The scientific and public debate on the potential for politics to exert influence over technological transformation is pervaded by a peculiar ambivalence. On the one hand, reference is made in many ways to the state's *limited* capacity for intervention as concerns modernization in industry and research. On the other hand, despite all the criticism of limitations on the political scope of action, whether imposed by the system or avoidable, the *fixation on the political system as the exclusive center of politics* continues to exist. Political discussion in science and in the public sphere over the past two or three decades indeed represents an intensification of this contrast. The advocacy of restrictive conditions on political action, which has gained new impetus with talk of the 'ungovernability' and the excesses of democracy, has never properly been questioned as to whether the *other* society might be coming into existence without plans, consent or consciousness from the workshops of techno-economic development. What remains instead are laments on the loss of the political, related to the normatively valid expectation that the decisions which change society should be concentrated in the institutions of the political system, even though they are no longer concentrated there.

Thus, already at an early stage the *decline of parliament* as a political center was criticized, and from quite different quarters. Decisions which according to the letter of the constitution were incumbent upon the parliament and the individual deputies, it was claimed, were increasingly being made either by the factional and party leadership, or by the governmental bureaucracy. This loss of parliamentary power is often interpreted as an inescapable consequence of the increasing complexity of conditions in modern industrial societies. At best, critical observers speak of a progressive autonomization of the state apparatus over against the will of the citizens, which however is already implicit in the principle of representative democracy.

With remarkable consonance they also determine that the shift of former parliamentary powers to factions and parties or the state bureaucracy would be overlain by two further developmental tendencies: the *technocratic* closing off of the scope for decision-making in the parliament and the executive, and the rise of power and influence groups organized *corporatively*. With the increasing scientization of political decisions, so the argument goes, political agencies only carry out what scientific expertise recommends (e.g. in the area of environmental policy, but also in the choice of large-scale technologies and their sites). In recent years attention has several times been called to the fact that the operative scope of the agents in question is still set too narrowly in this way. Politics is said to have migrated from the official arenas – parliament, government, political administration – into the *gray area of corporatism.* The organized power of the interest groups is said to produce prefabricated political decisions which others must then defend as their own creations.

The influence of such pressure groups, which in turn utilize bureaucratically organized offices, extends – as studies show – both to the decisions of the state executive and to 'will formation' in the political parties. According to one's standpoint, this process is in turn lamented as an undermining of the state by private pressure groups with a quasi-official character, or, by contrast, welcomed as a necessary corrective to the prior autonomization and consolidation of the governmental ruling apparatus.

In Marxist critiques and theory of the state, which after all do not have an autonomous concept of the political, this connection of state power to special interests is carried to the extreme. In the variants of this perspective the state, seen as the 'ideal total capitalist' in the sense of Marx's characterization, is completely reduced in scope to the function of a 'management committee of the ruling class'. The minimum of autonomy conceded to the state apparatus and its democratic institutions results in this view from the necessity of uniting the limited, short-term, conflicting and incompletely formulated 'individual capitalist' interests and enforcing them against resistance in their own camp. Here too, the political system is seen as the center of politics, but it loses all autonomy. The argument was always made against this thinking in the all too simple categories of 'base' and 'superstructure' that it misapprehends the degree of autonomization of political action in the developed parliamentary democracies. Similarly, it misunderstands the experiences of modern political history, which indicate that the organization of production in developed capitalist industrial society is quite compatible with extremely varied forms of political rule (as represented, say, by Sweden, Chile, France, and Germany).

In the seventies the main historical evidence for the 'relative autonomy' of the political system with regard to the principles and interests of the economic system was provided by the expansion of the social welfare state in Western European post-war development. In political theories of 'state capitalism' this interventionist power of the state is traced back to the fact that in the development of industrial capitalism 'the formation of system elements *alien* to the structure' occurs 'as a *necessary* part of [the system's (tr.)] existence' (Offe 1972: 38). In this view, the power of political decision-making draws its influence not only from the dysfunctional side effects of the market mechanism, but from the fact that 'the interventionist state jumps into the functional gaps of the market' (Habermas 1973: 51) – by improving the material and intangible infrastructure, expanding the educational system, protecting against unemployment risks and so on.

In the past ten years, this discussion has clearly receded into the background. It is not just that the generalized concept of crisis (economic, legitimation, motivational crises and so on) has lost its theoretical and political acuteness. From different quarters it has been unanimously stated that the project of the interventionist welfare state has lost its utopian energy as it has become established. Internally, the more successful it is, the more clearly the welfare state meets the resistance of private investors, who respond to rising wage and benefit costs with a diminishing willingness to make investments or with automation, which increasingly displaces human labor. At the same time, the drawbacks and side effects of the welfare state's achievements emerge ever more clearly:

> The legal and administrative means for the implementation of welfare state programs do not constitute a passive medium, without qualities, as it were. Rather, they are tied to a practice of the isolation of facts, normalization, and surveillance, whose reifying and subjectivizing power has been pursued by Foucault into the tiniest capillary branches of everyday communication . . . In short the contradiction between goal and method is inherent in the welfare state project as such. (Habermas 1985: 7f.)

Even externally, the nation state's scope of jurisdiction is overtaxed by historical developments – internationally interlocked markets and concentrations of capital – but also by the global exchange of pollutants and toxins and the accompanying universal health threats and natural destruction.

The more or less perplexed reactions to these developments are concentrated graphically in the phrase 'the new obscurity' (Habermas 1985). It also applies to two other states of affairs: first, the *weakening of the social structure and of voters' political behavior* that has become a disturbing factor in politics over the past ten years; second, the *mobilization of citizens and citizen protest* as well as a number of *social movements* that have been speaking out quite effectively on all matters of interest to them (Brand et al. 1983).

In all the Western democracies, party leaderships are puzzled by the *growing proportion of swing voters* who are making the political business unpredictable. If one found roughly 10 percent swing voters in Germany in 1963, for example, today their number is estimated by various studies at between 20 and 40 percent. Electoral researchers and politicians agree on the diagnosis: in view of the narrow majorities any party has been able to achieve, the swing voters with their 'mercurial flexibility' ([prominent pollster (tr.)] Noelle-Neumann 1991) will decide future elections.

Conversely, it also implies that parties can no longer count on 'regular voters' and must use all the means they have at their disposal to court the citizens – and recently women in particular (in summary form, see Radunski 1985). At the same time the citizens' initiative groups and new social movements gain political momentum and broad support from this visible gap between the demands of the citizenry and their representation in the spectrum of political parties.

Although the evaluation of all these 'dissonant' developments varies according to the political standpoint and although elements of an 'unbinding of politics' often come up in this 'demystification of the state' (Willke 1983), these diagnoses continue to be related implicitly or explicitly, actually or normatively, to the notion of a *political center* which has or should have its place and means of influence in the democratic institutions of the political and administrative system. In contrast to that, the view developed here will be that the preconditions for the separation of politics and non-politics are becoming fragile in the course of reflexive modernization.

Behind the phrase 'new obscurity' is concealed a profound *systemic transformation of the political*, in two respects. The first of these is the loss of power experienced by the centralized political system in the course of the *enforcement and utilization of civil rights* in the forms of a *new political culture*; the second lies in the changes of social structure connected with the transition from non-politics to *sub*-politics, a development that seems to lose its conditions of application in the hitherto prevailing 'harmonizing formula' – technical progress equals social progress. Both perspectives add up to an 'unbinding of politics', the possible consequences of which will be finally explored in three scenarios.[2]

Democratization as the Disempowerment of Politics

Not the failures of politics but its successes have led to the loss of state intervention power and to the delocalization of politics. One can even say, the more successfully political rights were fought for, pushed through and concretely realized in this century, the more emphatically the primacy of the political system was called into question, and the more fictitious became the simultaneously claimed concentration of decision-making at the top of the political and parliamentary system. In this sense political development is undergoing a rupture of continuity during the second half of this century, not only in its relationship to the fields of action of techno-economic development but also in its internal relationship. The concepts, foundations and instruments of politics (and non-politics) are becoming unclear, open and in need of a historically new determination.

The centering of decision-making authority in the political system, as planned in the relationship between *citoyen* and *bourgeois* in the project of the bourgeois industrial society, is based on the naive view that it would be possible on the one hand to enforce the democratic rights of the citizens, and on the other hand to preserve hierarchical authority relationships in reaching political decisions. Ultimately, the monopolization of democratically constituted decision-making rights is founded on the contradictory image of a *democratic monarchy*. The rules of democracy are limited to the choice of political representatives and to participation in political programs. Once in office, it is not only the 'monarch for a term' who develops dictatorial leadership qualities and enforces his decisions in authoritarian fashion from the top down; the agencies, interest groups and citizens' groups affected by the decisions also forget their rights and become 'democratic subjects' who accept without question the state's claims to dominance.

In the course of reflexive modernizations this perspective is undermined in several ways. It becomes increasingly clear that finding political 'solutions' becomes *contingent* precisely as democratic rights are established. In the fields of politics (and sub-politics) there is neither a single nor a 'best' solution, but always several solutions. As a consequence, political decision-making processes, no matter on what level they occur, can no longer be understood as the enforcement or implementation of a model determined in advance by some wise man or leader, whose rationality is not open to discussion and must be enforced even against the will and 'irrational resistance' of subordinated agencies, interests and citizens' groups. Both the formulation of the program and the decision-making process, as well as the enforcing of those decisions, must rather be understood as a process of *collective action* (Crozier and Friedberg 1979), and that means, even in the best case, collective learning and collective creation. This implies, however, that the official decision-making authority of political institutions is necessarily *de*centralized. The political-administrative system then can no longer be the only or the central locus of political events. In tandem *with* the democratization, networks of agreement and participation, negotiation, reinterpretation and possible resistance come into being *across* the formal horizontal and vertical structure of authorizations and jurisdictions.

The notion of a center of politics, as cultivated in the model of the industrial society, thus rests upon a peculiar *bisection of democracy*. On the one hand, the fields of sub-political action are exempt from the application of democratic rules (see above). On the other hand, even internally, politics still displays monarchical traits, according to the systematically incited external demands. The 'political leadership' must display a strong hand and dictatorial powers of enforcement over against the administration and the interest groups. With respect to the citizens, it must be an equal among equals and is supposed to listen to their voices and take their concerns and fears seriously.

This more than just reflects the constraint on all action to cut off questions, to shorten discussions and consultations. It also expresses inherent tensions and contradictions in the structure of the democratic political system: the relationship between parliamentary debate and the public sphere on one side and an executive branch on the other, which is responsible to the parliament and yet has its 'success' measured by the power with which it is able to carry out its decisions. The electoral campaign system in particular *forces* the mutual attribution of decision-making authorities – whether in proclaiming the successes of previous policies or in condemning them – which constantly nourishes and renews the actual *fiction* of the quasi-democratic 'dictator for a term'. Here the *system causes* the assumption to emerge that a government and the parties supporting it, once elected, are responsible for everything good and bad that happens during their term of office, which would obviously only be possible if this government were precisely not what it is – democratically elected and active in a society where all the citizens and the agencies possess numerous opportunities for consultation due to the establishment of democratic rights and obligations.

In this sense, democratization and *de*-democratization, modernity and *counter*-modernity have always been fused together in a contradictory way through the model of the specializability and monopolizability of politics within the political system as propagated in the project of industrial society. On the one hand, the centering and specialization of the political system and its institutions (parliament, executive branch, administration, etc.) is *functionally necessary*. Only in that way can processes of political will formation and the representation of citizen interests and citizens' groups be organized at all. That is also the only way it is possible to practice democracy in the sense of choosing a political leadership. In that respect, the staged events of politics bring about the *fiction of a steering center for modern society*, where the threads of political intervention ultimately run together through all the differentiations and interconnections. On the other hand, this authoritarian understanding of political leading positions and leadership becomes systematically *eviscerated and unreal* along *with* the establishment and observance of democratic rights. In this sense, democratization ultimately amounts to a kind of self-disempowerment and delocalization of politics, in any case to the differentiation of consultation, monitoring and possibilities of resistance.

Even if this path has by no means been followed to its end here, it is still valid in general to say that wherever rights are protected, social burdens redistributed, consultation made possible, wherever citizens become active, politics is unbound and generalized a bit more. Parallel to that, the notion of a centering of hierarchical decision-making power at the top of the political system is becoming a memory of the pre-, semi- or formal-democratic past. Crucially then, feedback effects *also* apply under certain conditions in legally protected democracies. The incremental amount of utilized democracy continually produces new standards and demands, which cause opinion to turn to dissatisfaction with the 'stand-off' and the 'authoritarian character' of the prevailing conditions, despite any expansions of democracy achieved. In that respect, 'successful' politics in democracy can lead to a situation where the institutions of the political system lose importance and see their substance vitiated. In this sense, *established* democracy, in which the citizens are aware of their rights and fill them with life, requires a different understanding of politics and different institutions than the society on the way to it.

Observance of Civil Rights and the Differentiation of Cultural Sub-Politics

In the developed democracies of the West a number of checks have been built up to limit the display of political power. Already in the nineteenth century, at the beginning of this development, there was the *separation of powers*, which ensures control functions for the *judiciary* alongside the parliament and the government. With the development of Germany the *autonomy of collective bargaining* has gained social and legal reality. The central questions of employment policy are thereby turned over to the regulated discussions of the competing parties in the labor market, and the state is obliged to be neutral in labor conflicts.

One of the last steps in this direction until now is the legal protection and substantive fulfillment of *freedom of the press*, which, in combination with the mass media (newspapers, radio, television) and new technological possibilities, brings about multiply graduated *forms of publicity*. Even if these certainly do not pursue the exalted goals of the Enlightenment, but are also and even primarily 'servants' of the market, of advertising and of consumption (whether of goods of all sorts or of institutionally fabricated information), and even if they possibly produce or exacerbate inarticulateness, isolation, even stupidity, there still remains an actual or potential monitoring function which media-directed publicity can perform with regard to political decisions. In this way, centers of sub-politics are created and stabilized along with the establishment of basic rights, and in the very same degree to which these rights are substantively completed and protected in their autonomy against the encroachments of political (or economic) power.

If one conceives of this process of the realization of civil and constitutional rights in all its stages as a process of political modernization, then the following seemingly paradoxical statement becomes comprehensible: *political modernization disempowers and unbinds politics and politicizes society.* More precisely, the modernization process furnishes the gradually emerging centers and fields of action it makes possible for sub-politics with opportunities for extra-parliamentary monitoring with and against the system. In this way, more or less clearly defined regions and means of partially autonomous cooperative and alternative politics are separated out which are based on rights that have been fought for and are now protected. And that also means that the power relationships within society have changed somewhat through the observance, expansive interpretation and elaboration of these rights. The 'heads' of the political system are confronted by cooperatively organized antagonists, with a 'definition-making power' of media-directed publicity, and so on, which can essentially codetermine and change the agenda of politics. Even the courts become omnipresent monitoring agencies of political decisions; paradoxically, this occurs in exactly the degree to which, on the one hand, the judges exercise their 'judicial independence' even against the grain of politics, and on the other, citizens transform themselves from the loyal addressees of political decrees into political participants and attempt to sue for their rights in court *against* the state, if need be.

It only *seems* paradoxical that this type of *structural democratization* occurs alongside the parliament and the political system. Here the *contradiction* entered into by democratization processes in the phase of reflexive modernization becomes tangible. First, against the background of *established* constitutional rights, opportunities for democratic codetermination and monitoring in diverse fields of sub-politics are differentiated and elaborated. Second, this development passes by the original home of democracy, the parliament. Rights and decision-making authorizations that continue to exist *pro forma* are diluted. Political life in the originally provided centers of political will formation loses its substance and threatens to become paralyzed.

Put another way: alongside the model of *specialized* democracy, forms of a *new political culture* are becoming reality, in which heterogeneous centers of sub-politics have an effect on the process of politically forming and enforcing decisions, on the basis of utilized constitutional rights. All of that obviously does not mean state politics is becoming devoid of influence. It retains its monopoly in the central areas of foreign and military policy and in the application of state power for the maintenance of 'internal security'. That this is a central area of influence of state politics becomes clear from the fact that since the revolutions of the nineteenth century there has been a *relatively close relationship between citizen mobilization and the techno-financial equipping of the police.* Even today it can be confirmed – with the example of disputes over large-scale technologies, for instance – that the exercise of state power and political liberalization are by all means mutually related.

New Political Culture

Constitutional rights in this sense are hinges for a decentralization of politics with long-term amplification effects. They offer multiple possibilities for interpretation and, in different historical situations, new starting points to break up formerly prevalent, restrictive and selective interpretations. Thus far, the final variant of this was demonstrated in the *broad political activation of citizens* – from initiative groups to the so-called 'new social movements', to forms of alternative critical professional practice (among physicians, chemists, nuclear physicists, etc.). With this multiplicity of forms undermining all previous political plans they took advantage of their previously only formal rights in extra-parliamentary direct action and filled them with the life they considered worth striving for. This very activation of the citizens on all sorts of topics receives a special meaning because the other central forums of sub-politics – the judiciary and media publicity – are *also* open to them. As the developments have shown, these can at least sometimes be used very effectively for protecting citizen interests (in environmental protection, in the anti-nuclear movement, or in the confidentiality of data).

In this, the 'amplification effect' shows itself: that the basic rights can be observed *successively* and expanded in a *mutually reinforcing way* and thus can amplify the 'resistance power' of the 'basis' and the 'subordinate agencies' against unwanted interventions 'from above'. The growing self-confidence and participatory interest of the citizens, which is reported just as impressively by numerous demographic surveys as by the variety of changing citizens' initiative groups and political movements, may look like 'resistance against state authority' to an authoritarian understanding of democracy. It may also appear to be an inadequate attempt at exerting political influence to the eyes of scientists who have followed their good old habits and fixed their gaze on the political system as the locus of politics. But it is the logical next step that follows the establishment of democratic rights and leads in the direction of *concrete* democracy. In these manifold developments, the *generalization* of political action announces itself, whose themes and conflicts are no longer determined only by the fight for rights, but also by their elaboration and utilization for the entire society.

Basic rights with a universalist validity claim, as established in Western societies over the past two centuries or more by fits and starts, but in a generally *directed* process (so far), thus form the hinges of political development. On the one hand, they have been fought for in parliaments;

on the other hand, centers of sub-politics can develop and differentiate themselves parallel to the parliaments, and through these a new page in the history of democracy can be opened. This can be shown firstly for two of the previously mentioned *sites and forms of sub-politics*: the judiciary and media publicity.

In the professional position of the *judge* as protected by civil service law in Germany, partially autonomous ranges of decision-making are coming into view, in part through new forms of observance and interpretation, in part through external changes. And as an astonished judiciary and public has been seeing recently, these are also being used in *controversial* ways. The rights reside originally in the long-standing legal principle of 'judicial independence'. Only recently, however, probably due among other things to generational changes and scientization processes, have the freedoms been actively used and self-confidently fleshed out by judges.

Among the many conditions which are decisive for this, two will be selected here: through reflexive scientization of the objects and decision-making processes of reaching verdicts, originally *prevailing objective constraint constructs have begun to crumble and have been opened to individual decisions, at least partially*. This applies first of all to scientific analysis of legal interpretation and judicial decision-making. These make visable and usable the *variants* of the administration of justice, within the framework provided by the letter of the law and the rules of interpreting it; these variants had hitherto been covered over by recruitment and the prevailing fundamental convictions. Thus, scientization has revealed usable techniques of argument here and in that way subjected the judicial profession to previously unknown, internal *pluralization in terms of professional policy*.

This tendency is supported by the fact that many topics and cases of conflict that are taken to court *have lost their social clarity*. In many central fields of conflict – particularly in reactor technology and environmental questions, but also in family and marriage law or labor law – experts and counter-experts confront each other in an irreconcilable battle of opinions. In this way the decision is handed back to the judge – partially because the choice of expert witnesses already contains a decision in advance, partially because it is his duty to weigh and reorder the arguments before reaching a verdict. The systematic cultivation of self-doubt in the sciences through the overproduction of hypothetical, isolated detailed results (see Chapter 7) leaves its mark on the judicial system and opens up decision-making leeway for the 'independent' judge; that is to say, it pluralizes and politicizes the process of reaching a verdict.

The consequence for the legislature is that it finds itself on the defendant's bench more and more frequently. By now judicial review procedures have become almost a part of the normal course of a controversial administrative action (e.g. deciding on if, how and where nuclear power plants will be built). Additionally, it is becoming more and more uncertain and more and more difficult to calculate how these procedures will arise on the way through the courts and above all, how long they will last. Correspondingly, gray areas of insecurity arise, which strengthen the impression of the state's lack of influence.

In a broader sense, this applies to legislative initiatives in general. No matter what, they soon collide with the limits of equivalent or higher jurisdictions, on the provincial, federal or European Community level. The judicial review procedures to be expected in cases of conflict provide the judge's potential verdict with an omnipresence in the political system (strengthening, it should be noted, the lawyers' monopoly on the administration) and narrow the leeway for arrangements.

Even the right to *freedom of the press*, with all its opportunities and problems of interpretation, offers numerous occasions for the differentiation of large and partial public spheres (from the global television network to the school newspaper) with individually very particularized, but overall considerable opportunities to influence the definition of social problems. These are limited and checked by the material conditions on the production of information and the general legal and social conditions. But they can also achieve considerable significance for the public – and thus the political – perception of problems, as the political boom of environmental issues and the rise and fall of social movements and subcultures illustrate. For instance, this becomes clear in the fact that expensive and extensive scientific investigations are often not really noticed in the agency that ordered them until television or a mass-circulation newspaper reports about them. People in the political administration read *Der Spiegel*, not investigation reports, and not only because the report would be unreadable, but because society is so designed that politically relevant matters are in *Spiegel*, quite independent of the contents and arguments. Suddenly the result loses any trace of research for private consumption; it haunts thousands of minds and thus demands personal responsibility and public (counter-)statements.

The power to define problems and priorities that can be developed under these conditions (and should under no circumstances be confused with a 'power of the editors', but coincides rather with the editorial work of employees) certainly relies at heart on circulation figures and ratings and the resulting fact that the political sphere can only ignore *published* public opinion at the risk of losing votes. It is therefore strengthened and stabilized by television viewing habits and new information technologies, but it also gains importance through the demystification of scientific rationality in risk society. From the wealth of hypothetical findings, publication in the mass media selects specific examples which thereby achieve the addition of familiarity and credibility that they can no longer attain as pure scientific results.

The consequence for politics is that reports on discoveries of toxins in refuse dumps, if catapulted overnight into the headlines, change the political agenda. The established public opinion that the forests are dying compels new priorities. When it has been scientifically confirmed on the European level that formaldehyde has carcinogenic effects, the previous chemical policy is threatened with collapse. It is necessary to react to all of this with staged political events – arguments or bills or financial plans. This defining power of media publicity can obviously never anticipate the political decision; and it remains for its part connected into the economic, legal and political presuppositions and concentrations of capital in the news business.

A final field of sub-politics should at least be mentioned here, that of *privacy*. The number of births is a key quantity for all areas of politics; likewise, the question of how people handle parenthood, for instance, whether the mother wishes to remain in her career or to withdraw completely back into the family. By nature, all the questions to which men and women must find an answer in their living situations have a political side. In that respect, the 'problem indicators' – rising divorce rates, declining birth rates, the increases in extramarital living situations – not only depict the situation of the familial and extrafamilial relationships between men and women, but also signal rapidly changing parameters for all political plans and directions. Decisions taken here (whether to have children, the number and the timing, for instance) are removed from external interventions even if serious turning points for retirement policy, labor market policy, welfare law and social policy are connected to them. And this is so precisely because according to the constitutionally guaranteed arrangement of family and privacy these decisions fall exclusively within the responsibility of the couples living together.

Legal protections for the private sphere have long existed. But they have not weighed so heavily for a long time. Only with the *detraditionalization* of lifeworlds do these free spaces come into existence, and along with them the uncertainty in the social foundations of politics. Women's achievement of equality in education and their rush into the labor market signify on the one hand only an extension to a previously excluded group of the equal opportunity that had always been guaranteed. The consequences, on the other hand, are that the situation is *changed all around*: in the family, marriage, parenthood; in the development of births and of unemployment; in welfare law; in the employment system; and so on. In this sense, individualization processes broaden the scope for sub-political structuring and decision-making in the private sphere, below the level where state influence is possible. In this sense too, the claim of the women's movement 'the personal is political' hits upon a state of affairs that is emerging more and more in history.

These different partial arenas of cultural and social sub-politics – media publicity, judiciary, privacy, citizens' initiative groups and the new social movements – add up to *forms of a new culture*, some extra-institutional, some institutionally protected. Such a politics escapes categorization, yet even in its fluid forms, or especially because of them, it has become an important factor influencing policy and the techno-economic development in Germany over the past two decades. The effectiveness of this political culture relies on filling the abstract rules of the law with social life; more precisely, on breaking open and overcoming the selective interpretation of universally valid basic laws piece by piece. A code word for this development is floating around in many disciplines of social science and in political discussion: *participation*. It is by no means necessary to glorify the development that has begun; one can decisively criticize its excesses tending toward a new mysticism and yet surmise with good reason that the quality and dissemination of this thinking have already changed the political landscape in Germany permanently and will do so even more clearly in the future.

Nor has the social and cultural differentiation of politics in the wake of its successes in the parliamentary system passed by political sociology without a trace. The rational-choice, hierarchical means–end model of politics (which was probably always fictitious, but was cultivated for a long time by bureaucracy research and decision theory) has begun to crumble. It is being displaced by theories that emphasize consultation, interaction, negotiation, network: in short, the *interdependency and process character* in the context of the responsible, affected and interested agencies and actors from the formulation of programs through the choice of measures to the forms of their enforcement. While the traditional understanding of politics proceeded with a certain naiveté from the assumption that the goals set can be reached by politics, provided the proper means are taken, politics in newer approaches is now viewed as the collaboration of different agents even *contrary* to formal hierarchies and *across* fixed responsibilities.

Thus, research has shown that the system of executive administrative agencies is often characterized by the lack of strict authority relationships and the dominance of horizontal connecting channels. Even in the case where formal hierarchical dependency relationships are present between superior and subordinate authorities, the possibilities of vertical influence are often not fully utilized (Mayntz 1980). In different stages of the political process quite different agents and groups of agents attain opportunities for consultation and cooperation. All of this emphasizes the *contingency* of the political sphere which has externally remained consistently hierarchical in the formal sense. At the same time this fluidization of politics into a *political process* is only being half-heartedly appreciated by social science. The directedness and structure of this process (in program, for instance, or in measures, enforcement, etc.) is still *assumed* (simply for reasons of the practicability of political science analysis). The fiction of the political-administrative system as the center for politics likewise continues to exist. In that way, however, the development which occupies the center of attention here cannot come into sight: the unbinding of politics.

Political Culture and Technical Development: the End of the Consensus on Progress?

Modernization in the political system constricts the scope of action in politics. Political utopias (democracy, the welfare state) that *have been established constrain* us, legally, economically and socially. In parallel to that, and alternatively, entirely new opportunities for intervention are opened up through modernization in the techno-economic system. Cultural constants and basic prerequisites of life and work to this point can be made inoperative with these. Microelectronics permits us to change the social constitution of the employment system. Gene technology puts humankind in an almost godlike position, in which it is able to create new materials and living creatures and revolutionize the biological and cultural foundations of the family. This generalization of the principle of design and constructibility, which now encompasses even the subject whom it was once supposed to serve, exponentiates the risks and politicizes the places, conditions and means of their origin and interpretation.

That the 'old' industrial society was obsessed with progress has often been emphasized. For all the criticism of that fact – from early Romanticism until today – there has never been a questioning of that *latent* faith in progress which has grown so precarious today with the growth of risks: the faith in the method of trial and error, the possibility of a systematic mastery of external and internal nature that was being gradually constructed. (Despite all the setbacks and secondary problems and all its critique of 'capitalistic faith in progress', this myth was obligatory until quite recently for the political left as well.) Additionally this background music of the critique of civilization has not deprived the social changes occurring under the sails of progress of *one iota of their momentum*. This points to the peculiarities of the process, in which social changes can occur 'incognito' as it were. 'Progress' is much more than an ideology; it is a 'normal' institutionalized *extra-parliamentary structure of action for the permanent changing of society*. Paradoxically enough, in the extreme case it can even push through the overthrow of previously prevailing relationships with the police power of the state against resistance that wishes to preserve the status quo.

In order to be able to understand this legitimating power of the consensus on progress, it is necessary to recollect a by now almost forgotten connection, that of the *relationship of social and political culture to techno-economic development*. At the beginning of this century the cultural influence on the system of labor, technology and business was the focus of a series of classical studies in social science. Max Weber demonstrated how important the Calvinist religious ethic and the 'inward asceticism' contained in it were in the rise and establishment of 'professionalism' and capitalistic business activity. More than a half century ago, Thorsten Veblen argued that the laws of economics are not constantly valid and cannot be understood independently, but are instead completely connected into the cultural system of society. If social forms of living and values change, then economic principles must also be transformed. If, for instance, the majority of the population rejects the values of economic growth (for whatever reason), then our thinking about the structuring of labor, the criteria of productivity and the direction of development will become dubious and a new type of pressure for political action will arise. In this sense, Weber and Veblen were arguing (each in his own way) that work, technological change and economic development are tied into the system of cultural norms, the prevailing expectations and the value orientations of people.

This basically evident insight, which was also advocated by a number of other authors,[3] has hardly attained any practical importance in the meantime beyond lip service. First of all, this is probably due to the fact that, to put it in an oversimplified way, social and political culture remained *stable* from the post World War II period into the sixties. A 'variable' that is constant does not enter the field of view; in that sense it is no longer a variable and can remain unrecognized in its significance. This changes instantly where the stability begins to crumble. Only retrospectively, so to speak, with the breakup of the normative background cultural consensus, does its significance for the development of the economy and technology become visible. In the boom of the post-war period in Germany (but also in other Western industrial states), *economic, technical and individual progress were obviously interlinked.* 'Economic growth', 'increases in productivity' or 'technological innovations' were not only economic objectives that suited the management's interests in the increase of capital. They also led, in a way visible to everyone, to the reconstruction of society, to growing opportunities for individual consumption, and to a 'democratization' of previously exclusive standards of living. The intermeshing of individual, social and economic interests in the pursuit of 'progress', understood in economic and technological terms, was successful against the background of the destruction left by the war to the extent that on the one hand the boom actually took hold, and on the other the extent of the technological innovations appeared calculable. Both conditions remain tied into the political hopes for the welfare state, and in that way they stabilize the spheres of policy and nonpolicy of 'technological transformation'. In detail this *social design of the consensus on progress in technology policy* is based on the following three preconditions, which have begun to crumble since the rise of a new political culture in the seventies, among other reasons (Braczyk et al. 1986).

Firstly, the consensus has its foundation in the harmonizing formula *technical progress equals social progress.* The assumption goes that technological development produces obvious use values that can literally be felt by everyone in the form of labor saving devices, improvements of life, rises in the standard of living, and so on.

Secondly, only this equation of technological and social progress permits negative effects (such as deskilling, restructuring, threats to job security, dangers to health, or destruction of nature) to be treated *separately*, and *retrospectively*, as 'social consequences of technological change'. 'Social consequences' are characteristically *injuries*, specifically, particular secondary problems for certain groups, which never call the socially evident value of the technological development itself into question. The talk of the social consequences here permits two things. For one, any claim for social and political structuring of the technological development is fended off. Additionally, controversies on the 'social consequences' can be fought out *without* harming the execution of the technological change. It is only possible and necessary to talk about *negative* 'social' consequences. The technological development itself remains undisputed, is closed to decision-making and follows its own inherent objective logic.

Thirdly, the carriers and producers of consensus on progress in technology policy are the industrial *bargaining parties*, the trade unions and the employers. Only indirect tasks fall upon the state – absorbing the 'social consequences' and monitoring the risks. Only the 'social consequences' are an object of controversy between the collective bargaining parties. Antagonisms in the assessment of the 'social consequences' always *presume* a *consensus* on how the technological development is carried out. This consensus over the central questions of technological development is fortified by a well rehearsed *common opposition* to 'hatred of technology', 'Ludditism', or 'critique of civilization'.

All the supporting pillars of this consensus on progress in technology policy – the separation of social and technological change, the imputation of systemic or objective constraints, the consensus formula that technological is equal to social progress, and the primary responsibility of the collective bargaining partners – have begun to disintegrate over the past twenty years, and not by chance or because of the machinations of cultural criticism, but in *consequence of reflexive modernization*. Latency and secondary effects have been ended by research on this matter (see above). As risks grow, the prerequisites for the harmonizing formula on the unity of technological and social progress have been canceled (see above). At the same time, groups enter the arena of the conflict over technology policy which are not provided for in the inter-organizational structure of interests and its forms of perceiving problems. In the conflicts over nuclear power plants or reprocessing facilities, for example, employers and labor unions, the supporters of the traditional technology consensus, have been forced into the spectators' gallery. The conflicts are now carried out directly between the state power and citizens' protest groups, and therefore in a *completely changed social and political scenario* and between agents who at first glance seem to have only a remoteness from technology in common.

Even this change between arenas and opponents is not coincidental. First off, it corresponds to the development of risk-intensive large-scale

technologies – nuclear power plants, reprocessing facilities, the universalization of chemical toxins – which enter into a direct mutual relationship to collective lifeworlds, outside the industrial arena. Additionally, the
growing interest of a new political culture in participation is expressed
there. From the conflict over reprocessing plants

> it is possible to learn that numerical minorities (e.g. 'opposing citizens' on the
> spot) must not be dismissed as trouble-makers and grumblers. The dissent they
> express has an *indicative value*. It indicates . . . a sweeping change of values
> and norms in society, or previously unknown differentiations between social
> groups. The established political organizations should take these signals at least
> as seriously as the election dates. A new form of political participation is
> announcing itself here. (Braczyk et al. 1986: 22)

Finally, science also fails as a source of legitimation. It is not the
uneducated or advocates of a new Stone Age culture who are warning of
the dangers, but more and more these activists are people who are
themselves scientists – nuclear engineers, physicians, geneticists or
computer scientists and the like – as well as countless citizens, for whom
subjection to danger and competence overlap. They know how to make
arguments, are well organized, in some cases possess their own
periodicals, and are in a position to provide the public and the courts with
arguments.

Thus an open situation is gradually coming into being; *techno-economic
development is losing its cultural consensus,* and at a point when the
acceleration of technological transformation and the accompanying social
changes are assuming an extent without parallel in history. This loss of
the previously accepted faith in progress changes nothing, however, of the
course of the technological transformation. This very misproportion is
what is meant by the concept of the techno-economic *sub-politics*: the
scope of the social changes varies inversely with their legitimation,
without changing anything of the enforcement power of the technological
transformation that has been transfigured into 'progress'.

The fear of the 'advances' in genetic technology is widespread today.
Hearings are held. Churches protest. Even scientists faithful to progress
cannot shake off their uneasiness. All of this takes place, however, like
an *obituary* for decisions taken long ago. Or rather, no decision ever
occurred. The question of 'whether' was never waiting at the door. No
committee ever let it in. It has always been on the way. The age of human
genetics, the reality of which people are debating today, actually started
long ago. One can say 'no' to progress, *but that does not change its
course at all.* Progress is a blank check to be honored *beyond* consent and
legitimation. The sensitivity of democratically legitimated politics to
criticism contrasts with the relative *immunity* to criticism of techno-
economic sub-politics which, unplanned, and closed to decision-making,
only becomes aware of itself as social change at the moment of its realization. This special structuring and accomplishment power of sub-politics
will now be pursued in an extreme case, medicine.

The Sub-Politics of Medicine – an Extreme Case Study

According to its avowed self-understanding, medicine serves health. In fact it has created entirely new situations, has changed the relationship of humankind to itself, to disease, illness and death, indeed it has changed the world. In order to recognize the *revolutionary effects* of medicine, it is not at all necessary to enter the thicket of evaluations ranging from medical promises of salvation to visions of immaturity.

One can argue whether medicine has actually improved the well-being of humanity. It is indisputable, however, that it has contributed to an increase in the number of human beings. The population of the Earth has risen by a factor of nearly ten. This is to be traced back primarily to a falling infant mortality and a rising life expectancy. Unless living conditions deteriorate dramatically in the coming years, members of socially unequal groups in Central Europe can count on reaching *on average* the age of seventy, which was still considered 'biblical' in the last century. This essentially reflects improvements in hygiene, which would have been unthinkable without the results of medical research. Mortality rates fell because nutritional and living conditions improved, and for the first time effective means were at hand to master infectious diseases. The consequences are a dramatic population growth especially in the poor countries of the Third World with the associated crucial political issues of hunger and misery, as well as radically growing inequalities on the world scale.

Quite a different dimension of the society-changing effects of medicine comes into view with the *divergence of diagnosis and therapy in the current development of medicine.*

> The apparatus of scientific diagnosis, the psycho-diagnostic theories and nomenclatures that have grown in great numbers, and a scientific interest that is penetrating ever further into the 'depths' of the human body and psyche – it is now obvious – have decoupled themselves from therapeutic competence, and have gradually . . . condemned it to 'lagging behind'. (Groß et al. 1985: 6)

The result is a *dramatic increase of so-called chronic illnesses,* that is to say, illnesses that can be diagnosed thanks to the more acute medical and technical sensory system, *without* the presence or even the prospect of any effective measures to treat them.

In its most advanced stage, medicine produces pathological conditions it defines as (for the time being or permanently) incurable, which represent totally new conditions of life and danger and *cross* the existing system of social inequalities. At the start of this century, 40 out of 100 patients died of *acute* illnesses. In 1980 these constituted only 1 percent of the causes of mortality. The proportion of those who died of *chronic* illnesses, on the other hand, rose in the same period from 46 to over 80 percent. In such cases, the end is preceded more and more often by a long period of illness. Of the 9.6 million West German citizens who were registered as having impaired health in the micro-census of 1982, nearly

70 percent were chronically ill. A cure in the original sense of medicine becomes more and more the exception as this development proceeds. Yet this is not the expression solely of a failure. Because of its *successes*, medicine also discharges people into illness, which it is able to diagnose with its high technology.

This development contains a medical and socio-political turn, which today is only beginning to become conscious and perceived in its far-reaching consequences. With its professionalized development in nineteenth century Europe, medicine has taken illness away from people by using technology, monopolized illness and administered it. Disease and illness were delegated wholesale to the institution of medicine for external mastery and were 'operated out' in one way or another by doctors in barracks-like 'hospitals', with the sick people largely remaining ignorant.

Today, conversely, the sick, who were systematically made and kept ignorant in dealing with their illness, are being left to themselves and other institutions, also totally unprepared for them: the family, the occupational world, schools or the public sphere. AIDS, the rapidly spreading immune system disorder, is only the most spectacular example of this. As a result of diagnostic 'progress' also, disease is being *generalized.* Anything and everything is 'sick' or can actually or potentially make one 'sick' – quite independently of how a person actually feels. Accordingly, the image of the 'active patient' is being brought out again; demands are being made for a 'working alliance' in which the patient becomes the 'auxiliary doctor' for the state of illness ascribed to him by medicine. The unusually high suicide rates show how poorly this about-face is being tolerated by the afflicted people. Among those suffering from chronic kidney disease for instance, whose lives depend on dialysis at regular intervals, the suicide rate is six times higher for all age groups than in the general public (on this see Stössel 1985).

The possibilities of *in vitro fertilization* and *embryo transplantation* that have recently been put into practice quite justifiably heat up emotions. The discussion is conducted in public under the misleading term 'test-tube baby'. This 'technological advance' consists essentially in the fact that

> the first forty-eight to seventy-two hours of human embryonic development, from the fertilization of the ovum to the first cell divisions, are transferred from the Fallopian tube of a woman to the laboratory (*in vitro* = in glass). The required ova are removed from the woman by an operative procedure. Prior to that, the ovaries are stimulated by hormones to produce several ova in a single menstrual cycle (superovulation). The ova are fertilized in a solution containing sperm and cultivated until the four- to eight-cell stage. Then, so long as their development is apparently normal, they are transplanted into the uterus. (Daele 1985: 17)[4]

The origin of the application of *in vitro* fertilization was the strong desire of many infertile women for children. To date, the treatment in most clinics is offered only to married couples. This restriction seems

rather anachronistic in view of the frequency of non-marital living relationships. On the other hand, opening this technology to single women
will lead to completely new types of social relationships, whose consequences cannot be predicted today at all. We are no longer dealing here
with the type of mother who is single following a divorce, but rather with
deliberate fatherless motherhood, which is historically unknown. It
presupposes male sperm donation *outside* any relationship. In that sense,
fatherless children would result, whose parents would be reduced to a
mother and an anonymous sperm donor. Ultimately this development
would lead to the retention of biological and the *abolition of social*
fatherhood (where all the equally social questions of *genetic* paternity
would be completely unresolved, such as descent, the inheritance of traits,
claims for support and inheritance, and so on).

An additional avalanche of problems is set free when one considers the
simple question of how the embryos should be handled *before* the implantation. When is the development of an embryo considered 'apparently
normal', so that it can be implanted into the uterus? From what point are
the embryos *not yet* or *already* unborn human life? '*In vitro* fertilization
makes human embryos available outside the body of a woman, and that
opens up a broad field of technical operations, some already realizable,
others which could become possible through further development' (Daele
1985: 19). Thus, following the example of the already existing sperm
banks, deep-frozen embryos could be stored and sold(?) in corresponding
'embryo banks'. The availability of embryos provides science with long-
hoped-for 'experimental objects' (language fails) for embryological,
immunological and pharmacological research. 'Embryos' – the word
stands for the beginning of human life – can be duplicated by division.
The resulting genetically identical twins can be utilized for determining the
sex or for the diagnosis of congenital or other diseases. Here are the starting points for new disciplines and practices: genetic diagnosis and therapy
on embryos, with all the associated fundamental questions. What constitutes a socially and ethically 'desirable', 'used' or 'healthy' genetic
substance? Who will perform this 'quality control of embryos' (this is
difficult to write) (Bräutigam and Mettler 1985), and by what right and
with what standards? What will happen to the 'low-quality embryos'
which do not satisfy the requirements of this prenatal 'entrance examination for the world'?

Many of the *ethical* problems raised by these developments in medical
technology (and others not mentioned here) which are nullifying traditional cultural constants have been recognized and competently discussed
(see also Jonas 1984; R. Löw 1983).[5]

A different aspect, however, will occupy the center of our attention
here, one that has so far been touched on only peripherally in the discussion: that is, *the analysis of medical progress as itself institutionalized, as
the institutionalized revolution of the lay public's social living conditions
without its consent*. How is it possible that all this can happen and that

only *subsequently* the questions regarding the consequences, goals and dangers of this *noiseless social and cultural revolution* must be pursued by a critical public against the professional optimism of the small clique of human genetic specialists, without real influence of their own and fixated entirely on their scientific conjecturing?

On the one hand, something incomparable is created here from what is seemingly comparable ('progress in medical technology'). One can admit that a degree of self-creation and self-change is inherent to human development. One can see that history presupposes and develops the ability to change and influence human nature, to produce culture, to manipulate the environment and to replace the constraints of natural evolution with self-created conditions. Still this should not deceive us that thrusts into new areas are occurring here. The talk of 'progress' presumes the subject whom all this is ultimately supposed to benefit. Unleashed thinking and acting in feasibility categories are oriented to the opposite, the object, the *mastery of nature* and the increase of social wealth it makes possible. When the principles of technological feasibility and arrangement encroach upon the subjects themselves in that way, then the very foundations of the model of progress are canceled. The bourgeoisie's pursuit of its own interests destroys the conditions of existence for the *citoyens*, who are ultimately supposed to hold all the democratic strings of development in their hands, according to the popular image of the division of labor in industrial society. *Surreptitiously, the mastery of nature becomes technical control of the subject in the truest sense of that word* – although, however, the cultural standards of enlightened subjectivity that this mastery was originally supposed to serve no longer exist.

This secret farewell to an epoch of human history takes place, on the other hand, without the necessity of crossing any barriers of consent. While the expert commissions all over the world are still drawing up their final report on the possible and unpredictable consequences of this step – which also means that political and social consequences lie far in the future – *the number of children produced in vitro is growing rapidly*. In Germany alone, more than seventy births were registered from 1978 to 1982. By early 1984 there were already over 500 with a total of more than 600 children. The clinics that conduct *in vitro* fertilizations have long waiting lists.

Thus, medicine possesses a *free pass* for the implementation and testing of its 'innovations', on the basis of the structure of its activity. The practitioner of medicine has always been able to undermine public debate and criticism of what a researcher may or may not do with a *policy of the fait accompli*. That no doubt also raises questions of scientific ethics. But such questions alone *foreshorten* the problem, like the attempt to reduce the 'power of monarchy' to the 'morality of the royal house'. This becomes even more important when one relates the *approach* and the *scope* of decision-making that changes society in politics to that in the sub-politics of medicine.

Despite all the criticism and skepticism regarding progress, what continues to be possible, even taken for granted, in the area of medicine would, if transferred to official politics, be equivalent to the scandal of simply implementing epoch-making fundamental decisions on the social future, while *bypassing* the parliament and the public sphere, and making debate on the consequences *unreal* by virtue of their realization in practice. This need not even express a failure of the moral quality of science. *According to medicine's social structure,* there is no parliament in the sub-politics of medicine, and no executive branch where the consequences of the decision could be investigated *in advance.* There is not even a social locus of decision making, and thus ultimately no firm decision and none that could be made firm. One must keep in view the fact that in the thoroughly bureaucratized, developed democracies of the West, anything and everything is scrutinized as to its legality, jurisdiction and democratic legitimation, while at the same time it is possible to abrogate the foundations of traditional life and living and bypass all bureaucratic or democratic monitoring and decision-making. This occurs under a storm of broadening criticism, but otherwise in extra-parliamentary normalcy.

In this way a complete *disequilibrium between external discussions and controls and the internal definition-making power of medical practice* comes into being and is preserved. According to their position, the public sphere and politics are always and necessarily 'uninformed', lagging hopelessly behind the developments, and thinking in terms of moral and social consequences which are alien to the thought and action of medical people. The most significant thing is, however, that they are of necessity talking about *unreal things*, about what cannot yet be seen. The consequences of external fertilization can indeed only be studied with empirical certainty *after* its implementation; beforehand everything remains speculation. The *direct* implementation on a living subject, which follows the inherent criteria and categories of 'medical progress', is confronted by fear and conjecturing on social consequences whose speculative substance rises in direct proportion to the depth of the encroachment on the prevailing stock of cultural certainties. Translated to politics, that means that deliberation over laws occurs *after* they take effect; only then are their consequences visible.

The collaboration of effectiveness and anonymity increases the structuring power of medical sub-politics. In this sphere it is possible to exceed limits with a self-assurance whose scope for social change on the one hand far surpasses the radius of influence of politics, and on the other could only attain realization in the realm of politics by passing through the parliamentary purgatory. In this sense the clinic and the parliament are quite comparable, even *functionally equivalent* with regard to the structuring and changing of social living conditions, but on the other hand they are not at all equivalent, since the parliament has *no* decisions of similar scope and *no* comparable opportunities for practically implementing them at its disposal. While the foundations of the family, marriage and relationships are being destroyed through research and practice in the clinics, the parliament and the government debate the 'crucial questions' of reducing costs in the health system, oriented to limitation and avoidance, although it is clear in any case that well intentioned plans and their actual implementation belong to two different worlds.

In the sub-politics of medicine, by contrast, the possibilities for thoughtless and unplanned exceeding of limits lie in the logic of 'progress'. Even *in vitro* fertilization was first tested in animal experiments. One can very well argue over whether that should be permitted. But certainly an essential barrier was crossed in applying this technique to people. This risk, which is after all not a risk for medicine, but for the next generation of people, for all of us, could and can be taken purely *immanently* in the circle of medical practice, and under the conditions and needs of a (global) competition for reputation which prevails there. This only seems to be a central 'ethical' problem of medicine, and is publicly perceived and discussed in such categories, *because* there already exists a social structure for the implementation of medical knowledge in practice without public consent or decision, which virtually excludes external monitoring and consultation.

One can formulate this central distinction between politics and sub-politics as: democratically legitimated politics, with its means of influence consisting of the law, funding and information (e.g. for consumers), possesses *in*direct sources of power, whose long 'implementation periods' offer additional possibilities for monitoring, correction and mitigation; the sub-politics of progress, by contrast, enjoys a *directness without implementation*. In it one could say that the legislative and executive branches lie united in the hands of medical research and practice (or related to industry, of management). It is the model of an undifferentiated authority to act, which does not yet know the separation of powers, and in which social goals only need be conceded to the affected parties retrospectively, as secondary consequences that have already become a reality.

This structure is of course most 'purely' defined in the medical profession. The doctors do not owe their structuring power to their special rationality or to their particular successes in the protection of the highly valued commodity, 'health'. Rather, it is the product and expression of a *successful professionalization* (at the turn of the twentieth century), and as a corresponding limiting case it is likewise of general interest for the conditions that give rise to the sub-political structuring power of professions (or in an 'incomplete' form, of occupations). There are several prerequisites. First, a professional group must succeed in protecting its access to *research* institutionally and thus opening for itself the sources of innovation. Second, it must succeed in essentially (co)determining the standards and contents of *training* and assuring in that way the transmission of professional norms and standards to the next generation. Third, the most essential and least often surmounted hurdle is taken where even the *practical application* of the knowledge worked out and the trained abilities occurs in professionally controlled organizations. Only then does a professional group possess an *organizational roof* under which *research, training and practice are interconnected*. Only in this constellation can substantively oriented structuring power be developed and affirmed without the necessity for social consent. The paradigm for this 'professional power circle' is the *clinic*. There the sources of influence for professional sub-politics are connected together in a historically unique manner in mutual affirmation and confirmation. Most other professional groups and organizations either do not control research as a source of innovation (social workers, nurses), or are cut off by nature from the application of their research findings (social sciences), or must apply them under extra-professional, industrial standards and controls (technology and the engineering sciences). Medicine alone possesses in the form of the clinic an organizational arrangement in which the development and application of research results to patients can be carried out and perfected autonomously and according to its own standards and categories in isolation from outside questions and monitoring.

In this way, medicine as a professional power has secured and expanded for itself a fundamental advantage against political and public attempts at consultation and intervention. In its fields of practice, clinical diagnosis and therapy, it not only controls the innovative power of science, but is at the same time its own parliament and its own government in matters of 'medical progress'. When it has to decide on 'malpractice', even the 'third force' of jurisprudence has to take recourse to medically produced and controlled norms and circumstances, which according to the social construction of rationality can ultimately be decided only by medical people and by no one else.

These are the conditions under which a 'policy of *faits accomplis*' can be conducted and extended to the cultural foundations of life and death. The medical profession thus finds itself in a position to subvert criticism, doubts and dictates from outside by the production of 'new facts'. Social expectations and standards of judgment are no longer pre-existent, but rather *reflexive*, that is to say, they are to be produced and defined in part by physicians in research, diagnosis and therapy, and are thus *changeable*. What is socially considered 'health' and 'disease' loses its pre-ordained 'natural' character in the framework of the medical monopoly and becomes a quantity that can be produced in the work of medicine. 'Life' and 'death' in this view are no longer permanent values and concepts beyond the reach of human beings. Rather, what is considered and recognized socially as 'life' and 'death' *becomes contingent in and through the work of medical people themselves*. It must be redetermined with all the foreseeable implications – and *against the background and on the foundation of circumstances, problems and criteria produced by medicine and biology*. Thus, following the advances in heart and brain surgery, it must again be decided and established whether a person 'is' dead if the brain fails but the heart is still beating, if the functioning of the heart can only be guaranteed artificially by corresponding complicated apparatus, or if certain brain functions fail (so that the patient is permanently 'unconscious') while other bodily functions remain intact, and so forth.

On the basis of the possibilities for genetic technology opened up by *in vitro* fertilization, life is no longer equal to life, and death is no longer equal to death. Once rather unambiguous fundamental categories and evident circumstances in humankind's understanding of itself and the world are being overrun by matters of fact that can be and have been produced, unasked, by medicine, and they then become contingent and changeable. New situations requiring a decision that were not present during the earlier evolution are being continually produced and (at least in part) they have always been answered in advance in medical practice for the benefit of research-oriented medicine. The decision patterns can themselves be 'mastered' politically and legally only on the basis of medical diagnoses (certainly in collaboration with other professions). In this way the medical view of things *objectivizes* itself and expands ever more deeply and broadly into all aspects of life and areas of human existence. In more and more fields of action a *reality* defined and thoroughly structured by medicine is becoming the prerequisite of thought and action. A medically shaped law, 'medically evaluated' labor technologies, environmental data, and norms for environmental protection or eating habits come into existence. In this way, not only is the spiral of medical formation and decision-making twisted deeper and deeper into the second reality of the risk society, but an *insatiable appetite for medicine* is produced, a permanently expanding market for the services of the medical profession whose ramifications echo into the distant depths.

An occupational group that has managed such an interconnection of science, training and practice possesses more than just a certain 'professional strategy' to protect the market for its offerings – a legal monopoly or exclusive access to training or certification and the like (on this see Beck and Brater 1978). Far beyond that, it possesses a golden goose, so to speak, 'laying' possible market strategies. This professional organizational setting is the equivalent of a *reflexive market strategy*, because it puts the professional group in a position to *produce continually new professional strategies* from its control of the cognitive development in the field of activity it monopolizes. Thus it is able to profit from self-produced risks and hazardous conditions and to extend its own area of activity continually through related techno-therapeutic innovations.

This professional dominance of medicine must *not*, however, be confused with or equated to *personal* power of the physician. Medical structuring power is exercised instead in professional form and there is a characteristic built-in barrier between the private interests of those active in the profession and the maintenance and exercise of political and social functions. The police, judges, or the administrative officials are also not able to employ the powers of domination delegated to them like a prince in his kingdom in order to increase their personal power, and not only because legal regulations, monitors and supervisors prevent them. They are also unable to do this because in the very form of the profession there is an embedded indifference of their private economic interests (income, career and so on) with respect to the substantive goals and side effects of their work. Individual doctors are cut off from the socially transforming scope of their interventions. The latter do not even fall within their horizon of reference; they are shifted off in any case into the side effects of medical practice. What is of primary and central importance for physicians is 'medical progress', as internally defined and controlled within the profession. Of course, successes in this direction do not register directly, but only *translated*, into career opportunities, salary, or position in the hierarchy. In this sense, salaried physicians conducting research into human genetics are *dependent like every other employee*. They can be discharged, replaced, monitored by others as to the 'professional' performance of their task, and they are subject to external directions and regulation (Beck 1979).

A further characteristic of sub-politics expresses itself here, which is elaborated in different ways in different fields of activity. Whereas in politics consciousness and influence can coincide, at least in theory, with the functions and tasks performed, *in the field of sub-politics, consciousness and actual effects, social change and influence systematically diverge*. To put it differently, the scope of the social changes set loose need not be correlated at all with commensurate gains in power, but conversely can even coincide with a lack of influence. Thus a relatively small group of researchers and practitioners of human genetics are promoting an upheaval in social circumstances, unconsciously and unplanned, in the apparent normalcy of their professional practice as employees.

The Dilemma of Technology Policy

Now one can say that the justification of techno-economic sub-politics is *derived from the legitimacy of the political system*. The fact that no *direct* decisions are made about technology in the political system ought to encounter little controversy. The side effects for which responsibility must be shared there are not caused by the politician. Nevertheless, technology policy controls the levers of financial support and the legislative channeling and cushioning of undesirable effects. Decision-making on techno-scientific development and its economic exploitation, however, escapes the reach of research policy. In relations to the state, industry possesses a double advantage, that of the *autonomy of investment decisions* and the *monopoly on the application of technology*. The strings controlling the modernization process in the form of economic planning, of the economic yield (or risk) and of the technological structure in the firms themselves all lie in the hands of economic sub-politics.

This division of labor in the power structure of modernization discharges the state into a multiple belatedness. First it struggles to catch up with the technological development, which was decided upon elsewhere. Despite all its support of research, its influence on the goals of technological development remains secondary. No votes are taken in parliament on the employment and development of microelectronics, genetic technology or the like; at most it might vote on *supporting* them in order to protect the country's economic future (and jobs). It is precisely the intimate connection between decisions on technological development and those on investment which forces the industries to forge their plans in secret for reasons of competition. Consequently, decisions only reach the desks of politicians and the public sphere after being taken.

Once decisions on technological developments under the cloak of investment decisions have been taken, they acquire and develop, of course, a considerable weight of their own. Now they come into the world with the constraint that investments have about them – they must *make money*. Fundamental objections would endanger capital (and, of course, jobs). Anyone who now points out the side effects harms the enterprises that have invested their future and that of their employees in these plans, and thus ultimately endangers even the economic policy of the government.

Therein lies a double limitation. Firstly, estimation of side effects occurs under the pressure of investment decisions taken in order to make a profit. Secondly, this is relieved by the fact that consequences are difficult to assess in any case, and governmental counter-measures require a long path and a long time for implementation. The consequence is the typical situation that 'industrially produced problems of the present, being based on *yesterday's* investment decisions and the technological innovations of the *day before yesterday*, will at best meet with counter-measures *tomorrow*, which will perhaps become effective *the day after tomorrow*' (Jaenicke 1979: 33). In this sense, politics therefore becomes specialized through the legitimation of consequences it has neither caused nor really been able to avoid. According to the design of the division of powers, politics remains responsible in a double sense for decisions taken in industry. The pseudo-political, industrial 'sovereignty' in matters of technological development possesses only borrowed legitimacy. It must be socially restored in retrospect again and again in the eyes of a public sphere grown critical. This need for the political legitimation of decisions that were not made is strengthened by the political and official responsibility for side effects. The division of labor thus leaves the industries with the primary decision-making power but *without* responsibility for side effects, while politics is assigned the task of democratically legitimating decisions it has *not* taken and of 'cushioning' technology's side effects.

At the same time, the demonstration of side effects (at least at an early date) collides with the economic and economic policy interests that are invested in the chosen path of technological development. The more the side effects (or public sensitivities to them) grow and the greater the interest in economic recovery becomes (also in view of mass unemployment), that much narrower becomes the freedom of action for technology policy, which is caught between the millstones of a critical public and economic priorities.

Relief is offered here by the model of progress. 'Progress' can be understood as *legitimate* social change *without* democratic political legitimation. *Faith in progress replaces voting*. Furthermore: it is a substitute for questions, a type of consent in advance for objectives and consequences that remain unknown and unmentioned. Progress is a blank page as a political program, to which wholesale agreement is demanded, as if it were the earthly road to heaven. The fundamental demands of democracy have been turned on their heads by the model of progress. Even the fact that one is concerned in progress with social change must be pointed out retrospectively. Officially, one is dealing with something quite different and always the same – economic priorities, competition in the global market, or jobs. Social change takes place only in *displaced* form. Progress is the inversion of rational action as a 'rationalization process'. It is the continuous changing of society into the unknown, without a program or a vote. We assume that things will go well, that in the end everything we have brought down upon ourselves can be turned back into progressiveness. But even asking about why or wherefore has something heretical about it. Consent without knowledge of wherefore is the prerequisite. Everything else is heresy.

Here the *counter-modernity* of faith in progress becomes clear. It is a type of *secular religion of modernity*. All the features of a religious faith apply to it, such as trust in the unknown and the intangible or trust against one's own better judgment, without knowing the way or the 'how'. Faith in progress is the self-confidence of modernity in its own technology that has become creativity. The productive forces, along with those who develop and administer them, science and business, have taken the place of God and the Church.

The fascination the ersatz god of progress exercises on people in the epoch of industrial society becomes all the more astonishing, the more closely one examines its earthly design. The *non*-responsibility of science corresponds to the *implicit* responsibility of the businesses and the *mere responsibility for legitimation* of politics. 'Progress' is social change institutionalized into a position of *non*-responsibility. The fatefulness of the faith in an absolute imperative transfigured into progress is, however, *manufactured*. The 'anarchy of side effects' corresponds to a governmental policy which is only able to give its blessings to prescribed decisions, to an economy that leaves the social consequences in the latency of the cost-intensifying factors, and to a science that introduces the process with the clear conscience of its theoretical attitude and wishes to remain oblivious to the consequences. Where the belief in progress becomes a *tradition* of progress that subverts modernity just as it created it, the *non-*

politics of the techno-economic development transforms itself into a *sub-politics* in need of legitimation.

The Sub-Politics of Industrial Automation

Functionalist and neo-Marxist analyses, as well as those of the sociology of organizations, are still thinking in terms of the 'certainties' of large organization and hierarchy, Taylorism and economic crisis, which have long been undermined by the developments in plants and the developmental possibilities in the enterprises. Along with the automation possibilities of microelectronics and other information technologies, with the environmental issues and the politicization of risks, *uncertainty* has even penetrated into the cathedrals of the economic dogmas. What seemed solid and mandated only a short while ago is becoming mobile: temporal, spatial and legal standardizations of wage labor (on this see Chapter 6 for a detailed discussion); the power hierarchy of large organizations; the possibilities of rationalization; all of these no longer conform to the traditional plans and relations. They reach across the rigid limits of divisions, plants and sectors; the structure of the production sectors can be renetworked electronically; technical production systems can be changed independently of human labor structures; in view of the requirements for flexibility dictated by the market, ecological morality and the politicization of production, notions of profitability are becoming fluid; and new forms of 'flexible specialization' (Piore and Sabel 1985) compete effectively with the old 'hulks' of mass production.

This surplus of possibilities to change structures need by no means be applied as part of organizational policy immediately, all at once or in the near future. And yet this confusion on future development among the interwoven influences of ecology, new technologies and a transformed political culture has already changed conditions today.

> In the prospering fifties and sixties it was still possible to predict the development of national economies with relative precision. Today it is no longer even possible to forecast the changing directions of economic indicators from one month to the next. Corresponding to the uncertainty about changes in the national economies is the confusion on the outlooks of individual sales markets. Management is unsure which products should be produced and what technologies should be employed for that purpose – indeed, it is not even certain how authority and jurisdiction should be distributed within the company. Anyone who talks with industrialists or reads the business press will probably reach the conclusion that many corporations would have difficulties arriving at comprehensive strategies for the future, even without governmental intervention. (Piore and Sabel 1985: 22)

Of course, risks and uncertainties are a 'quasi-natural' constitutive element of economic activity. But the present confusion displays new traits. It is all too clearly different from the Great Depression of the thirties. In those days, fascists, communists and capitalists were striving everywhere to emulate the technological example of one country: the United States. Ironically, at that time, when society as a whole appeared extremely fragile and susceptible to change, no one seemed willing to doubt those very principles of industrial organization which appear exceedingly dubious today. The current confusion over how technologies, markets and hierarchies are to be organized is the visible sign of the collapse of decisive, yet scarcely understood, elements of the familiar system of economic development. (Piore and Sabel 1985: 22f.)

The range of organizational social changes that are becoming *possible* through microelectronics is considerable. Structural unemployment represents a major fear, but only an intensification that still meets the criteria of the traditional categories for the perception of problems. In the medium term it ought to become of equal importance that the use of microcomputers and microprocessors *falsifies* the traditional organizational premises of the economic system. To put it bluntly, microelectronics is introducing a stage of technological development which *refutes technically* the myth of technological determinism. For one thing, computers and control devices are programmable, that is they are functional for the broadest variety of purposes, problems and situations. Thus, technology no longer prescribes how it is to be employed in detail; quite to the contrary, this can and must be fed into the technology. Hitherto existing legitimatory possibilities for arranging social structure according to 'objective technical constraints' are diminishing, or even being reversed. One must know what type of social organization in its horizontal and vertical dimensions one *wants*, in order to use the networking possibilities of electronic control and information technologies at all. On the other hand, microelectronics permits the *decoupling* of labor and production processes. That is to say, the system of human labor and the system of technological production can be varied *independently* of one another (Kommissionsbericht 1983: 167ff.).

In all the dimensions and on all levels of the organization new patterns are becoming possible – across the boundaries of divisions, plants and sectors. The basic premise of the industrial system on this point, that cooperation is *spatially bound* in an 'organizational structure' serving that purpose, is losing the technical basis for its necessity. But that implies, however, that the 'building blocks' upon which traditional notions and theories of organization are based are being exchanged. The latitude for organizational variations being opened up in this way cannot yet even be imagined. That is not the least important reason why they certainly will not be exhausted overnight. We are living at the beginning of an *experimental phase of organizational planning*, which hardly takes a back seat to the constraints to experiment with new ways of living in the private sphere.

It is important to assess the dimensions correctly. The model of *primary* rationalization, which is marked out by changes in the categories of job, skill and technical system, is being displaced by *reflexive* rationalizations directed at the premises and invariants of change to this point. The emerging latitudes for organizational arrangement can accordingly be circumscribed by the traditionally prevalent guiding principles of industrial society, among others, the *plant paradigm*, the *arrangement of production sectors*, and the constraint to *mass production*.

In discussions on the social consequences of microelectronics, a certain view is still predominant in research and the public sphere. It is asked and investigated whether in the final account *jobs* are lost or not, whether *skills* and their hierarchies change, whether new *professions* arise and old ones become superfluous, and so on. People still think in the categories of the good old industrial society and can hardly imagine that the latter no longer capture the emerging 'possible realities'. Often enough, such investigations issue a sort of 'all clear bulletin' such as that jobs and skills will change within an expectable range. The categories of the plant and the division, the assignment of the labor and production systems, and the like are held constant in this process. But the specific potential of 'intelligent' electronics for automation which is only gradually becoming visible, falls through this grid in which industrial society and sociology think and conduct research. We are concerned with rationalization of the *system*, which makes the seemingly ultra-stable organizational boundaries *within* and *between* plants, divisions, sectors, etc. appear malleable.

The characteristic of the impending waves of rationalization, then, is their *boundary-crossing* and *boundary-changing* potential. The paradigm of the firm and its embedding in the sectoral structure are up for grabs, including the structure of divisions in plants, the interaction of organization and cooperation, the coexistence of plant organizations – quite apart from the fact that entire divisions (in assembly for instance, but also in administration) can be automated, brought together in data banks and even directly connected electronically to the customer. In this is concealed an important opportunity for company policy to change *the governance of the workplace with an (initially) unchanged job structure*. The intra- and interorganizational structure can, so to speak, be changed under the cover (now more abstract) of the corporation around the jobs – thus bypassing the trade unions (Altmann et al. 1986).

The *organizational configurations* that can be produced in this way are not so 'top-heavy', consisting of fewer elements which can perhaps be recombined in a quite different way at different times. Each individual 'organizational element' then possibly possesses its own relations to the external world and pursues its own 'organizational foreign policy' specific to its function. The prescribed goals can be pursued without consulting the central organization about everything in advance – so long as certain effects (e.g. profitability, quick adaptations to changed market conditions, attention to market diversification) are met in a way that *can be monitored*. 'Domination', which was organized in the large industrial plants and the bureaucracy as a chain of command that could be directly experienced socially, is being delegated here to the united functional principles and effects. Systems come into being in which perceivable 'rulers' are becoming a rarity. The place of orders and obedience is being taken by the electronically monitored 'self-coordination' of 'functional elements' under presumed and that much more strictly enforceable principles of efficiency. In this sense the *transparent organization* with respect to performance monitoring and personnel policy may exist in the foreseeable future – probably with the effect, however, that this change in the form of monitoring mechanisms will accompany a *horizontal autonomization* of subordinate, subsidiary and coordinate organizations.

The microelectronic metamorphosis of the control structure will make the direction and monopolization of information flows a central problem in the 'plants' of the future. It is the case not only that the employees could become 'transparent' for the plants (management), but also that the plant could become 'transparent' for the employees and the interested environment. To the extent that the localization of production becomes worn and frayed, information becomes the central means that enables the connection and coherence of the production unit. Thus it becomes a key question who gets what information, by what means, and in what order, about whom and what, and for what purpose. It is not difficult to predict that in the organizational disputes of the future these *power struggles over the distribution and the distribution coefficient of information flows* will become an important source of conflict. This significance is further emphasized by the fact that, as a result of decentralized production, first the legal ownership of the means of production, and then the actual disposition over them is beginning to become more differentiated and the control of the production process is coming to hang by the thin thread of the manageability of information and information networks. This would only reinforce the monopolization of decision-making authority due to control of ever more concentrated capital.

The continuing constraints in the direction of concentration and centralization can be seized and organized in a new way through the help of telecommunications. It remains correct that modernity is dependent on the concentration of decision-making and on highly complex possibilities of coordination for the exercise of its tasks and functions. But these need not be carried out in the form of mammoth organizations. They can also be delegated through information technology, worked on in decentralized data, information and organizational networks, or provided by (semi-)automatic services in direct 'interactive cooperation' with the receivers, as has already been exemplified by automated teller machines.

Here a completely new sort of trend arises, one that is contradictory according to conventional concepts. The concentration of data and information is accompanied by the *dismantling* of hierarchically organized mega-bureaucracies and administrative apparatus based on the division of labor. The centralization of functions and information interpenetrates with *de*bureaucratization. Concentration of decision-making authority and the decentralization of labor organizations and service institutions both become possible. Irrespective of distances, the 'middle' level of bureaucratic organizations (in the administration, the service sector and the production sphere) is fused together in 'direct' interaction via video display terminals made possible by information technology. Numerous tasks of the welfare state and the state administration – but also of customer service, jobbing, and repair shops – can be transformed into a type of electronic self-service store, even if all this means is that the 'chaos of the administration' is transmitted in objectified form by electronic means directly to the 'mature citizen'. In this case the person entitled to a service no longer interacts directly with an administrative official, customer adviser or the like, but rather chooses the desired treatment, service or authorization according to a procedure whose rules can be looked up electronically. It may be that this objectification via data processing technologies is not possible, sensible, or socially realizable for certain central areas of service. For a broader realm of routine activities, however, that is not the case, so that in the near future a large part of the administrative and service routine can be performed in this way – saving personnel costs.

At least two organizational premises of the economic system in industrial society have been shown in these semi-empirical trend forecasts, in addition to the plant paradigm and the sectoral structure. The first is the *outline of the production sectors*, and the second is the basic assumption that industrial capitalist production must of necessity follow the norms and forms of *mass production* in the long run. It can already be foreseen today that the impending rationalization processes are taking aim at the sectoral structure as such. What is emerging is *neither* industrial *nor* familial production, *neither* the service *nor* the informal sector; it is a *third entity*, a blurring or a subversion of the boundaries in sector-spanning forms of combination and cooperation, for the peculiarities and problems of which we have yet to develop a conceptual and empirical sensitivity.

Already through self-service shops, and in particular through automatic teller machines and services provided via video display terminals (but also through citizens' or self-help groups and the like), there has been a redistribution of labor across sectoral boundaries. At the same time the labor force of consumers is mobilized *outside the labor market* and integrated into the commercially organized production process. On the one hand, this inclusion of unpaid consumer labor is certainly part of the free-market plan to lower wage and production costs. On the other hand, areas of overlap arise at the boundary of automation which can be understood neither as self-help nor as a service. The machines permit banks, for example, to delegate paid labor of tellers to the consumers who are 'compensated' with access to their accounts at all times.

In the redistributions between production, services and consumption, which are made possible by technology and are socially desirable, there is a bit of *clever self-abrogation of the market*, to which economists committed to the market turn a blind eye. One often hears talk today of 'shadow labor' or the 'shadow economy' and so on. It generally goes unrecognized, however, that shadow labor is spreading *within* market-mediated industrial and service-sector production, not just outside of it. The wave of automation sparked by microelectronics produces *hybrid forms* between paid and unpaid labor, in which the proportion of labor mediated by the market is *decreasing*, but the proportion of unpaid consumer labor is increasing. The wave of automation in the service sector can thus be understood as a transfer of labor from production to consumption, from the specialist to the general public, from compensation to self-participation.

As insecurity and risks increase, the interest of employers in *flexibility* is growing – a demand that has always existed, but is gaining competitive urgency today in view of the intermeshing of political culture and technical development on the one hand, and the possibilities for electronic organization of work, developments in production and market fluctuations on the other. The *organizational prerequisites of standardized mass production are beginning to crumble.* This overproduction model of industrial society still retains its spheres of application (e.g. long production runs in the cigarette, textile, electric lamp or food industries), but is supplemented and displaced by new types of hybrids, mass-produced *and* individualized products, as can already be observed in the electrical industry, among certain automobile firms and in communications. Different circuits or different combinations are produced and offered here, following a modular principle.

The adjustment of plants to the *de*standardization of the markets and to internal product diversification, as well as the accompanying requirements for rapid organizational adjustments in view of markets that are saturated or change due to the identification of risks, can either not be accomplished, or only awkwardly and cost-intensively with the traditional rigid plant organization. Such changes must always be pushed through from the top down, with a great expenditure of time, following a plan and in the form of orders (against resistance). In mobile, loose or fluid organizational networks, by contrast, these varying adaptation feats can be *incorporated into the structure*, so to speak. But then the struggle between mass and craft production, which history seemed to have decided, starts a new historical round. The victory of mass production, presented as eternal, could be revised through new forms of 'flexible specialization' on the basis of computer-controlled, innovation-intensive products in small production runs (Piore and Sabel 1985).

The era of the factory, the 'cathedral of the industrial age', is probably not coming to an end, but its monopoly on the future is being broken. These gigantic, hierarchical organizations, subject to the dictates of the machinery's rhythms, may have been suited to produce the same products and reach the same decisions over and over again in a comparatively stable industrial environment. But, to borrow a word from the language that grew up with those organizations, they are becoming 'dysfunctional' today for a number of reasons. They are no longer in harmony with the demands of an industrialized society in which the development of the self encroaches on the world of work. As 'organizational giants' they are incapable of reacting flexibly to the rapidly changing, self-revolutionizing technologies, product variations and politico-culturally conditioned market fluctuations in a public sphere that is sensitized to risks and destruction. Their mass products no longer meet the needs of the sub-markets that are splitting off. They are also incapable of properly utilizing the great inventive gifts of the most modern technologies for individualizing products and services.

The decisive point here is that this turn away from the 'giant organizations' with their constraints to standardize, their chains of command and the like *does not* collide with the fundamental principles of industrial production – maximization of profits, property relationships, ruling interests – but rather is forced by them.

Not all of the 'pillars' of the industrial system – the plant paradigm, the outline of the production sectors, the forms of mass production and the temporal, spatial and legal standardizations of wage labor – are being loosened or abolished all at once and across the board. Still, there remains a *systemic transformation* of labor and production which is putting the compulsory unity of industrial society's organizational forms of the economy and capitalism into its relative context as a historically transitory intermediary phase of roughly 100 years' duration.

This development – if it does indeed occur – will cause spring to break forth in the 'Antarctica' of the organizational premises from organizational sociology and (neo-)Marxism. Expectations for the change of industrial labor that had appeared to be cast in iron are being turned on their heads:[6] not of course as a new edition of a legalistic evolution of organizational forms with seemingly 'intrinsic superiority' on the road to capitalistic economic success, but as the *product of struggles and decisions about forms of labor, organization and operation*. That one is always centrally concerned here with power in production and the labor market, its presuppositions and the rules for exercising it, is obvious. As a result of the sub-political organizing spaces that open up in the operational rationalization process, the social fabric of the operation becomes *politicized*: less in the sense that a new edition of class struggles results, but more in the sense that the apparent 'single way' of industrial production becomes configurable, sacrificing its organizational unity, becoming *destandardized* and *pluralized*.

In the disputes between management, works council, trade unions and the rank and file workers, decisions on alternative models of work relations will be on the agenda in coming years. These models of work relations will be conceived along the lines of visions of everyday life. They will afford the possibility of a democratic socialism of everyday life – or the alternative of an authoritarian rule, the basis of existing property relationships. What is characteristic here perhaps lies in the fact that these two alternatives no longer exclude one another since the conceptualizations in which they are formulated no longer apply. The essential thing is that from one enterprise to another, from one sector to another, different models and policies can be propagated and tested. This could simply mean the proliferation of a succession of meaningless 'fads' in labor relations policy. All together, the tendency towards pluralization of forms of living is spreading to the production sphere. A *pluralization of the milieus and forms of labor* results, in which 'more conservative' and 'more socialistic', or 'more rural' and 'more urban' variants are locked in competition.

But that means that operational activity comes under *pressure for legitimation* to a degree previously unknown. It acquires a new political and moral dimension, which had seemed alien to economic action. This *moralization of industrial production*, which reflects the dependence of operations on the political culture in which they produce, ought to become one of the most interesting developments of the coming years. It is based not only on external moral pressure, but also on the intensity and effectiveness with which opposing interests (also those of social movements) have organized themselves, on their skill in presenting their interests and viewpoints to a public that is becoming more sensitive, on the market significance of risk definitions and on the competition of the plants with each other, where the legitimation problems of one party become the advantages of the other. In a certain way, the public gains influence on the plants in the course of the 'tightening of the legitimation screws'. The organizational power of the plants is not abolished, *but it is deprived of its a priori objectivity, its necessity, and its charitable nature*; in short, it becomes a *sub*-politics.

This development is what must be understood. Techno-economic action remains shielded from the demands of democratic legitimation by its own constitution. At the same time, however, it loses its non-political character. It is *neither politics nor non-politics, but a third entity: economically guided action in pursuit of interests.* This pursuit of interests, for one thing, has attained the scope to change society as the latency of risks has disappeared, and additionally has lost its façade of objective necessity in the pluralism of its decisions and revisions of decisions. Risk-laden consequences and alternative possible arrangements are bursting forth everywhere. The *one-sided* interest relation of operational analysis stands out in equal measure.

Wherever *several* decisions with quite *divergent* implications for *different* affected parties or for the general public are possible, business activity in all its forms (even extending into details of technical production and cost accounting) becomes liable to public accusations and therefore in need of justification. Even business activity thus becomes discursive – or it suffers in the market. Not just packaging but *arguments also* are part of the basic prerequisites for self-assertion in the market. If one wished, one could say that Adam Smith's optimism that self-interest and the public welfare would automatically coincide in market-dependent activity has been thrown out the window. The changes in political culture already mentioned are also reflected here. Through the influence of various centers of sub-politics – media publicity, citizens' initiatives, new social movements, critical engineers and judges – operational decisions and production methods can be publicly denounced instantaneously, and forced with the cudgel of lost market shares to give a *non*-economic, *discursive* justification of their measures.

If this has not yet appeared today, or done so only in embryonic form (for instance in disputes with the chemical industry, which has by now seen itself forced to issue full-page whitewashes in answer to public accusations), then that is once again a reflection of mass unemployment and the relief and market opportunities it offers to corporations. In that respect, the effect of the alternative political culture on techno-economic decision-making processes in the firms remains concealed in the abstract primacy of economic recovery.

Scenarios of a Possible Future

The modern religion of progress, no matter how contradictory it might be, has had its era and still exists in those areas where its promises encounter conditions that prevent their fulfillment. These were and are tangible material poverty, underdeveloped productive forces, or class-based inequities which determine political disputes. Two historical developments ended this epoch at the end of the seventies in the developed Western countries. While politics runs up against inherent limits with the expansion of the welfare state, the possibilities for social change from the collaboration of research, technology and science accumulate. *In this way, with institutional stability and unchanged jurisdictions, the organizational power migrates from the domain of politics to that of sub-politics.* In contemporary discussions, the 'alternative society' is no longer expected to come from parliamentary debates on new laws, but rather from the application of microelectronics, genetic technology and information media.

Political utopias have given way to speculation about side effects. Correspondingly, the utopias have turned negative. The structuring of the future is taking place indirectly and unrecognizably in research laboratories and executive suites, not in the parliament or in political parties. Everyone else – even the most responsible and best informed people in politics and science – more or less lives off the crumbs of information that fall from the planning tables of technological sub-politics. Research laboratories and plant managements in the future-oriented industries have become 'revolutionary cells' under the cloak of normality. Here the structures of a new society are being implemented with regard to the ultimate goals of progress in knowledge, outside the parliamentary system, not in opposition to it, but simply ignoring it.

The situation threatens to turn ugly with non-politics beginning to take over the leading role of politics. Politics is becoming a publicly financed advertising agency for the sunny sides of a development it does not know, and one that is removed from its active influence. The general unawareness of this development is exceeded only by the necessity with which it impends. With their gestures of preserving the status quo, politicians promote the transformation to an alternative society of which they cannot have even an inkling, and at the same time they blame 'anti-cultural agitation' for the systematically incited fears of the future. Businessmen and scientists, who occupy themselves in their everyday work with plans for the revolutionary overthrow of the present social order, insist with the innocent face of objectivity that they are not responsible for any of the issues decided in these plans.

But it is not just the people who lose their credibility, but also the role structure in which they are trapped. Where the side effects take on the extent and the forms of an epochal social change, the naturalness of progress comes into view with all its threatening character. The division of powers in the modernization process itself is becoming fluid. Gray zones of a political arrangement of the future are coming into being, which in conclusion will be sketched in three (by no means mutually exclusive) variants. The first is *back to industrial society* (reindustrialization); the second is the *democratization* of technological transformation; and the third is *differential politics*.

Back to Industrial Society

This option is being pursued today by the overwhelming majority in politics, the sciences and the public sphere – *across* the lines of political opposition and across the borders of nations. And in fact a number of solid foundations can be cited for it. First of all is its *realism*, which believes it has drawn the lessons from the past 200 years of criticism of progress and civilization, and is also based on an assessment of immutable market constraints and economic conditions. Arguing or acting contrary to these presumes – in this assessment – massive ignorance or masochistic character traits. According to this view, we are dealing today with a revival of 'anti-modernist' movements and arguments, which have always accompanied industrial development like a shadow – *without* ultimately being able to hinder its progress. At the same time, the economic necessities – mass unemployment or industrial competition – drastically narrow any room to maneuver politically. The consequence is that things will carry on in the same way anyway (with a couple of 'ecological corrective measures') as the knowledge of 'post-history', of the inevitability of the developmental path of industrial society, appears to confirm. Even the relief that counting on 'progress' has always offered seems to speak in favor of this option. The question 'What should we do?', which is asked anew by each generation, is answered by faith in progress: 'The same as ever, only bigger, faster, and more.' In that respect there is much to suggest that in this scenario we are dealing with the probable future.

The scenario determining action and thought is clear. It is a reprint from the experiences of industrial society since the nineteenth century, projected onto the society of the twenty-first century. According to this script, the risks produced by industrialization do not really represent a new threat. They were and are the self-made challenges of tomorrow; they mobilize new scientific and technological creative forces, and in that way they represent rungs on the ladder of progress. Many people sense the market opportunities opening up here, and trusting the old logic, they consign the dangers of the present to the status of items to be mastered technically in the future. They misunderstand two things here: first, the character of industrial society as a *semi*-modern society; second, that the categories in which they think – modernization of the *tradition* – and those in which we live – modernization of *industrial society* – belong to two different centuries, in which the world was changed as never before. In other words, they fail to see that in modernization – i.e. the putative constancy of innovations – a qualitative discontinuity appears in the guise of continuity. Let us look first at the consequences implied if we carry on in the present epoch with the mentality of the initial century of modernity.

Economic priorities occupy the foreground here. Their imperative radiates out into all the other issues and problems. This is even true where the leading role is given to economic expansion *for the sake of* employment policy. Now this basic interest seems to force one into a blind march with investment decisions that are made, through which the technological and thus the social development is set and kept in motion without an opportunity to make decisions, and with no knowledge of why and where things are going. This throws two switches. In the fields of technological sub-politics that power potential to overthrow social conditions accumulates which Marx had once ascribed to the proletariat – except that it can be used under the protection of state power (and under the critical eyes of the labor union alternative power and an uneasy public). On the other hand, politics is shunted off to the role of legitimating protector of external decisions that change society from the bottom up.

This cutback to mere legitimation is strengthened under conditions of mass unemployment. The more emphatically economic policy sets the course and the more clearly the combating of mass unemployment gains impetus, the greater the discretionary possibilities of the plants become and the less room the government has to act in economic policy. The consequence is that politics moves onto the slippery slope of *self-disempowerment*. At the same time, its inherent contradictions sharpen. Even in the full brilliance of all its democratic powers it limits itself to the role of advocacy for a development, whose official tendency to euphemism has always been called into question by the unchallenged elemental force with which it comes over society.

In dealings with risks, this public advocacy of something that one cannot know at all becomes open to doubt and turns into a danger for voter approval. The risks fall under the jurisdiction of governmental action, and that would, if applied, in turn require interventions in the contexts from which they originate, industrial production – interventions one has just forsworn as part of the coordination of industrial policy. Accordingly, one advance decision determines another so that actual existing risks are not supposed to exist. To the same degree as sensitivity to risks *grows* in the public, a political need for *minimization* research arises. This is supposed to guarantee the legitimatory representative role of politics scientifically. Where risks nevertheless pass the social process of origination (e.g. the dying forests) and the cry for politically responsible remedies gains a significance that could perhaps decide elections, the self-prescribed impotence of politics emerges openly. It constantly stays the hand with which it claims to want to create a political remedy. The tug of war over the introduction of the catalytic converter, speed limits on freeways, or legislation to reduce pollutants and toxins in food, air and water provide numerous exemplary illustrations.

This 'course of things' is by no means so unalterable as is often alleged. Nor does the alternative lie in the antagonism between capitalism and socialism, which has dominated this century and the last. What is decisive is, rather, that both aspects in the transition to the risk society, dangers and opportunities, have been misunderstood. The 'original mistake' of the reindustrialization strategy, which attempts to prolong the nineteenth century into the twenty-first, lies in the fact that the *antagonism* between industrial society and modernity remains unrecognized. The indissoluble equation of developmental conditions of modernity in the nineteenth century, which are gathered together in the project of industrial society, with the developmental program of modernity, blocks the view of two different things: first, that in central areas the project of industrial society amounts to a bifurcation of modernity in many respects; and second, that the adherence to the experiences and maxims of modernity offers the continuity and the opportunity to overcome the restrictions of industrial society.

Concretely, this means that in the rush of women into the labor market, in the demystification of scientific rationality, in the disappearance of the belief in progress, in the changes of political culture accomplished outside parliament, the demands of modernity are asserted *against* their bifurcation in industrial society even in those areas where thus far new livable, institutionalizable answers are not in the offing. Even the potentials for danger which modernity has systematically set free as industrial society, without any foresight and counter to the demand for rationality to which it is itself subject, *could* represent a challenge to creative fantasy and the human ability to shape the world, if they were finally taken seriously.

This historical misjudgment of situations and developmental tendencies now takes effect in detail. It may be that in the epoch of industrial society the previously mentioned 'blind march' between business and politics was possible and necessary. Under the conditions of the risk society, acting like this would mean confusing the basic multiplication table with a polynomial equation. The *structural* differentiation of situations *across* the institutional boundaries of business and politics would then be as invisible as the *distinct* interests of particular sectors and groups. In this way, for instance, *it is impossible to speak of a uniformity of economic interests with respect to the definition of risks*. On the contrary, risk interpretations drive *wedges* into the business camp. There are always *losers*, but also *winners*, from risks. But that implies that risk definitions do not deprive us, but rather make political decisions *possible*. They are a highly effective instrument for steering and selecting economic developments. In that respect the statistically well documented assessment is correct that perceptions of risk contradict economic interests only *selectively*, so that an ecological alternative would not necessarily run aground on its high costs.

The division of situations that cause risks between economic interests and politics lies along the same line. As side effects the risks fall under the responsibility of politics and not business. That is to say, business is not responsible for something it causes, and politics is responsible for something over which it has no control. As long as this remains the case, the side effects will also persist. This redounds to the structural disadvantage of politics, which not only has its frustrations (with the public, health care costs and the like) but is also continually being held responsible for something that is becoming more and more difficult to deny, but whose causation and change lies outside of the scope of its direct influence.

This circle of self-disempowerment and loss of credibility, however, can be broken. The key lies in the responsibility for side effects itself. Alternatively, political action gains influence in parallel to the *detection and perception* of risk potential. Risk definitions activate responsibilities and create zones of *illegitimate* systemic conditions, which cry out for change in the interest of the general public. Thus they do not cripple political action and need not be covered up at all costs against a systematically upset public with the help of a science that is either blind or externally controlled. On the contrary, risk definitions *open up* new political options which can be used to win back and strengthen democratic parliamentary influence.

Conversely, denial does not eliminate risks. On the contrary, what was intended as a policy of stabilization can very quickly turn into a general *destabilization*. The concealed risks themselves can suddenly change into social risk situations of such seriousness that it becomes inconceivable how the thoughtlessness of industrial society could have been handled so poorly – politically, and not just techno-scientifically. The sensitivity for appropriate action which has grown as democratic rights have become internalized cannot be satisfied in the long run by demonstrations of political futility and cosmetic, symbolic operations. At the same time, insecurities are growing in all regions of social life: professions, the family, gender relations, marriage and so on.

A society attuned to minimizing the problems is without preparation when the 'future shock' (Toffler 1980) hits it. Under the influence of that shock, political apathy and cynicism can grow rapidly in the populace, and the already existing gap between the social structure and politics, or the political parties and the electorate, can widen rapidly. Perhaps the rejection of 'politics' will then tend to affect not just individual representatives and parties, but the system of democratic rules as a whole. The old coalition between insecurity and radicalism would be revived. The call for *political leadership* would once again resound ominously. The longing for a 'strong hand' would grow to exactly the degree as people see the world crumbling around them. The hunger for order and reliability would revive the spectres of the past. The side effects of a politics that ignores side effects would threaten to destroy politics itself. Ultimately, it could not be ruled out that the still undigested past [of Germany (tr.)] might become a *possible* developmental option for the future although in a different form.

The Democratization of Techno-Economic Development

In this model of development, a connection is made to the tradition of modernity, which aims at expanding the degree of self-determination. The starting point is the assessment that in the innovation process of industrial society the opportunities for democratic self-determination were *institutionally truncated*. From the outset, techno-economic innovations as a motor for permanent social change have been excluded from the possibility of democratic consultation, monitoring and resistance. Therefore a number of contradictions are built into the design of the innovation process, and these are opening up today.

Modernization is considered 'rationalization', although something is happening to the system here that is beyond our conscious knowledge and control. On the one hand, industrial society can only be conceived of as a democracy; yet on the other hand, it has always held the possibility that the society may turn from the lack of knowledge, which moves it, into the opposite of its assumed claim to enlightenment and progress. To the degree that this is a threat, faith and skepticism in the progressiveness of the unleashed movement once again come into opposition to a social form that more than any other has made knowledge and the ability to get it the basis of its development. Doctrinal conflicts and the associated tendencies to brand some as heretics and rebuild the piles for burning them come to determine a social development that had once relied on the rational solution of conflicts.

Science, which played an essential part in setting everything in motion, has excused itself from the consequences and takes refuge for its own part in decision-making, into which modernity transforms everything anyway. Therefore, what matters now – the conclusion goes – is to make this basis for decision-making publicly accessible, according to the rules provided for such things in the recipe book of modernity: *democratization*. The proven instruments of the political system are to be expanded to conditions outside it. Many variants of this are conceivable and under discussion. The palette of suggestions extends from parliamentary checks on corporate technology development, to special 'modernization parliaments' in which interdisciplinary groups of experts would look through, evaluate and approve plans, all the way to inclusion of citizens' groups in technological planning and the decision-making processes in research policy.

The basic thought runs like this: the auxiliary and alternative governments of techno-economic sub-politics – science and research – could be brought under parliamentary responsibility. If they are to function as an auxiliary government by virtue of their freedom of investment and research, then they should at least be compelled to justify themselves before the democratic institutions on basic decisions of the 'rationalization process'. But this simplistic transfer is precisely where the *cardinal problem* of this cognitive and political approach is located. In its prescriptions it continues to be related to the epoch of industrial society, even through the opposite demand of the reindustrialization strategy. The nineteenth century understanding of 'democratization' presumes centralization, bureaucratization and the like, and thus connects up to conditions which have historically become to some degree antiquated and to some degree questionable.

The goals that are to be achieved through democratization are clear enough; the practice of having public political discussions only after research and investment decisions are made is to be broken up. The demand is that the consequences and organizational freedom of action of microelectronics or genetic technology belong in parliament *before* the fundamental decisions on their application have been taken. The consequences of such a development can easily be forecast: bureaucratic-parliamentary obstacles to plant automation and scientific research.

This is, however, only one variant of this model of the future. For the other one, the expansion of the welfare state serves as the exemplar. In crude terms, one argues in relation to the poverty risk of the nineteenth and the first half of the twentieth century. Poverty risks and technological risks are side effects of the industrialization process in different historical phases of its development. Both types of industrialization risks follow a similar political trajectory – shifted in time – so that it is possible to learn from experience in dealing with poverty risks socially and politically for the treatment of technological risks. The political and historical trajectory of the poverty risk – bitter denial; the struggle for perception and recognition; the political and legal consequences of the expansion of the welfare state – seems to be repeating itself in the case of global risk situations on a new level and in a new field. Precisely as the expansion of the welfare state in this century shows, denial is not the only option with regard to industrially produced risk situations. They can also be converted into an *expansion* of opportunities for political action and of democratic rights to protection.

The representatives of this development envision an *ecological variant of the welfare state*. This can even provide answers to *two* fundamental problems, destruction of nature and mass unemployment. Appropriate legal regulations and political institutions will be created along the pattern of welfare policy laws and institutions. Agencies would have to be created and equipped with the appropriate jurisdictions in order to combat the exploitation of nature effectively. By analogy to old-age insurance, an insurance system could be established against health damage from environmental and nutritional pollution. Of course, for that it would be necessary to change the legal basis so as not to afflict the victim with the difficult burden of causal proof, on top of all his or her other problems.

The limitations and collateral problems of welfare state interventions that have by now appeared need not necessarily apply equally to the extension to ecology. Here too, there will be resistance from private investors. In the case of welfare state protections, these had their objective basis in the rising wage and fringe benefit costs. Similar wholesale burdens that affect all enterprises *are absent* in technology policy initiatives. They also register as costs for some, but they open up new markets for others. The costs and opportunities for expansion are unequally distributed between sectors and plants, one might say. From that fact, opportunities result for the establishment of a correspondingly ecology-oriented policy. The interest bloc of business falls apart under the impression of risk selectivity. Coalitions can be created which in turn help politics to bring the anonymous creative power of progress into the realm of political democratic action. Wherever the presence of toxins threatens the lives of people and nature, or where the foundations of traditional social life and cooperative work are threatened by automation measures, expectations of politics are systematically produced that can be converted into an expansion of political democratic initiatives. The dangers of such an ecologically oriented state interventionism can be derived from the parallels to the welfare state: *scientific authoritarianism* and an excessive *bureaucracy*.

In addition to that, this way of thinking is based on an error that also characterizes the project of reindustrialization in that it is assumed that modernity has, or should have, a guiding political control center, through all its reproductions and obscurities. The control strings ought to be pulled together in the political system and its central organs – that is the argument here. Everything that runs counter to that is viewed and valued as a *failure* of politics, democracy and the like. On the one hand, it is implied that modernization means autonomy, differentiation, or individualization. On the other hand, the 'solution' of the sub-processes that fall apart there is sought in a *recentralization* in the political system, according to the model of parliamentary democracy. In the process, it is not only the dark sides of a bureaucratic centralism and interventionism which are excluded (they have by now become clear enough). Even before that, the basic state of affairs is *ignored, to wit, that modern society has no control center.* One may ask of course how the autonomization tendencies are to be prevented from being or becoming larger than the possible self-coordination of the subsystems or units. This question should not deceive us, however, as to the reality of the lack of a center or direction in modernity.

Neither is it necessary for alternatives produced in the process of modernization to lead down the one-way street of anomie. It is also possible to conceive of new intermediate forms of mutual control that avoid parliamentary centralism and yet create comparable compulsory justification. The development of political culture in Germany over the past two decades provides models for this, such as media publicity, citizens' action groups, protest movements and the like. The latter remain meaningless, as long as they are related to the premises of an institutional center of politics. Then they seem unsuitable, insufficient, unstable, or they may even appear to be operating on the margins of non-parliamentary legality. But if one puts the fundamental state of affairs at the center of analysis, the *unbinding* of politics, then the meaning of those phenomena as forms of experimental democracy reveals itself. Against the background of established basic rights and differentiated sub-politics, they are exploring new forms of direct consultation and shared control beyond the fictions of centralized direction and progress.

Differential Politics

The starting point for this plan of the future is the *unbinding* of politics, that is, the spectrum of mainstream politics, secondary politics, sub-politics and alternative politics that has arisen under the conditions of developed democracy in a thoroughly differentiated society. The assessment is that this lack of a center for politics can no longer be reversed, even by the demand for democratization. Politics *has generalized itself in a certain sense*, and has therefore become 'centerless'. The unalterability of this transition of executive politics into a *political process*, which has lost its uniqueness, its opposite number, its concept and its mode of acting all at the same time, is, however, not only an occasion for sadness. In it a *different epoch of modernization* announces itself, one which was characterized here by the concept of *reflexivity*. The 'law' of functional differentiation is subverted and nullified by *dedifferentiations* (risk conflicts and cooperation, the moralization of production, the differentiation of sub-politics). In this *second-degree* rationalization the principles of centralization and bureaucratization, along with the associated rigidity of social structures, come into conflict with the principles of *flexibility*. The latter gain increasing priority in the situations of risk and uncertainty that are coming into being, but also presuppose new, as yet unforeseeable, forms of *externally monitored self-coordination* of subsystems and decentralized units of action.

Starting points for a much more manageable *structural democratization* lie concealed within the historical transformation. This had its beginnings in the principle of the separation of powers (and in that sense it is already contained in the model of industrial society) and was further extended by freedom of the press, among other things. Today at the very least it is becoming obvious that the economic system also is a field in which not only are advances produced as the unseen results of self-interest and technical constraints, but also concrete sub-politics is conducted, in the sense of social change that could also go differently. Suddenly the 'techno-economic necessity' of pollutant emissions is shriveling under public pressure into one decision among several.

The historically aware person suspected that the conditions inside the walls of the private sphere need not follow the traditional patterns of marriage and family, or male and female roles, but not until the general detraditionalization was he or she given the knowledge of this or, what is more, the decision for it. The legislature has neither the right nor the opportunity to intervene governmentally here. The 'auxiliary government of the private sphere' can change the conditions of how people live together *here and now*, without proposed laws and resolutions, and is doing so, as the rapidly increasing variety of shifting modes of living illustrates.

Our view of this development is still being obstructed by the façade of intact reality which has been preserved from industrial society. The assessment presented here is that, today, monopolies which arose with industrial society and were built into its institutions are breaking up. *Monopolies are breaking up* – the monopolies of science on rationality, of men on professions, of marriage on sexuality, and of politics on policy – *but worlds are not collapsing*. All these are beginning to crumble for the most varied of reasons with manifold, unpredictable and ambivalent results. But each of these monopolies also stands in contradiction to the principles that were established along with modernity. Science's monopoly on rationalism excludes self-skepticism; the professional monopoly of men stands in contrast to the universalist demands for equality, under which modernity entered the scene; and so on. This also means, however, that many risks and issues arise within the *continuity* of modernity and are asserted *against* the bifurcation of its principles in the project of industrial society. The other side of the uncertainty that the risk society brings upon tormented humanity is the *opportunity* to find and activate the increase of equality, freedom and self-expression promised by modernity, *against* the limitations, the functional imperatives and the fatalism of progress in industrial society.

Perceiving and understanding the situation and the development has been essentially distorted because the external and the internal, the arranged and the actual role-playing, *systematically* diverge. In many areas, we are still acting out the play according to the script of industrial society, although we can no longer play the roles it prescribes in the actual conditions under which we live, and we act them out for ourselves and others although we know that everything actually runs quite differently. *The gesture of 'as if' has ruled the scene from the nineteenth to the twenty-first century.* Scientists act *as if* they held a lease on truth, and they must do this for the outside world, because their entire position depends on it. Politicians are obliged – especially during campaigns – to simulate a decision-making power which they know better than anyone else is a *myth created by the system*, and one that can be thrown right back in their faces at the next opportunity.

These fictions have their reality in the functional role-playing and the power structure of industrial society. But they also have their *unreality* in the jungle of obscurity which is precisely the *result* of reflexive modernizations. Whether misery is caused or alleviated by this is difficult to decide, not least of all because the defining system of concepts is affected and begins to blur. In order to describe or understand the achieved level of differentiated (sub-)politics at all, a *different understanding of politics* is required than that which is the basis for the specialization of politics in the political system. Politics has certainly not been generalized in the sense of a widespread democracy. But in what sense is this true? What losses and gains does the unbinding of politics signify for the political sphere and the networks of sub- and alternative politics, or, to put it more cautiously, might it imply?

The initial insight is that *politics must catch up with the self-limitation that has been carried out historically.* Politics is no longer the only or even the central place where decisions are made on the arrangement of the political future. What is at stake in elections and campaigns is not the election of a 'leader of the nation' who then holds the reins of power and is to be held responsible for everything good and bad that happens during his term of office. If this were so, we would be living in a dictatorship that elects its dictator, but not in a democracy. One can go so far as to say that all notions of centralization in politics are inversely proportional to the degree of democratization of a society. It is so important to recognize this because the compulsion to operate with the fiction of centralized state power creates the background of expectations against which the reality of political interdependence appears as a weakness, a failure, which can only be corrected by a 'strong hand', even though it is the exact opposite, a sign of universalized citizen rebelliousness in the sense of active cooperation and opposition.

The same applies to the other side of the same relationship, the varied fields of sub-politics. Business, science and the like can no longer act as if they were not doing what they are doing, that is, changing the conditions of social life and hence making policy *by their own means*. There is nothing disreputable about this, nothing that need be hidden or kept secret. Rather, it is the conscious arrangement and use of the scope of action that has been opened up by modernity. Where everything has become controllable, the product of human efforts, the *age of excuses is over*. There are no longer any dominant objective constraints, unless we allow them and make them dominate. That certainly does not mean that everything can be arranged exactly as we like. But it certainly does mean that the cloak of objective constraints must be discarded and thus interests, standpoints and possibilities must be balanced. Nor can the accumulated privileges to create *faits accomplis* that were previously shielded behind the optimistic promises of progress continue to hope for transplanetary validity. That raises the question of how research that redefines death and life, for instance, is to be controlled, if not through regulations or parliamentary decisions. To put it concretely: how can we prevent human genetic escapism in the future without choking off freedom of inquiry in research, which we cannot live without?

My answer is, *through the extension and legal protection of certain possibilities for sub-politics to exert influence*. Essential background conditions for this certainly include strong and independent courts, as well as strong and independent media, with everything that presumes. Those are, one might say, two of the main pillars in the system of sub-political controls. But as the past teaches us, they are not sufficient in themselves. A supplementary step is required. The possibilities of self-control that are held up by all possessors of monopolies must be supplemented by opportunities for *self-criticism*. That is to say, things that until now have only been able to make their way with great difficulty against the dominance of professions or operational management must be *institutionally protected*: alternative evaluations, alternative professional practice, discussions within organizations and professions of the consequences of their own developments, and repressed skepticism. In this case, Popper is really correct; criticism does mean progress. Only when medicine opposes medicine, nuclear physics opposes nuclear physics, human genetics opposes human genetics or information technology opposes information technology can the future that is being brewed up in the test-tube become intelligible and evaluable for the outside world. Enabling self-criticism in all its forms is not some sort of danger, but probably the *only way* that the mistakes that would sooner or later destroy our world can be detected in advance.

What kinds of regulations and protections this will require in individual cases cannot yet be foreseen in detail. Much would be gained, however, if the regulations that make people the opinion slaves of those they work for were reduced. Then it would also be possible for engineers to report on their experiences in organizations and on the risks they see and produce, or at least they would not have to forget them once they leave work. The right to criticism within professions and organizations, like the right to strike, ought to be fought for and protected in the public interest. This institutionalization of self-criticism is so important because in many areas neither the risks nor the alternative methods to avoid them can be recognized without the proper technical know-how.

For research, this would certainly have the consequence that it would be necessary to engage in *controversial and alternative* discussions on the risks of certain steps and plans in advance, and not only in intradisciplinary circles but also in *interdisciplinary partial public spheres* that would need to be created institutionally. Considering that this is as yet a completely unwritten page, it seems unnecessary to think in detail about the form in which this could be organized or what monitoring possibilities these interprofessional and supraprofessional agencies would be capable of carrying out.

Considerable opportunities to exert influence would be connected to this in turn, for official politics. Imagine how the discussion on reducing costs in health care could be enlivened, if we possessed an effective alternative medicine with strong arguments. Of course, that would also mean that politics could not re-establish its monopoly either. There would nevertheless exist a decisive difference from the various fields of sub-politics, which would probably increase in importance. While the battles over particular interests and viewpoints rage and should rage in business (and also in the sciences), politics could lay down the overall (juridical) conditions, check the general applicability of regulations and produce consensus.

That means that the *preserving, settling, discursive functions of politics* – which quietly are already dominant, but remain overshadowed by fictitious power constructions – could become the core of its tasks. By comparison with the centers of sub-politics, then, politics would exhibit a more *preserving* effect. The level of social and democratic rights already achieved would have to be protected from encroachments (even from the ranks of politics itself) and expanded. Innovations, by contrast, would have to continue down the paradoxical path of self-disempowerment, in which legal and institutional conditions would be created to enable ongoing processes of social learning and experimentation to continue against existing restrictions. Such processes include the development of new forms of living in the course of individualization processes, or pluralization and criticism within professions. Behind the façades of the good old industrial society that are still being propped up, could it be that, alongside the many risks and dangers, forms of this new division of labor and power between politics and sub-politics are already beginning to stand out and be practiced today?

Notes

1 Beck (1988: Part II) the *politics of risk* has been further developed, especially the politics of institutions and organizations.
2 Here the argument of this chapter is based on a *limited* concept of politics. The center of interest is occupied by the *structuring and changing of living conditions*, while politics as conventionally understood is viewed as the defense and legitimation of domination, power and interests.

3 Alongside Weber and Veblen, one should also mention here, among social scientists, Emile Durkheim, Georg Simmel, and more recently, John Kenneth Galbraith and Daniel Bell.

4 In the scientific experiments made possible in this way, the development *in vitro* is not limited *technically* to the stage at which the implantation in the uterus normally takes place. 'Theoretically, complete embryonic development *in vitro* could be attempted, with the goal of making a genuine test-tube baby possible. Embryonic cells could be utilized to make *chimeras*, hybrids with twins of other species. Chimeras are especially well suited for the experimental investigation of embryonic development. Finally, it is conceivable that one could 'clone' human embryos, perhaps by replacing the nucleus of the embryonic cell with the cell of another individual. This has already been done successfully with mice. For people, it could serve to produce genetically identical offspring or embryonic tissue that could be used as organ transplantation material without danger of an immune reaction in the donor of the cell nucleus. Of course, all of this is mere fantasy so far' (Daele 1985: 21).

5 To cite only one additional example, completely new complexes of problems and conflicts have also been created by *prenatal diagnosis and fetal surgery*, that is, the possibility of performing operative procedures on the embryonic child inside its mother's body. *The vital interests of mother and child are already split apart in this way before birth, while they are still corporally united.* As diagnostic and surgical possibilities grow, the definition of illnesses is extended to unborn life. Quite independently of the consciousness and volition of the therapists and their object, the risks of the operation and its consequences create *contradictory states of risk* for the mother (or the paid surrogate?) and the growing child in her womb. This is also an example of how, through developments in medical technology, social differentiations can be extended beyond the limits of the unity of the body into a psycho-physical relationship.

6 This applies, for instance, to the 'functional necessity' of fragmented industrial labor. As is known, it found its prophet in Fredric Taylor, who surrounded it with the aura of 'scientific management'. Even the Marxist critics of Taylor are deeply convinced of the inherent systemic necessity of this 'philosophy of the organization of labor'. They criticize the resulting meaningless, alienated forms of labor; paradoxically, however, they *defend* its 'realism' at the same time against the 'naive utopianism' of trying to break through this Tayloristic 'magic of necessity' and fully exploiting here and now the existing scope for 'more humane' organizations of labor. To put it rather pointedly: by now Taylor's *Marxist* critics are among the most resolute *advocates* of Taylorism. Blinded by the total penetrating power of capitalism, they fail to see that where Taylorism is still flourishing (or flourishing again) – which is the case in all too many places – this must by no means be interpreted as a confirmation of a 'governing necessity of the system'. Instead it is an expression of the unbroken power of a conservative managerial elite, whose historically obsolescent Tayloristic monopoly claims they are implicitly helping to stabilize.

BIBLIOGRAPHY

Preface

Adorno, T. W. (ed.) (1969) *Spätkapitalismus oder Industriegesellschaft?* Frankfurt.

Anders, G. (1980) *Die Antiquiertheit des Menschen. Uber die Zerstörung des lebens im Zeitalter der dritten Industriellen Revolution.* Munich.

Beck, U. (1985) 'Von der Vergänglichkeit der Industriegesellschaft', in T. Schmid (ed.), *Das pfeifende Schwein.* Berlin.

Bell, D. (1976) *Die Zukunft der westlichen Welt – Kultur und Technik im Widerstreit.* Frankfurt.

Berger, J. (ed.) (1986) *Moderne oder Postmoderne.* Special issue 4 of *Soziale Welt.* Göttingen.

Berger, P., B. Berger, H. Kellner (1975) *Das Unbehagen in der Modernität.* Frankfurt.

Brand, G. (1972) 'Industrialisierung, Modernisierung, gesellschaftliche Entwicklung', *Zeitschrift für Soziologie*, no. 1: 2–14.

Dahrendorf, R. (1979) *Lebenschancen.* Frankfurt. In English (1979) *Life Chances.* London.

Eisenstadt, S. N. (1979) *Tradition, Wandel und Modernität.* Frankfurt.

Etzioni, A. (1983) *An Immodest Agenda.* New York.

Fourastié, J. (1969) *Die Grosse Hoffnung des zwanzigsten Jahrhunderts.* Cologne.

Gehlen, A. (1963) 'Uber die kulturelle Kristallisation', in his *Studien zur Anthropologie und Soziologie.* Neuwied.

Giddens, A. (1990) *The Consequences of Modernity.* Stanford.

Giddens, A. (1991) *Modernity and Self-Identity in the Late Modern Age.* Cambridge.

Habermas, J. (1985a) *Der philosophische Diskurs der Moderne.* Frankfurt.

Habermas, J. (1985b) *Die Neue Unübersichtlichkeit.* Frankfurt.

Horkheimer, M., T. W. Adorno (1969) *Dialektik der Aufklärung.* Frankfurt. In English (1972) *Dialectic of Enlightenment.* New York.

Jonas, H. (1984) *Das Prinzip Verantwortung – Versuch einer Ethik für die technologische Zivilisation.* Frankfurt.

Koselleck, R. (1979) *Vergangene Zukunft.* Frankfurt.

Lash, S. (1992) 'Reflexive modernization: the aesthetic dimension', *Theory, Culture & Society*, 10, no. 3.

Lepsius, M. R. (1977) 'Soziologische Theoreme über die Sozialstruktur der "Moderne" und der "Modernisierung"', in R. Koselleck (ed.) *Studien zum Beginn der modernen Welt.* Stuttgart.

Lodge, D. (1977) *Modernism, Antimodernism and Postmodernism.* Birmingham.

Luhmann, N. (1989) *Ecological Communication.* Cambridge: Polity Press.

Schelsky, H. (1965) 'Der Mensch in der wissenschaftlichen Zivilisation', in his *Auf der Suche nach Wirklichkeit.* Dusseldorf.

Toffler, A. (1980) *Die dritte Welle – Zukunftschancen, Perspektiven für die Gesellschaft des 21. Jahrhunderts.* Munich.

Touraine, A. (1983) 'Soziale Bewegungen', *Soziale Welt*, 34, no. 1.

Chapters 1 and 2

Alexander, J., P. Sztompka (1990) (eds) *Rethinking Progress*. Boston.

Anders, G. (1983) *Die atomare Bedrohung*. Munich.

Bauman, Z. (1989) *Modernity and the Holocaust*. Cambridge.

Bechmann, G. (ed.) (1984) *Gesellschaftliche Bedingungen und Folgen der Technologie-politik*. Frankfurt/New York.

Beck, U. (1988) *Gegengifte: Die organisierte Unverantwortlichkeit*. Frankfurt. In English (1992) *Counter-Poisons*. Cambridge.

Beck, U. (1991) *Politik in der Risikogesellschaft*. Frankfurt. In English (1993) New York.

Beck, U. (1992) 'From industrial society to risk society', *Theory, Culture & Society*, 9(1): 97-123.

Berger, J. (ed.) (1986) *Die Moderne – Kontinuitäten und Zäsuren*. Special issue 4 of *Soziale Welt*.

Brooks, H. (1984) 'The resolution of technically intensive public policy disputes', *Science, Technology, Human Values*, 9, no. 1.

Conrad, J. (1978) *Zum Stand der Risikoforschung*. Frankfurt. Battelle.

Corbin, A. (1984) *Pesthauch und Blütenduft*. Berlin.

Daele, W. v.d. (1986) 'Technische Dynamik und gesellschaftliche Moral – Zur soziologischen Bedeutung der Gentechnologie', *Soziale Welt*, 37, nos 2/3.

Douglas, M., A. Wildavsky (1982) *Risk and Culture*. New York.

Eisenstadt, S. (1979) *Tradition, Wandel and Modernität*. Frankfurt.

Eppler, E. (1981) *Wege aus der Gefahr*. Reinbek.

Etzioni, A. (1968) *The Active Society*. New York.

Friedrichs, G., G. Bechmann, F. Gloede, (1983) *Großtechnologien in der gesellschaftlichen Kontroverse*. Karlsruhe.

Glotz, P. (1984) *Die Arbeit der Zuspitzung*. Berlin.

Habermas, J. (1971) *Towards a Rational Society*. London.

Jänicke, M. (1979) *Wie das Industriesystem von seinen Mißständen profitiert*. Cologne.

Jänicke, M., U. E. Simonis, G. Weegmann (1985) *Wissen für die Umwelt. 17 Wissenschaftler bilanzieren*. Berlin/New York.

Jungk, R. (1977) *Der Atomstaat. Vom Fortschritt in die Unmenschlichkeit*. Hamburg.

Kallscheuer, O. (1983) 'Fortschrittsangst', *Kursbuch*, 74.

Keck, O. (1984) *Der schnelle Brüter – Eine Fallstudie über Entscheidungsprozesse in der Großtechnologie*. Frankfurt.

Kitschelt, H. (1984) *Der ökologische Diskurs. Eine Analyse von Gesellschaftskonzeptionen in der Energiedebatte*. Frankfurt.

Koselleck, R. (ed.) (1977) *Studien über den Beginn der modernen Welt*. Stuttgart.

Kruedener, J. v., K. v. Schulert (eds) (1981) *Technikfolgen und sozialer Wandel*. Cologne.

Lahl, U., B. Zeschmer (1984) *Formaldehyd – Porträt einer Chemikalie: Kniefall der Wissenschaft vor der Industrie?* Freiburg.

Leipert, C., U. E. Simonis (1985) *Arbeit und Umwelt, Forschungsbericht*. Berlin.

Lepsius, R. (1977) 'Soziologische Theoreme über die Sozialstruktur der "Moderne" und der "Modernisierung"', in R. Koselleck (ed.), *Studien zum Beginn der modernen Welt*. Stuttgart.

Mayer-Tasch, P. C. (1985) 'Die Internationale Umweltpolitik als Herausforderung für die Nationalstaatlichkeit', *Aus Politik und Zeitgeschichte*, 20.

Moscovici, S. (1982) *Versuch über die menschliche Geschichte der Natur*. Frankfurt.

Nelkin, D., M. S. Brown (1984) *Workers at Risk*. Chicago.

Nelkin, D., M. Pollok (1979) 'Public participation in technological decisions: reality or grand illusion?', *Technology Review*, August/September.

Novotny, H. (ed.) (1985) *Vom Technology Assessment zur Technikbewertung. Ein europäischer Vergleich*. Vienna.

O'Riordan, T. (1983) 'The cognitive and political dimension of risk analysis', *Journal of Environmental Psychology*, 3: 345-354.

Otway, H., P. D. Pahner (1976) 'Risk assessment', *Futures*, 8: 122–134.

Otway, H., K. Thomas (1982) 'Reflections on risk perception and policy', *Risk Analysis*, 2, no. 2.

Perrow, C. (1984) *Normal Accidents: Living with High Risk Technologies*. New York.

Rat der Sachverständigen für Umweltfragen (1985) *Sondergutachten Umweltprobleme der Landwirtschaft*. Abridged, unpublished ms. Bonn.

Renn, O. (1984) *Risikowahrnehmung in der Kernenergie*. Frankfurt.

Ropohl, G. (1985) *Die unvollkommene Technik*. Frankfurt.

Rowe, W. D. (1975) *An Anatomy of Risk*. New York.

Schumm, W. (1985) *Die Risikoproduktion kapitalistischer Industriegesellschaften*. Unpublished ms. Frankfurt.

Schütz, R. (1984) *Okologische Aspekte einer naturphilosophischen Ethik*. Unpublished ms. Bamberg.

Short, J. F. (1984) 'The social fabric of risk: towards the social transformation of risk analysis', *American Sociological Review*, 49, December: 711–725.

Späth, L. (1985) *Wende in die Zukunft: Die Bundesrepublik in die Informationsgesellschaft*. Reinbek.

Starr, C. (1965) 'Social benefit versus technological risk', *Science*, 165: 1232–1238.

Stegmüller, W. (1970) *Probleme und Resultate der Wissenschaftstheorie*. Berlin/New York.

Strasser, J., K. Traube (1984) *Die Zukunft des Fortschritts. Der Sozialismus und die Krise des Industrialismus*. Berlin.

The Council for Science and Society (1977) *The Acceptability of Risks*. London.

Thompson, M., A. Wildavsky (1982) 'A proposal to create a cultural theory of risk', in H. Kunreuther and E.V. Ley (eds), *The Risk Analysis Controversy*. New York.

Touraine, A. et al. (1982) *Die antinukleare Prophetie. Zukunftsentwürfe einer sozialen Bewegung*. Frankfurt.

Umweltbundesamt (1985) *Berichte*, vol. 5. Berlin.

Urban, M. (1985) 'Wie das Sevesogift wirkt', *Süddeutsche Zeitung*, April 30.

Wambach, M. M. (ed.) (1983) *Der Mensch als Risiko. Zur Logik von Prävention und Früherkennung*. Frankfurt.

Chapter 3

Abelshauser, W. (1983) *Wirtschaftsgeschichte der Bundesrepublik Deutschland 1945–1980*. Frankfurt.

Alber, J. (1982) *Vom Armenhaus zum Wohlfahrtsstaat. Analysen zur Entwicklung der Sozialversicherung in Westeuropa*. Frankfurt/New York.

Allerbeck, K. R., H. R. Stork (1980) 'Soziale Mobilität in Deutschland 1833–1970. Eine Reanalyse', in *Kölner Zeitschrift für Soziologie und Sozialpsychologie*, 32: 13ff.

Badura, B. (ed.) (1981) *Soziale Unterstützung und chronische Krankheit*. Frankfurt.

Bahrdt, H. P. (1975) 'Erzählte Lebensgeschichten von Arbeitern', in M. Osterland (ed.), *Arbeitssituation, Lebenslage und Konfliktpotential*. Frankfurt.

Ballerstedt, E., W. Glatzer (1979) *Soziologischer Almanach*. Frankfurt.

Balsen, W., H. Nakielski, K. Rössel, R. Winkel (1984) *Die neue Armut – Ausgrenzung von Arbeitslosen aus der Arbeitslosenunterstützung*. Koln.

Beck, U. (1983) 'Jenseits von Stand und Klasse?', in R. Kreckel (ed.), *Soziale Ungleichheiten*. Special issue 2 of *Soziale Welt*. Göttingen.

Beck, U. (1984) 'Jenseits von Stand und Klasse', *Merkur*, 38, no. 5: 485–497.

Beck-Gernsheim, E. (1983) 'Vom "Dasein fur andere" zum Anspruch auf ein Stuck "eigenes Leben"', *Soziale Welt*, 34: 307–340.

Bellmann, L., K. Gerlach, O. Hübler (1984) *Lohnstruktur in der Bundesrepublik Deutschland. Zur Theorie und Empirie der Arbeitseinkommen*. Frankfurt/New York.

Bendix, R., S. M. Lipset (1959) *Social Mobility in Industrial Society*. Berkeley/Los Angeles.

Berger, J. (1983) 'Das Ende der Gewißheit – Zum analytischen Potential der Marxschen Theorie', *Leviathan*, 11: 475ff.

Berger, P. (1986) *Entstrukturierte Klassengesellschaft? Klassenbildung und Strukturen sozialer Ungleichheit im historischen Wandel*. Opladen.

Berger, P., B. Berger, H. Kellner (1975) *Das Unbehagen in der Modernität*. Frankfurt.

Bernstein, B. (1971) *Class, Codes and Control*, vol. 1. London.

Bischoff, J. et al. (1982) *Jenseits der Klassen? Gesellschaft und Staat im Spätkapitalismus*. Hamburg.

Blossfeld, P. (1984) 'Bildungsreform und Beschäftigung der jungen Generation im öffentlichen und privaten Sektor. Eine empirisch vergleichende Analyse', *Soziale Welt*, 35: 159ff.

Bolte, K. M. (1983) 'Anmerkungen zur Erforschung sozialer Ungleichheit', in R. Kreckel (ed.), *Soziale Ungleichheiten*. Special issue 2 of *Soziale Welt*. Göttingen.

Bolte, K. M., S. Hradil (1984) *Soziale Ungleichheit in der Bundesrepublik Deutschland*. Opladen.

Bonß, W., H. G. Heinze (eds) (1984) *Arbeitslosigkeit in der Arbeitsgesellschaft*. Frankfurt.

Borchardt, K. (1985) 'Nach dem "Wunder". Uber die wirtschaftliche Entwicklung der Bundesrepublik', *Merkur*, 39: 35ff.

Bourdieu, P. (1979) *La Distinction*. Paris. In English (1984) *Distinction: a Social Critique of the Judgment of Taste*, tr. R. Nice. Cambridge, Mass.

Bourdieu, P. (1982) *Die feinen Unterschiede*. Frankfurt.

Bourdieu, R., J.-C. Passeron (1971) *Die Illusion der Chancengleichheit*. Stuttgart.

Brock, D., H. R. Vetter (1982) *Alltägliche Arbeitsexistenz*. Frankfurt.

Buchtemann, C. F. (1984) 'Der Arbeitsprozeß. Theorie und Empirie strukturierter Arbeitslosigkeit in der Bundesrepublik Deutschland', in W. Bonß and H.G. Heinze (eds), *Arbeitslosigkeit in der Arbeitsgesellschaft*. Frankfurt.

Bundesminister der Sozialordnung (1983) *Arbeits- und Sozialstatistik: Hauptergebnisse*. Bonn.

Cohen, J. L. (1982) *Class and Civil Society: the Limits of Marxian Critical Theory*. Amherst.

Conze, W., M. R. Lepsius (eds) (1983) *Sozialgeschichte der Bundesrepublik Deutschland. Beiträge zum Kontinuitätsproblem*. Stuttgart.

Cottrell, A. (1984) *Social Classes in Marxist Theory*. London.

Dahrendorf, R. (1957) *Soziale Klassen und Klassenkonflikt in der industriellen Gesellschaft*. Stuttgart.

Engelsing, R. (1978) *Zur Sozialgeschichte deutscher Mittel- und Unterschichten*. Göttingen.

Feher, F., A. Heller (1983) 'Class, democracy and modernity', *Theory and Society*, 12: 211ff.

Flora, P. et al. (1983) *State, Economy and Society in Western Europe 1815–1975. A Data Handbook in Two Volumes. Vol. I: The Growth of Mass Democracies and Welfare States*. Frankfurt/London/Chicago.

Fuchs, W. (1983) 'Jugendliche Statuspassage oder individualisierte Jugendbiographie?', *Soziale Welt*, 34: 341–371.

Geiger, T. (1969) *Die Klassengesellschaft im Schmelztiegel*. Koln/Hagen.

Giddens, A. (1973) *The Class Structure of Advanced Societies*. London. In German (1979) Frankfurt.

Glatzer, W., W. Zapf (eds) (1984) *Lebensqualität in der Bundesrepublik. Objektive Lebensbedingungen und subjektives Wohlbefinden*. Frankfurt/New York.

Goldthorpe, J. H. (1980) *Social Mobility and Class Structure in Modern Britain*. Oxford.

Goldthorpe, J. H. et al. (1970) *Der 'wohlhabende' Arbeiter in England*, 3 vols. Munich. In English (1968) *The Affluent Worker*. London.

Gorz, A. (1980) *Abschied vom Proletariat*. Frankfurt.

Gouldner, A. W. (1980) *Die Intelligenz als neue Klasse*. Frankfurt. In English (1979) *The Future of Intellectuals and the Rise of the New Class*. London.

Haller, M., W. Müller (1983) *Beschäftigungssystem im gesellschaftlichen Wandel*. Frankfurt/New York.

Handl, J., K. U. Mayer, W. Müller (1977) *Klassenlagen und Sozialstruktur. Empirische Untersuchungen für die Bundesrepublik Deutschland*. Frankfurt.

Heinze, R. G., H. W. Hohn, K. Hinrichs, T. Olk (1981) 'Armut und Arbeitsmarkt: Zum Zusammenhang von Klassenlagen und Verarmungsrisiken im Sozialstaat', *Zeitschrift für Soziologie*, 10: 219ff.

Herkommer, S. (1983) 'Sozialstaat und Klassengesellschaft – Zur Reproduktion sozialer Ungleichheit im Spätkapitalismus', in R. Kreckel (ed.), *Soziale Ungleichheiten*. Special issue 2 of *Soziale Welt*. Göttingen.

Hondrich, K. (ed.) (1982) *Soziale Differenzierungen*. Frankfurt.

Hondrich, K. O. (1984) 'Der Wert der Gleichheit und der Bedeutungswandel der Ungleichheit', *Soziale Welt*, 35: 267ff.

Honneth, A. (1981) 'Moralbewußtsein und soziale Klassenherrschaft. Einige Schwierigkeiten in der Analyse normativer Handlungspotentiale', *Leviathan*, 9: 555ff.

Hörning, K. (ed.) (1971) *Der 'neue' Arbeiter – Zum Wandel sozialer Schichtstrukturen*. Frankfurt.

Hradil, S. (1983) 'Die Ungleichheit der "Sozialen Lage"', in R. Kreckel (ed.), *Soziale Ungleichheiten*. Special issue 2 of *Soziale Welt*. Göttingen.

Huck, G. (ed.) (1980) *Sozialgeschichte der Freizeit. Untersuchungen zum Wandel der Alltagskultur in Deutschland*. Wuppertal.

Kaelble, H. (1983a) *Industrialisierung und soziale Ungleichheit. Europa im 19. Jahrhundert. Eine Bilanz*. Göttingen.

Kaelble, H. (1983b) *Soziale Mobilität und Chancengleichheit im 19. und 20. Jahrhundert. Deutschland im internationalen Vergleich*. Göttingen.

Kickbusch, I., B. Riedmuller (eds) (1984) *Die armen Frauen. Frauen in der Sozialpolitik*. Frankfurt.

Kocka, J. (1979) 'Stand – Klasse – Organisation. Strukturen sozialer Ungleichheit in Deutschland vom späten 18. bis zum frühen 20. Jahrhundert im Aufriß', in H.-U. Wehler (ed.), *Klassen in der europäischen Sozialgeschichte*. Göttingen.

Kocka, J. (1983) *Lohnarbeit und Klassenbindung*. Bonn.

Kocka, J. (1983) 'Diskussionsbeitrag', in R. Kreckel (ed.), *Soziale Ungleichheiten*. Special issue 2 of *Soziale Welt*. Göttingen.

Kreckel, R. (1983) 'Theorie sozialer Ungleichheit im Übergang', in R. Kreckel (ed.), *Soziale Ungleichheiten*. Special issue 2 of *Soziale Welt*. Göttingen.

Landesregierung Baden-Württemberg (1983) *Bericht der Kommission 'Zukunftsperspektiven Gesellschaftlicher Entwicklung'*. Stuttgart.

Langewiesche D., K. Schönhoven (eds) (1981) *Arbeiter in Deutschland. Studien zur Lebensweise der Arbeiterschaft im Zeitalter der Industrialisierung*. Paderborn.

Lederer, E. (1979) 'Die Gesellschaft der Unselbständigen. Zum sozialpsychischen Habitus der Gegenwart', in J. Kocka (ed.), *Kapitalismus, Klassenstruktur und Probleme der Demokratie in Deutschland*. Göttingen.

Lepsius, M. R. (1979) 'Soziale Ungleichheit und Klassenstruktur in der Bundesrepublik Deutschland', in H.-U. Wehler (ed.), *Klassen in der europäischen Sozialgeschichte*. Göttingen.

Lutz, B. (1983) 'Bildungsexpansion und soziale Ungleichheit – Eine historisch-soziologische Skizze', in R. Kreckel (ed.), *Soziale Ungleichheiten*. Special issue 2 of *Soziale Welt*. Göttingen.

Lutz, B. (1984) *Der kurze Traum immerwährender Prosperität. Eine Neuinterpretation der industriell-kapitalistischen Entwicklung im Europa des 20. Jahrhunderts*. Frankfurt/New York.

Maase, K. (1984) 'Betriebe ohne Hinterland? Zu einigen Bedingungen der Klassenbildung im Reproduktionsbereich', in Institut für Marxistische Studien und Forschungen, *Marxistische Studien. Jahrbuch des IMSF 7*. Frankfurt.

Marx, K. (1971) *Die Frühschriften*. Stuttgart.

Marx, K. (1982) 'Der 18te Brumaire des Louis Napoleon', in *Marx Engels Werke*, vol. 8. Berlin.

Meja, V., D. Misgeld, N. Stehr (eds) (1987) *Modern German Sociology*. New York.

Miegel, M. (1983) *Die verkannte Revolution. Einkommen und Vermögen privater Haushalte*. Stuttgart.

Mommsen, W. J., W. Mock (eds) (1982) *Die Entstehung des Wohlfahrtsstaates in Großbritannien und Deutschland 1850–1950*. Stuttgart.

Moore, B. (1982) *Ungerechtigkeit – Die sozialen Ursachen von Unterordnung und Widerstand*. Frankfurt. In English (1978) *Injustice: the Social Basis of Obedience and Revolt*. London.

Mooser, J. (1983) 'Auflösung proletarischer Milieus. Klassenbildung und Individualisierung in der Arbeiterschaft vom Kaiserreich bis in die Bundesrepublik Deutschland', *Soziale Welt*, 34: 270ff.

Mooser, J. (1984) *Arbeiterleben in Deutschland 1900–1970. Klassenlagen, Kultur und Politik*. Frankfurt.

Müller, W., A. Willms, J. Handl (1983) *Strukturwandel der Frauenarbeit*. Frankfurt/New York.

Osterland, M. (1973) *Materialien zur Lebens- und Arbeitssituation der Industriearbeiter in der Bundesrepublik Deutschland*. Frankfurt.

Osterland, M. (1978) 'Lebensbilanzen und Lebensperspektiven von Industriearbeitern', in M. Kohli (ed.), *Soziologie des Lebenslaufes*. Darmstadt.

Pappi, F. U. (1979) 'Konstanz und Wandel der Hauptspannungslinien in der Bundesrepublik', in J. Matthes (ed.), *Sozialer Wandel in Westeuropa*. Frankfurt.

Reulecke, J., W. Weber (eds) (1978) *Fabrik, Familie, Feierabend. Beiträge zur Sozialgeschichte des Alltags im Industriezeitalter*. Wuppertal.

Schelsky, H. (1961) 'Die Bedeutung des Klassenbegriffs für die Analyse unserer Gesellschaft', in Seidel and Jenker (eds), *Klassenbildung und Sozialschichtung*. Darmstadt.

Schneider, R. (1982) 'Die Bildungsentwicklung in den westeuropäischen Staaten, 1870–1975', *Zeitschrift für Soziologie*, 11, no. 3.

Smith, G. (1982) 'Nachkriegsgesellschaft im historischen Vergleich', Kolloquium des Instituts für Zeitgeschichte, Munich/Vienna.

Statistisches Bundesamt (1983) *Bildung im Zahlenspiel*. Wiesbaden/Stuttgart.

Teichler, U., D. Hartung, R. Nuthmann (1976) *Hochschulexpansion und Bedarf der Gesellschaft*. Stuttgart.

Thompson, E. P. (1963) *The Making of the English Working Class*. Harmondsworth.

Touraine, A. (1983) 'Soziale Bewegungen', *Soziale Welt*, 34, no. 1.

Voigt, R. (ed.) (1980) *Verrechtlichung*. Königstein.

Weber, M. (1972) *Wirtschaft und Gesellschaft*, 3rd edn. Tübingen.

Wehler, H.-U. (ed.) (1979) *Klassen in der europäischen Sozialgeschichte*. Göttingen.

Westergaard, J. (1965) 'The withering away of class: a contemporary myth', in P. Anderson (ed.), *Towards Socialism*. London.

Wiegand, E., W. Zapf (eds) (1982) *Wandel der Lebensbedingungen in Deutschland. Wohlfahrtsentwicklung seit der Industrialisierung*. Frankfurt/New York.

Zapf, W. (ed.) (1977) *Lebensbedingungen in der Bundesrepublik. Sozialer Wandel und Wohlfahrtsentwicklung*. Frankfurt/New York.

Chapter 4

Allerbeck, K., W. Hoag (1984) *Jugend ohne Zukunft*. Munich.

Ariès, P. (1984) 'Liebe in der Ehe', in P. Ariès, A. Béjin, M. Foucault et al. (eds), *Die Masken des Begehrens und die Metamorphosen der Sinnlichkeit – Zur Geschichte der Sexualität im Abendland*. Frankfurt.

Beck, U., E. Beck-Gernsheim, (1990) *Das ganz normale Chaos der Liebe*. Frankfurt. In English (1993). Cambridge.

Beck-Gernsheim, E. (1983) 'Vom "Dasein für andere" zum Anspruch auf ein Stuck "eigenes Leben"', *Soziale Welt*, 34: 307–340.

Beck-Gernsheim, E. (1984) *Vom Geburtenrückgang zur Neuen Mütterlichkeit? Über private und politische Interessen am Kind*. Frankfurt.

Beck-Gernsheim, E. (1985) *Das halbierte Leben. Männerwelt Beruf, Frauenwelt Familie*, 2nd edn. Frankfurt.

Beck-Gernsheim, E. (1986) 'Von der Liebe zur Beziehung? Veränderungen im Verhältnis von Mann und Frau in der individualisierten Gesellschaft', in J. Berger (ed.), *Moderne oder Postmoderne*. Special issue 4 of *Soziale Welt*. Göttingen.

Beck-Gernsheim, E. (1988) *Die Kinderfrage: Frauen zwischen Kindern und Unabhängigkeit*. Munich.

Béjin, A. (1984) 'Ehen ohne Trauschein heute', in P. Ariès, A. Béjin, M. Foucault et al. (eds), *Die Masken des Begehrens und die Metamorphosen der Sinnlichkeit – Zur Geschichte der Sexualität im Abendland*. Frankfurt.

Berger, B., P. L. Berger (1983) *The War over the Family*. New York. In German (1984) Reinbek.

Berger, P., H. Kellner (1965) 'Die Ehe und die Konstruktion der Wirklichkeit', *Soziale Welt*, 16: 220–241.

Bernardoni, C., V. Werner (eds) (1983) *Der vergeudete Reichtum – Über die Partizipation von Frauen im öffentlichen Leben*. Bonn.

Beyer, J. et al. (eds) (1983) *Frauenlexikon – Stichworte zur Selbstbestimmung*. Munich.

Biermann, I., C. Schmerl, L. Ziebell (1985) *Leben mit kurzfristigem Denken – Eine Untersuchung zur Situation arbeitsloser Akademikerinnen*. Weilheim und Basel.

Brose, H.-G., M. Wohlrab-Sahr (1986) 'Formen individualisierter Lebensführung von Frauen – ein neues Arrangement zwischen Familie und Beruf', in H.-G. Brose (ed.), *Berufsbiographien im Wandel*. Opladen.

Buchholz, W. et al. (1984) *Lebenswelt und Familienwirklichkeit*. Frankfurt.

Bundesminister für Bildung und Wissenschaft (1982/83, 1984/85) *Grund- und Strukturdaten*. Bonn.

Bundesminister für Jugend, Familie und Gesundheit (1981) *Frauen 80*. Cologne.

Bundesminister für Jugend, Familie und Gesundheit (1985) *Nichteheliche Lebensgemeinschaften in der Bundesrepublik Deutschland*. Cologne.

Degler, C. N. (1980) *At Odds – Women and the Family in America from the Revolution to the Present*. New York.

Demos, J., S. S. Boocock, (eds) (1978) *Turning Points – Historical and Sociological Essays on the Family*. Chicago.

Diezinger, A., R. Marquardt, H. Bilden (1982) *Zukunft mit beschränkten Möglichkeiten, Projektbericht*. Munich.

Ehrenreich, B. (1983) *The Hearts of Men*. New York. In German (1985) Reinbek.

Erler, G. A. (1985) 'Erdöl und Mutterliebe – von der Knappheit einiger Rohstoffe', in T. Schmid (ed.), *Das pfeifende Schwein*. Berlin.

Frauenlexikon (1983). Munich.

Gensior, S. (1983) 'Moderne Frauenarbeit', in *Karriere oder Kochtopf: Jahrbuch für Sozialökonomie und Gesellschaftstheorie*. Opladen.

Gilligan, C. (1984) *Die andere Stimme. Lebenskonflikte und Moral der Frau*. Munich.

Glick, P. C. (1984) 'Marriage, divorce, and living arrangements', *Journal of Family Issues*, 5, no. 1: 7–26.

Hoff, A., J. Scholz (1985) *Neue Männer in Beruf und Familie: Forschungsbericht*. Berlin.

Imhof, A. E. (1981) *Die gewonnenen Jahre*. Munich.

Imhof, A. E. (1984) *Die verlorenen Welten*. Munich.

Institut für Demoskopie Allensbach (1985) *Einstellungen zu Ehe und Familie im Wandel der Zeit*. Stuttgart.

Jurreit, M.-L. (ed.) (1979) *Frauenprogramm. Gegen Diskriminierung. Ein Handbuch*. Reinbek.

Kamerman, S. B. (1984) 'Women, children poverty: public policies and female-headed families in industrialized countries', in *Signs: Journal of Women in Culture and Society*. Special issue *Women and Poverty*. Chicago.

Kommission (1983) *Zukunftsperspektiven gesellschaftlicher Entwicklungen, Bericht (erstellt im Auftrage der Landesregierung von Baden-Württemberg)*. Stuttgart.

Lasch, C. (1977) *Haven in Heartless World: the Family Besieged*. New York.

Metz-Gockel, S., U. Müller (1985) 'Der Mann', *Brigitte–Untersuchung*, ms. Hamburg.

Müller, W., A. Willms, J. Handl (1983) *Strukturwandel der Frauenarbeit*. Frankfurt.
Muschg, G. (1976) 'Bericht von einer falschen Front', in H.P. Piwitt (ed.), *Literaturmagazin 5*. Reinbek.
Offe, C. (1984) *Arbeitsgesellschaft*. Frankfurt.
Olerup, A., L. Schneider, E. Monod (1985) *Women, Work and Computerization - Opportunities and Disadvantages*. New York.
Ostner, J., B. Piper (eds) (1986) *Arbeitsbereich Familie*. Frankfurt.
Pearce, D., H. McAdoo (1981) *Women and Children: Alone and in Poverty*. Washington.
Pross, H. (1978) *Der deutsche Mann*. Reinbek.
Quintessenzen (1984) *Frauen und Arbeitsmarkt*. IAB. Nürnberg.
Rerrich, M. S. (1983) 'Veränderte Elternschaft', *Soziale Welt*, 34: 420–449.
Rerrich, M. S. (1986) *Balanceakt Familie*. Freiburg.
Rilke, R. M. (1980) *Briefe*. Frankfurt.
Rubin, I. B. (1983) *Intimate Strangers. Men and Women Together*. New York.
Schulz, W. (1983) 'Von der Institution "Familie" zu den Teilbeziehungen zwischen Mann, Frau und Kind', *Soziale Welt*, 34: 401–419.
Seidenspinner, G., A. Burger (1982) *Mädchen 82, Brigitte-Untersuchung*. Hamburg.
Sennett, R. (1976) *The Fall of Public Man*. London. In German (1983) Frankfurt.
Statistisches Bundesamt (1983) *Datenreport*. Bonn.
Wahl, K. et al. (1980) *Familien sind anders!* Reinbek.
Weber-Kellermann, I. (1975) *Die deutsche Familie. Versuch einer Sozialgeschichte*. Frankfurt.
Wiegmann, B. (1979) 'Frauen und Justiz', in M.-L. Jurreit (ed.), *Frauenprogramm. Gegen Diskriminierung. Ein Handbuch*. Reinbek.
Willms, A. (1983) 'Grundzüge der Entwicklung der Frauenarbeit von 1800 bis 1980', in W. Müller, A. Willms, J. Handl (eds), *Strukturwandel der Frauenarbeit*. Frankfurt.

Chapter 5

Adorno, T. W. (1982) *Minima Moralia*. Frankfurt.
Anders, G. (1980) *Die Antiquiertheit des Menschen*. Munich.
Baethge, M. (1985) 'Individualisierung als Hoffnung und Verhängnis', *Soziale Welt*, 36: 299ff.
Beck-Gernsheim, E. (1986) *Geburtenrückgang und Neuer Kinderwunsch*. Postdoctoral thesis. Munich.
Bolte, K. M. (1983) 'Subjektorientierte Soziologie', in K.M. Bolte (ed.), *Subjektorientierte Arbeits- und Berufssoziologie*. Frankfurt.
Brose, H.-G. (1982) 'Die Vermittlung von sozialen und biographischen Zeitstrukturen', in *Kölner Zeitschrift für Soziologie und Sozialpsychologie*, special issue 29: 385ff.
Deizinger, A., H. Bilden et al. (1982) *Zukunft mit beschränkten Möglichkeiten*. Munich.
Durkheim, E. (1982) *Über die Teilung der sozialen Arbeit*. Frankfurt.
Elias, N. (1969) *Über den Prozeß der Zivilisation*. Bern/Munich. In English (1978) *The Civilizing Process*. Oxford.
Fuchs, W. (1983) 'Jugendliche Statuspassage oder individualisierte Jugendbiographie?', *Soziale Welt*, 34: 341–371.
Fuchs, W. (1984) *Biographische Forschung*. Opladen.
Geulen, D. (1977) *Das vergesellschaftete Subjekt*. Frankfurt.
Gross, P. (1985) 'Bastelmentalität: Ein postmoderner Schwebezustand', in T. Schmid (ed.), *Das pfeifende Schwein*. Berlin.
Hornstein, W. (1985) 'Jugend. Strukturwandel in gesellschaftlichen Wandlungsprozess', in S. Hradil (ed.), *Sozialstruktur im Umbruch*. Opladen.
Imhof, A. E. (1984) 'Von der unsicheren zur sicheren Lebenszeit', *Vierteljahresschrift für Sozial- und Wirtschaftsgeschichte*, 71: 175–198.
Kohli, M. (1985) 'Die Institutionalisierung des Lebenslaufes', *Kölner Zeitschrift für Soziologie und Sozialpsychologie*, 1, 1–29.

Kohli, M., J. W. Meyer (eds) (1985) *Social Structure and Social Construction of Life Stages*. Symposium with contributions from M. W. Riley, K. U. Mayer, T. Held, T. K. Hareven. *Human Development*, 18.

Kohli, M., G. Robert (eds) (1984) *Biographie und soziale Wirklichkeit*. Stuttgart.

Ley, K. (1984) 'Von der Normal- zur Wahlbiographie', in M. Kohli and G. Robert (eds), *Biographie und soziale Wirklichkeit*. Stuttgart.

Landmann, T. (1971) *Das End des Individuums*. Stuttgart.

Luhmann, N. (1985) 'Die Autopoiesis des Bewußtseins', *Soziale Welt*, 36: 402.

Maase, K. (1984) 'Betriebe ohne Hinterland?', in Institut für Marxistische Studien und Forschungen, *Marxistische Studien. Jahrbuch des IMSF 7*. Frankfurt.

Mooser, J. (1983) 'Auflösung proletarischer Milieus', *Soziale Welt*, 34.

Nunner-Winkler, G. (1985) 'Identität und Individualität', *Soziale Welt*, 36: 466ff.

Rosenmayr, L. (ed.) (1978) *Die menschlichen Lebensalter. Kontinuität und Krisen*. Munich.

Rosenmayr, L. (1985) 'Wege zum Ich vor bedrohter Zukunft', *Soziale Welt*, 36: 274ff.

Shell Youth Study (n.d.)

Simmel, G. (1958a) *Philosophie des Geldes*. Berlin. In English (1978) *The Philosophy of Money* (ed. D. Frisby). London.

Simmel, G. (1958b) *Soziologie*. Berlin.

Vester, H. G. (1984) *Die Thematisierung des Selbst in der postmodernen Gesellschaft*. Bonn.

Chapter 6

Althoff, H. (1982) 'Der Statusverlust im Anschluß an eine Berufsausbildung', *Berufsbildung in Wissenschaft und Praxis*, 5: 16ff.

Altmann, N. et al. (1986) 'Ein neuer Rationalisierungstyp', *Soziale Welt*, 37, nos 2/3.

Arendt, H. (1981) *Vita activa oder Vom tätigen Leben*. Munich.

Beck, U., M. Brater, H. J. Daheim (1980) *Soziologie der Arbeit und der Berufe*. Reinbek.

Blossfeld, H.-P. (1984) 'Bildungsreform und Beschäftigung der jungen Generation im öffentlichen Dienst', *Soziale Welt*, 35 no. 2.

Buck, B. (1985) 'Berufe und neue Technologien', *Soziale Welt*, 36, no. 1: 83ff.

Bundesminister für Bildung und Wissenschaft (1983) *Grund- und Strukturdaten 1982/83*. Bonn.

Dahrendorf, R. (1980) 'Im Entschwinden der Arbeitsgesellschaft. Wandlungen der sozialen Konstruktion des menschlichen Lebens', *Merkur*, 34: 749ff.

Dahrendorf, R. (1982) 'Wenn der Arbeitsgesellschaft die Arbeit ausgeht', in J. Matthes (ed.), *Krise der Arbeitsgesellschaft*. Frankfurt.

Dierkes, M., B. Strümpel (eds) (1985) *Wenig Arbeit, aber viel zu tun*. Cologne.

Dombois, R., M. Osterland (1982) 'Neue Formen des flexiblen Arbeitskräfteeinsatzes: Teilzeitarbeit und Leiharbeit', *Soziale Welt*, 33: 466ff.

Handl, J. (1984) *Zur Veränderung der beruflichen Chancen von Berufsanfängern zwischen 1950 und 1982*. Thesis paper. Nürnberg.

Heinze, R. G. (1984) *Der Arbeitsschock*. Cologne.

Hirschhorn, L. (1979) 'The theory of social services in disaccumulationist capitalism', *International Journal of Health Services*, 9, no. 2: 295–311.

Hornstein, W. (1981) 'Kindheit und Jugend im Spannungsfeld gesellschaftlicher Entwicklung', in *Jugend in den achtziger Jahren: Eine Generation ohne Zukunft?*. Schriftenreihe des Bayrischen Jugendrings. Munich.

Jürgens, U., F. Naschold (eds) (1984) *Arbeitspolitik. Materialien zum Zusammenhang von politischer Macht, Kontrolle und betrieblicher Organisation der Arbeit*. Opladen.

Kaiser, M. et al. (1984) 'Fachhochschulabsolventen – zwei Jahre danach', *MittAB*: 241ff.

Kern, H., M. Schumann (1984) *Ende der Arbeitsteilung?* Munich.

Kloas, P.-W. (1984) *Arbeitslosigkeit nach Abschluß der betrieblichen Ausbildung*. Thesis paper. Nürnberg.

Kommission (1983) *Zukunftsperspektiven gesellschaftlicher Entwicklungen*. Stuttgart.

Kubicek, H., A. Rolf (1985) *Mikropolis mit Computernetzen in der 'Informations-gesellschaft'*. Hamburg.

Kutsch, T., F. Vilmar (eds) (1983) *Arbeitszeitverkürzung*. Opladen.

Mertens, D. (1984) 'Das Qualifikationsparadox. Bildung und Beschäftigung bei kritischer Arbeitsmarktperspektive', *Zeitschrift für Pädagogik*, 30.

Müller, C. (1982) 'Ungeschützte Beschäftigungsverhältnisse', in C. Hagemann-White (ed.), *Beiträge zur Frauenforschung*. Bamberg.

Negt, O. (1984) *Lebendige Arbeit, enteignete Zeit*. Frankfurt.

Offe, C. (1984) *Arbeitsgesellschaft: Strukturprobleme und Zukunftsperspektiven*. Frankfurt/New York.

Offe, C., H. Hinrichs, H. Wiesenthal (eds) (1982) *Arbeitszeitpolitik*. Frankfurt.

Schelsky, H. (1942) 'Die Bedeutung des Berufs in der modernen Gesellschaft', in T. Luckmann and W. Sprondel (eds), *Berufssoziologie*. Cologne.

Sklar, M. (1968) 'On the proletarian revolution and the end of political-economic society', *Radical America*, 3: 3–28.

Chapter 7

Adorno, T. W., M. Horkheimer (1970) *Dialektik der Aufklärung*. Frankfurt.

Beck, U. (1974) *Objektivität und Normativität – Die Theorie-Praxis Debatte in der modernen deutschen und amerikanischen Soziologie*. Reinbek.

Beck, U. (ed.) (1982) *Soziologie und Praxis, Erfahrungen, Konflikte, Perspektiven*. Special issue 1 of *Soziale Welt*. Göttingen.

Beck, U., W. Bonß (1984) 'Soziologie und Modernisierung. Zur Ortsbestimmung der Verwendungsforschung', in *Soziale Welt*, 35: 381ff.

Böhme, G., W. v.d. Daele, W. Krohn (1972) 'Alternativen in der Wissenschaft', *Zeitschrift für Soziologie*: 302ff.

Böhme, G., W. v.d. Daele, W. Krohn (1973) 'Die Finalisierung der Wissenschaft', *Zeitschrift für Soziologie*: 128ff.

Bonß, W. (1982) *Die Einübung des Tatsachenblicks. Zur Struktur und Veränderung empirischer Sozialforschung*. Frankfurt.

Bonß, W., H. Hartmann (1985) 'Konstruierte Gesellschaft, rationale Deutung. Zum Wirk-lichkeitscharakter soziologischer Diskurse', in W. Bonß and H. Hartmann (eds), *Entzauberte Wissenschaft. Zur Relativität und Geltung soziologischer Forschung*. Special issue 3 of *Soziale Welt*. Göttingen.

Campbell, D. T. (1985) 'Häuptlinge und Rituale. Das Sozialsystem der Wissenschaft als Stammesorganisation', in W. Bonß and H. Hartmann (eds), *Entzauberte Wissenschaft. Zur Relativität und Geltung soziologischer Forschung*. Special issue 3 of *Soziale Welt*. Göttingen.

Carson, R. (1962) *Silent Spring*. New York.

Commoner, B. (1963) *Science and Survival*. New York.

Duerr, H. P. (ed.) (1981) *Der Wissenschaftler und das Irrationale*, 2 vols. Frankfurt.

Feyerabend, P. (1980) *Erkenntnis für freie Menschen*, rev. edn. Frankfurt.

Gouldner, A., S. M. Miller (1965) *Applied Sociology: Opportunities and Problems*. New York.

Hartmann, H. (1970) *Empirische Sozialforschung*. Munich.

Hartmann, H., E. Dübbers (1984) *Kritik in der Wissenschaftspraxis. Buchbesprechungen und ihr Echo*. Frankfurt.

Hartmann, H., M. Hartmann (1982) 'Vom Elend der Experten: Zwischen Akademisierung und De-Professionalisierung', *Kölner Zeitschrift für Soziologie und Sozialpsychologie*, 193ff.

Hollis, M., S. Lukes (eds) (1982) *Rationality and Relativism*. Oxford.

Illich, I. (1979) *Entmündigung durch Experten. Zur Kritik der Dienstleistungsberufe*. Reinbek.

Knorr-Cetina, K. (1984) *Die Fabrikation von Erkenntnis*. Frankfurt.
Knorr-Cetina, K., M. Mulkavy (eds) (1983) *Science Observed. Perspectives on the Social Study of Science*. London.
Kuhn, T. (1970) *Die Struktur wissenschaftlicher Revolutionen*. Frankfurt. In English (1970) *The Structure of Scientific Revolutions*. Chicago.
Küppers, G., P. Lundgreen, P. Weingart (1978) *Umweltforschung – die gesteuerte Wissenschaft?* Frankfurt.
Lakatos, I. (1974) 'Methodologie der Forschungsprogramme', in I. Lakatos and A. Musgrave (eds), *Kritik und Erkenntnisfortschritt*. Braunschweig.
Lau, C. (1984) 'Soziologie im öffentlichen Diskurs. Voraussetzungen und Grenzen sozialwissenschaftlicher Rationalisierung und gesellschaftlicher Praxis', *Soziale Welt*, 35: 407ff.
Lindbloom, C. E. (1959) 'The science of muddling through', *Public Administration Review*, 19: 79ff.
Matthes, J. (1985) 'Die Soziologen und ihre Wirklichkeit. Anmerkungen zum Wirklichkeitsverhältnis der Soziologie', in W. Bonß and H. Hartmann (eds), *Entzauberte Wissenschaft. Zur Relativität und Geltung sozialogischer Forschung*. Special issue 3 of *Soziale Welt*. Göttingen.
Mayntz, R. (ed.) (1980) *Implementationsforschung*. Cologne.
Meja, V., N. Stehr (1982) *Der Streit um die Wissenssoziologie*, 2 vols. Frankfurt.
Meyer-Abich, K. M. (1980) 'Versagt die Wissenschaft vor dem Grundrecht der Freiheit? Gründe der Vertrauenskrise zwischen Wissenschaft und Öffentlichkeit', *Zeitschrift für Didaktik der Philosophie*, no. 1.
Mitchell, R. C. (1979) *Science, Silent Spring; Science, Technology and the Environment Movement in the United States*. Ms. Washington.
Novotny, H. (1979) *Kernenergie: Gefahr oder Notwendigkeit*. Frankfurt.
Overington, M. A. (1985) 'Einfach der Vernunft folgen: Neuere Entwicklungstendenzen in der Metatheorie', in W. Bonß and H. Hartmann (eds), *Entzauberte Wissenschaft. Zur Relativität und Geltung soziologischer Forschung*. Special issue 3 of *Soziale Welt*. Göttingen.
Pavelka, F. (1979) 'Das Deprofessionalisierungsspiel. Ein Spiel für Profis', *Psychosozial*, 2: 19ff.
Popper, K. R. (1968) *Logik der Forschung*, 6th edn. Tübingen. In English (1989) *The Logic of Scientific Discovery*. London.
Popper, K. R. (1972) *Objektive Erkenntnis. Ein evolutionärer Entwurf*. Hamburg.
Scott, R., A. Shore (1979) *Why Sociology does not Apply: a Study of the Use of Sociology in Public Policy*. New York.
Shostak, A. B. (ed.) (1974) *Putting Sociology to Work*. New York.
Stehr, N., R. Konig (eds) (1975) *Wissenschaftssoziologie. Studien und Materialien*. Special issue 18 of *Kölner Zeitschrift für Soziologie und Sozialpsychologie*. Cologne/Opladen.
Stehr, N., V. Meja (1981) *Wissenschaftssoziologie*. Special issue 22 of *Kölner Zeitschrift für Soziologie und Sozialpsychologie*. Opladen.
Struening, E. L., B. Brewer (eds) (1984) *The University Edition of the Handbook of Evaluation Research*. London/Beverly Hills.
Weber, M. (1982) 'Vom inneren Beruf zur Wissenschaft', in J. Winkelmann (ed.), *Max Weber: Soziologie, weltgeschichtliche Analysen*. Stuttgart.
Weingart, P. (1979) *Das 'Harrisburg-Syndrom' oder die De-Professionalisierung der Experten*.
Weingart, P. (1983) 'Verwissenschaftlichung der Gesellschaft – Politisierung der Wissenschaft', *Zeitschrift für Soziologie*: 225ff.
Weingart, P. (1984) 'Anything goes – rien ne va plus', *Kursbuch*, 78: 74.
Weiss, C. H. (ed.) (1977) *Using Social Research for Public Policy Making*. Lexington.
Wissenschaftszentrum Berlin (1977) *Interaktion von Wissenschaft und Politik*. Frankfurt.

Chapter 8

Alemann, U. v. (ed.) (1981) *Neokorporatismus*. Frankfurt/New York.

Alemann, U. v., R. C. Heinze (eds) (1979) *Verbände und Staat*. *Vom Pluralismus zum Korporatismus*. Opladen.

Altmann, N. et al. (1986) 'Ein ''Neuer Rationalisierungstyp''', *Soziale Welt*, 37.

Arendt, H. (1981) *Macht und Gewalt*. Munich.

Beck, U. (1979) *Soziale Wirklichkeit als Produkt gesellschaftlicher Arbeit*. Unpublished postdoctoral thesis. Munich.

Beck, U. (1988) *Gegengifte: Die organisierte Unverantwortlichkeit*. Frankfurt. In English (1992) *Counter-Poisons*. Cambridge.

Beck, U. (1991) *Politik in der Risikogesellschaft*. Frankfurt. In English (1993) New York.

Beck, U., M. Brater (1978) *Berufliche Arbeitsteilung und soziale Ungleichheit*. Frankfurt/New York.

Berger, J. (ed.) (1986) *Moderne oder Postmoderne*. Special issue 4 of *Soziale Welt*. Göttingen.

Berger, S. 'Politics and Anti-Politics in Western Europe in the Seventies', *Daedalus*, 108: 27–50.

Bergmann, J., G. Brandt, K. Korber, O. Mohl, C. Offe (1969) 'Herrschaft, Klassenverhältnis und Schichten', in T. W. Adorno (ed.), *Spätkapitalismus oder Industriegesellschaft?* Stuttgart.

Braczyk, H. J. et al. (1986) 'Konsensverlust und neue Technologien – Zur exemplarischen Bedeutung des Konfliktes um die Wiederaufarbeitungsanlage für die gesellschaftliche Steuerung technischen Wandels', *Soziale Welt*, 37, nos 2/3.

Bräutigam, H. H., L. Mettler (1985) *Die programmierte Vererbung*. Hamburg.

Brand, K. W. (ed.) (1985) *Neue soziale Bewegungen in Westeuropa und in den USA*. Frankfurt.

Brand, K. W., D. Büsser, D. Rucht (1983) *Aufbruch in eine neue Gesellschaft*. Frankfurt.

Bühl, W. (1983) *Die Angst des Menschen vor der Technik*. Düsseldorf.

Crozier, M., E. Friedberg (1979) *Macht und Organisation*. Königstein.

Crozier, M., S. P. Huntington, J. Watanuki (1975) *The Crisis of Democracy*. New York.

Daele, W. v.d. (1985) *Mensch nach Maß*. Munich.

Daele, W. v.d. (1986) 'Technische Dynamik und gesellschaftliche Moral', *Soziale Welt*, 37, nos 2/3.

Donati, P. R. (1984) 'Organization between Movement and Institution', *Social Science Information*, 23, (4/5): 837–859.

Elster, J. (1979) 'Risk, uncertainty, and nuclear power', *Social Science Information*.

Flora, P., J. Alber (1981) 'Modernization, democratization, and the development of welfare states in Western Europe', in P. Flora and A.J. Heidenheimer (eds), *The Development of Welfare States in Europe and America*. New Brunswick.

Freeman, J. (ed.) (1983) *Social Movements in the Sixties and Seventies*. New York/London.

Gershuny, J. I. (1978) *After Industrial Society? The Emerging Self-Service-Economy*. London.

Grew, R. (ed.) (1978) *Crises of Political Development in Europe and the United States*. Princeton.

Gross, P. (1984) *Industrielle Mikrobiologie*. *Sonderheft Spektrum der Wissenschaft*. Heidelberg.

Groß, P., R. Hitzler, A. Honer (1985) 'Zwei Kulturen? Diagnostische und therapeutische Kompetenz im Wandel', in *Österr. Zeitschrift für Soziologie. Sonderheft Medizinsoziologie*.

Habermas, J. (1973) *Legitimationsprobleme im Spätkapitalismus*. Frankfurt. In English (1975) *Legitimation Crisis*. London.

Habermas, J. (1981) *Theorie des kommunikativen Handelns*, vol. 2, Frankfurt. In English (1984 and 1988) *The Theory of Communicative Competence*, 2 vols. London.

Habermas, J. (1985) *Die neue Unübersichtlichkeit*. Frankfurt.

Hirschmann, A. O. (1981) *Shifting Involvements. Private Interests and Public Action.* Princeton.

Inglehart, R. (1977) *The Silent Revolution. Changing Values and Political Styles among Western Publics.* Princeton.

Institute for Contemporary Studies (1976) *The Politics of Planning. A Review and Critique of Centralized Economic Planning.* San Francisco.

Jaenicke, M. (1979) *Wie das Industriesystem von seinen Mißständen profitiert.* Cologne.

Japp, K. P. (1984) 'Selbsterzeugung oder Fremdverschulden. Thesen zum Rationalismus in den Theorien sozialer Bewegungen', *Soziale Welt*, 35.

Jonas, H. (1984) *Technik, Ethik und Biogenetische Kunst.* Ms.

Kitschelt, H. (1985) 'Materiale Politisierung der Produktion', *Zeitschrift für Soziologie*, 14, no. 3: 188–208.

Kommissionsbericht (1983) *Zukunftsperspektiven gesellschaftlicher Entwicklung.* Stuttgart.

Kreß, K., K. G. Nikolai (1985) *Bürgerinitiativen – Zum Verhältnis von Betroffenheit und politischer Beteiligung der Bürger.* Bonn.

Lipset, S. M., S. Rokkan (1967) 'Cleavage structures, party systems, and voter alignments: an introduction', in S.M. Lipset and S. Rokkan (eds), *Party Systems and Voter Alignments.* New York.

Löw, R. (1983) 'Gen und Ethik', in P. Koslowski (ed.), *Die Verführung durch das Machbare.* Munich.

Luhmann, N. (1981) *Politische Theorie im Wohlfahrtsstaat.* Munich.

Mayer-Tasch, C. P. (1976) *Die Bürgerinitiativbewegung.* Reinbek.

Mayntz, R. (ed.) (1980) *Implementationsforschung.* Cologne.

Melacci, A. (1984) 'An end to social movements? Introductory paper to sessions on new movements and change in organizational forms', *Social Science Information*, 23, nos 4/5: 819–835.

Neidhardt, F. (1985) 'Einige Ideen zu einer allgemeinen Theorie sozialer Bewegungen', in S. Hradil (ed.), *Sozialstruktur im Umbruch.* Opladen.

Noelle-Neumann, E. (1991) *Öffentliche Meinung.* Berlin.

Offe, C. (1972) *Strukturprobleme des kapitalistischen Staates.* Frankfurt.

Offe, C. (1980) 'Konkurrenzpartei und politische Identität', in R. Roth (ed.), *Parlamentarisches Ritual und politische Alternativen.* Frankfurt.

Offe, C. (1986) 'Null-option', in J. Berger (ed.), *Moderne oder Postmoderne.* Special issue 4 of *Soziale Welt.* Göttingen.

Piore, M. J., C. F. Sabel (1985) *Das Ende der Massenproduktion.* New York/Berlin. In English (1985) *The Second Industrial Divide.* New York.

Radunski, P. (1985) 'Die Wähler in der Stimmungsdemokratie', *Sonde*, 2: 3ff.

Schenk, M. (1984) *Soziale Netzwerke und Kommunikation.* Tübingen.

Sieferle, R. P. (1985) *Fortschrittsfeinde? Opposition gegen Technik und Industrie von der Romantik bis zur Gegenwart.* Munich.

Stössel, J.-P. (1985) 'Dem chronisch Kranken hilft kein Arzt', *Süddeutsche Zeitung*, November 21, 1985.

Toffler, A. (1980) *Die dritte Welle.* Munich.

Touraine, A. (1977) *The Self-Production of Society.* Chicago.

Willke, H. (1983) *Entzauberug des Staates. Überlegungen zu einer sozietalen Steuerungstheorie.* Königstein.

INDEX

modernization, reflexive, *cont.*
  and technological progress 202
monarchy, democratic 191, 192
Mooser, J. 129
morality, *see* ethics
movements, new social 11, 90, 190, 195,
  223, 231
Müller, Carola 147
myth of industrial society 11

nation states, undermining of borders 2,
  23, 36, 47–8, 189
nature
  human consciousness of 55, 74
  mastery 24–5, 81, 200, 207
  and society 80–4, 87, 154
needs, and risk production 56
neutrality, in science 170, 174
nitrates, threat to water 33
nuclear risk
  effects 22
  and fallibilism 177–8
  perception 75
  trivialization 60
nuclear weapons 48, 75
Nunner-Winckler, G. 137 n.2
nutrition, and risk avoidance 35–6,
  179

objectification of errors 159
objectivity
  and risk definition 29
  in science 29, 174
obscurity, new 190
occupation
  and risk distribution 35
  see also labor; labor market; work
Offe, C. 110, 189

parenthood 105, 108–9, 110–13, 116,
  118–19, 125, 198
parliament
  decline as political center 188, 192, 194,
    195, 223, 226–7
  and democratization 229
  and medical technology 208–9
participation, political 183, 185, 192, 195,
  199, 202–3
particularism, in science 167
parties, political, and social change 188,
  190
people
  consequences of pollution for 24–6
  effect of toxins on 68–9
  and effects of risk recognition 77

perception of risk 21, 27, 44–6, 55, 57–9,
  75, 227
  and social identity 99
pesticides
  definition 65–6
  safety limits 25, 54, 137
  Third World use 42, 44
Pesticides Advisory Committee (UK) 4–5
Piore, M.J. & Sabel, C.F. 215–16
plant species, threat to 37–8, 56, 83
Plato 73
pluralism, liberal
  biographical 114–15, 119–20
  and risk 4, 48
politics
  alternative 194
  autonomy 186–7, 189, 223
  and class society 91
  as contingent 191, 199
  differential 231–5
  disempowerment 186–7, 191–9, 223–8
  and employment 141, 146, 149
  and gender relations 99, 119
  loss of function 187–90
  and medical technology 208–9
  new political culture 190, 194, 195–9,
    200–3
  and politicization of nature 80–4
  and pollution 24
  and private sphere 24, 105–6, 109,
    116–17, 119, 126, 132, 198
  rational choice model 199
  recentralization 230–1
  reflexive 76–80, 154, 183
  and risk 78, 225–7
  and science 81–2, 170, 172–4, 188
  as source of solutions 31, 48–50, 191
  sub-politics 14, 190, 192–4, 203, 223,
    233–4
    differentiation 193–8
    of industrial automation 215–23
    of medicine 204–12
    of techno-economics 183–7, 199,
      200–3, 212–15, 223–5, 228–31
  unbinding 154, 185, 190–9, 231–3
  and voting behavior 190
  see also business; democracy
polluter pays principle 39, 63
pollution, industrial 21
  distribution 24–6
  limitation 64–8
  as supra-national 23, 40
  visibility 55
Popper, Karl 141, 165–6, 234
population levels 204